THE TIMES

Big Book of Quick Crosswords

Book 1

300 world-famous crossword puzzles

Published in 2016 by Times Books

First printed as 978-0-00-711078-0,
978-0-00-712615-6, 978-0-00-712269-1
and 978-0-00-714495-2

HarperCollins Publishers
Westerhill Road
Bishopbriggs
Glasgow G64 2QT
www.harpercollins.co.uk

10 9 8

© Times Newspapers 2016

The Times® is a registered trademark
of Times Newspapers Limited

ISBN 978-0-00-819576-2

Layout by Davidson's Publishing
Solutions

Printed and bound by
CPI Group (UK) Ltd, Croydon, CR0 4YY

The contents of this publication
are believed correct at the time of
printing. Nevertheless the publisher
can accept no responsibility for
errors or omissions, changes in the
detail given or for any expense or loss
thereby caused.

A catalogue record for this book is
available from the British Library.

If you would like to comment on any
aspect of this book, please contact us
at the given address or online.
E-mail: puzzles@harpercollins.co.uk

 facebook.com/collinsdictionary
 @collinsdict

THE PUZZLES

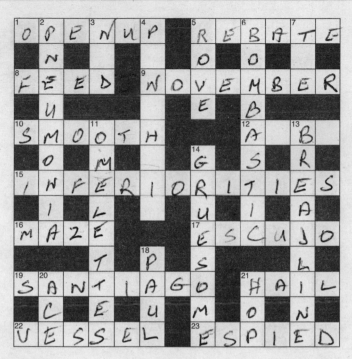

ACROSS

1 Make accessible; speak more freely (4,2)

5 Refund of excess (6)

8 Give meal to (4)

9 Remember its Fifth (8)

10 Level, polished (6)

12 French clerical title, e.g. Liszt's (4)

15 Points, levels of being less good (13)

16 Labyrinth (4)

17 Money of Portugal (6)

19 Capital of Chile (8)

21 Greet; falling stones (4)

22 Ship; liquid holder (6)

23 Caught sight of (6)

DOWN

2 Inflamed-lung illness (9)

3 Show agreement; Cain's land (3)

4 Bat in emergency (*baseball*) (5-3)

5 Wander (4)

6 Pompously high-flown (in speech) (9)

7 Digit; sounds like *haul* (3)

11 Egg dishes (9)

13 Subsistence level (9)

14 Inspiring horror, disgust (8)

18 Missionary apostle; – Jones, dance (4)

20 Champion; point winning serve (3)

21 Jump; beer ingredient (3)

ACROSS

1 Self-controlled (after Greek philosophers) (5)
7 Charged (with crime) (7)
8 Deep red shade (7)
9 Smokers' saucer (7)
11 Draw out (6)
13 K, Q, or **J** (5,4)
15 Friction-reducing substance (9)
19 Of the French (6)
21 Sleep (*colloq.*) (4-3)
23 Trace; tiny remnant (7)
24 Bravery (7)
25 Animal track (5)

DOWN

1, 20 Paris basilica (5,5)
2 Source (6)
3 Of the universe (6)
4 Water-into-wine miracle town (4)
5 Of the countryside (6)
6 Restoration work; goes (7)
10 Twine (6)
12 Sensitive to slights (6)
14 Snooker-table edge (7)
16 Lab vessel; sharp reply (6)
17 Heel/ankle bones (6)
18 Creature with missing pigment (6)
20 See 1*dn*
22 Level (4)

ACROSS

1 Daffodils (8)
5 Capital of Norway (4)
8 Filthy look; overbrightness (5)
9 (Rocket) start to rise (4,3)
11 Tiny –, *Christmas Carol* cripple (3)
12 Riddle (9)
13 Join the forces (6)
15 Creeks of the sea (6)
18 Health, vitality (4-5)
19 Poor –, Edgar's disguise *(Lear)* (3)
20 Localised speech (7)
21 Wall-painting (5)
22 Get clean (4)
23 Uneven (contest) (3-5)

DOWN

1 Woman's bedwear (7)
2 Kingdom (5)
3 Not to be forgiven (11)
4 Unspeaking (6)
6 Whip; one harassing (7)
7 Foreign-aid charity (5)
10 Exciting activity (3,3,5)
14 Burns's Scottish 20 (7)
16 Tasted; took specimens (7)
17 Pay attention (6)
18 Victoria, *the – at Windsor (Kipling)* (5)
19 Weary (5)

ACROSS

1 Place of light confinement (4,6)
8 Dissolve (team) (7)
9 Greek A (5)
10 Make tea, beer (4)
11 Useless item; failure (4,4)
13 Water behind reef (6)
15 Unconscious (6)
17 Feeling gratitude (8)
18 Piece of money (4)
21 Social grouping (5)
22 Property theft (7)
23 Aggrieved, bitter feelings (10)

DOWN

2 Ski course (5)
3 Minimum type of tide (4)
4 Africa/Arabia divider (3,3)
5 Carelessly quick (8)
6 Roman god of 19 (7)
7 Naughty, dishonest behaviour (5-5)
8 Make feeble (10)
12 (Given) permanently (3,5)
14 River of ice (7)
16 Exhibiting 23 (6)
19 Large body of water (5)
20 Looking stern, harsh (4)

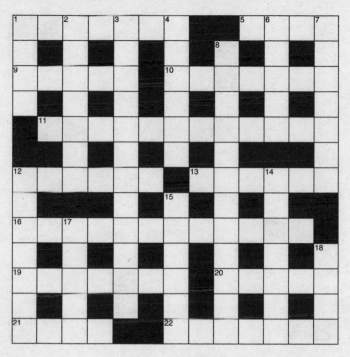

ACROSS

- **1** Newborn to pride (4,3)
- **5** Mutilate (4)
- **9** Burdened (5)
- **10** Two-line verse (7)
- **11** Impossible to stomach (12)
- **12** Language group including Gaelic, Welsh (6)
- **13** *Last Theorem* mathematician (6)
- **16** Have to retract (statement) (3,4,5)
- **19** Highly influential; able to develop (7)
- **20** Jewelled headdress (5)
- **21** Completed (4)
- **22** Park wardens (7)

DOWN

- **1** Temporarily inactive period (4)
- **2** Service book; type of number (7)
- **3** Teaching to respond to stimulus (12)
- **4** Pail (6)
- **6** Off-the-cuff (2-3)
- **7** Annual car check-up (3,4)
- **8** Kick one who is down (3,3,4,2)
- **12** Needing ironing (7)
- **14** Intervene to reconcile (7)
- **15** Block of building stone (6)
- **17** Athenian misanthrope *(Shakespeare)* (5)
- **18** Spoils; Roman god (4)

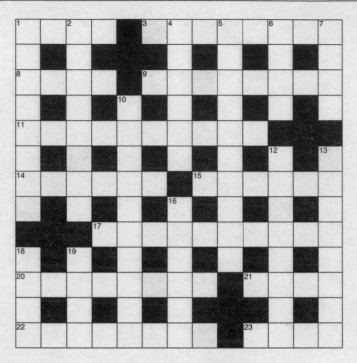

ACROSS

1 Daybreak (4)
3 Israel tribe; Jacob's youngest (8)
8 Cheat of payment (4)
9 Inclination, bent (8)
11 Unpleasantly modern (10)
14 Out of one's mind (6)
15 Predicament; just pass (exam) (6)
17 Prerequisite (4,3,3)
20 (Impractical) perfection seeker (8)
21 Fail to achieve (4)
22 Peripatetic drinking session (3,5)
23 Incline; thin (4)

DOWN

1 Carefree, urbane (8)
2 19th century US frontier zone (4,4)
4 Vigour (6)
5 Racing ruling body (6,4)
6 Sound mournful (4)
7 Observe; brief jotting (4)
10 Analgesic (10)
12 Yellow-skin disease (8)
13 *In Memoriam* poet (8)
16 Up-and-down plaything (3-3)
18 Thin scrap (cloud, material) (4)
19 Plant for flavouring (4)

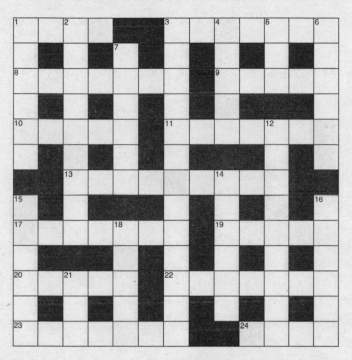

ACROSS

1 An army; a party-giver (4)
3 Small falcon (7)
8 Prince, chose gold casket *(Merchant of Venice)* (7)
9 E.g. potato root (5)
10 Name (of e.g. book) (5)
11 Engagingly attractive (7)
13 Gangster chief (9)
17 Rips veil off (7)
19 A parable; *worse (anagram)* (5)
20 Chinese black/white animal (5)
22 Tribal chief (7)
23 Member of white-rose party (7)
24 Gaming stake (4)

DOWN

1, 15 Egg that sat on a wall (6,6)
2 Ploy (9)
3 Be worldly wise (4,5,4)
4 The Devil (5)
5 Difficulty; polish (3)
6 Pantry (6)
7 Smooth cement floor (6)
12 Lady rower (9)
14 Light cavalryman (6)
15 See 1*dn*
16 An alloy; an Age; a statue (6)
18 Hindu holy man (5)
21 And not (3)

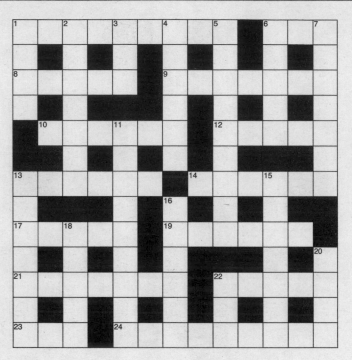

ACROSS

1 Be indecisive (9)
6 Tedious task; cigarette (3)
8 Clever; with a cutting edge (5)
9 Innate; unaffected (7)
10 Curving outwards (6)
12 Show as untrue (5)
13 A tree; neat (6)
14 Parliament clock tower (3,3)
17 Put lid on (5)
19 Immoral; sacrilegious (6)
21 Surround; envelop (7)
22 Divided into areas (5)
23 Agent (3)
24 Sleepy (9)

DOWN

1 Flower receptacle (4)
2 Outcry (7)
3 Part of face; cheek (3)
4 Building extension (6)
5 Found; ascertain (9)
6 Running wild (animal) (5)
7 Spanish treasure ship (7)
11 Done through another (9)
13 Achievement of aim (7)
15 Equilibrium (7)
16 Exhibition building (6)
18 Petain's capital (5)
20 Having lost fizz (4)
22 Animal exhibition (3)

ACROSS

1 Hobby (7)
5 Boring; cloudy (4)
8 Silk strip for tying, etc. (6)
9 Filthy (stables Hercules cleaned) (6)
10 Sheath for sword (8)
12 Portent (4)
13 With which not to touch the hated (9)
17 Huge (4)
18 Posh dance hall (8)
20 Spasmodic, intermittent (6)
21 Consternation (6)
23 Earth; to make dirty (4)
24 Navigation instrument (7)

DOWN

2 For each person (6)
3 Vessel; Swift's *Tale* of one (3)
4 Miraculous food; unexpected gift (5)
5 Priest's neckwear (3,6)
6 One taking charge (6)
7 Short of money (4,2)
11 Delighting the eye (9)
14 Eat fast; make turkey noise (6)
15 Gambling house (6)
16 Area of land, of knowledge (6)
19 House at drive entrance (5)
22 Relax; take (exam) (3)

ACROSS

1 Good-luck charm (6)
5 Seize (4)
9 Where Don John of Austria beat Turks *(Chesterton)* (7)
10 Reason for action (6)
11 Light-hearted repartee (8)
12 Servants' uniform (6)
15 It is *a lovesome thing, God wot (T. E. Brown)* (6)
18 Sheriff's officer (8)
20 Unrivalled (6)
22 Orgy of destruction (7)
23 Entrance; number attending match (4)
24 Speckled hen; a county (6)

DOWN

2 Muslim scholar (6)
3 Unbalanced (8)
4 Indian two-wheeler; Friendly Islands (5)
6 Humiliating defeat (4)
7 Dam-building rodent (6)
8 Unpretentious; (US) ugly (girl) (6)
13 Provisions of food (8)
14 Detain (enemy aliens) (6)
16 Canvas shelter (6)
17 Weak; over-refined (6)
19 Presses for information; shoes (5)
21 Abandon; resign (4)

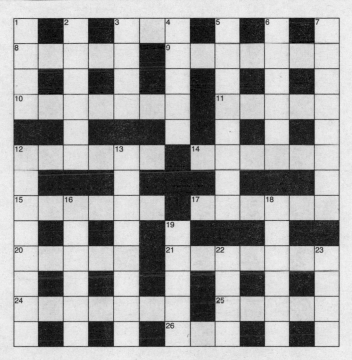

ACROSS

3 Club; protected mammal (3)

8 Road to house; compel (5)

9 One without illusions (7)

10 One without credulity (7)

11 Wood-shaping machine (5)

12 Grass-cutter (6)

14 Breathe painfully; bright idea (6)

15 Esoteric (6)

17 Rival of classical Athens (6)

20 *Manfred, Don Juan* poet (5)

21 Contented (7)

24 Spouse's child, not one's own (7)

25 Calls; feature of Saturn (5)

26 Element Sn (3)

DOWN

1 Probability (4)

2 Best clothes (6)

3 Disposition; warped (4)

4 Stretch of land (5)

5 High-masted vessel (4,4)

6 Not much (6)

7 And so on (2,6)

12 Looking down on "inferiors" (8)

13 Sanctity (8)

16 Membrane over eye (6)

18 Getting up; revolt (6)

19 Exhausted (5)

22 Make (money) (4)

23 Sleep rough (4)

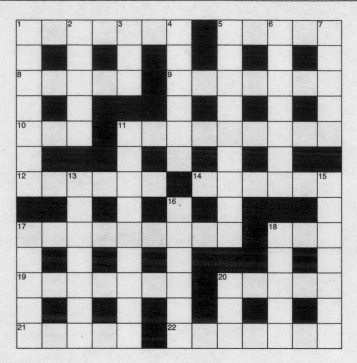

ACROSS

1 Free from blame (7)
5 Rugby formation (5)
8 Cavalry unit (5)
9 Claude –, French composer (7)
10 Silent; act in mime (3)
11 Dancer's twirl (9)
12 Suicide bird *(Mikado)* (3-3)
14 Magician (6)
17 Birnam Wood came to it *(Macbeth)* (9)
18 Fasten; (golf) hole marker (3)
19 Insufficient attention (7)
20 Sphere (5)
21 Swell; sudden increase (5)
22 Muslim fast (7)

DOWN

1 Endeavour (7)
2 Great fuss, wind (5)
3 Drink with tongue; circuit (3)
4 Tolerate (6)
5 Not for discussion outside court (3,6)
6 Egypt town, hieroglyph key stone (7)
7 Perhaps (5)
11 Special benefit, immunity (9)
13 Department head (7)
15 Deep, dismal cell (7)
16 Divisor; business agent (6)
17 Sand hills (5)
18 Sticking out; arrogant (5)
20 Type of tree; part of mouth (3)

ACROSS

1 War/disaster relief agency (3,5)
5 Part of hand; trophy (4)
9 Be all one deserves (5,3,5)
10 Stabiliser; sounds like *benefit cheque* (4)
11 Hazardous polar mass, may calve (7)
13 Rudderless (6)
15 Old and useless (4,2)
18 Holder of responsible post (7)
20 Two of Henry VIII's wives (4)
23 Trouble in store (especially for Faust) (3,5,2,3)
24 Be excessively fond (4)
25 Falstaff's red-nosed crony (8)

DOWN

1 Iron rot (4)
2 Unclean (5)
3 Recite rapidly, easily (4,3)
4 Penalty box (hockey) (3,3)
6 To increase (7)
7 Lessen severity of (8)
8 Unconfined (4)
12 Strangled by wire (8)
14 Think; bounce back (7)
16 Modified (7)
17 Three-horse Russian vehicle (6)
19 Head cook (4)
21 Gurkha homeland (5)
22 Popular but false idea (4)

ACROSS

1 Tiny bit (of learning) (10)
8 Siegfried –, war poet (7)
9 Deeper; ring on target (5)
10 Well-ventilated (4)
11 How the unprepared are caught (2,3,3)
13 John –; – Beardsley (6)
15 Indelible skin picture (6)
17 Ceremonious Catholic service (4,4)
18 Amongst (4)
21 A small whale (5)
22 Diplomat; sort of case (7)
23 Methodical (10)

DOWN

2 Tightwad (5)
3 Stepped; "generations have –" *(Hopkins)* (4)
4 Pacific warming current (2,4)
5 One from Emerald Isle (8)
6 Firing of bullet (7)
7 Barset bishop's wife *(Trollope)* (3,7)
8 One disliking going out (4-2-4)
12 With no visible join (8)
14 Past misdemeanours (forgiven) (7)
16 Condition; lands (6)
19 Speed of sound (4,1)
20 Sicilian volcano (4)

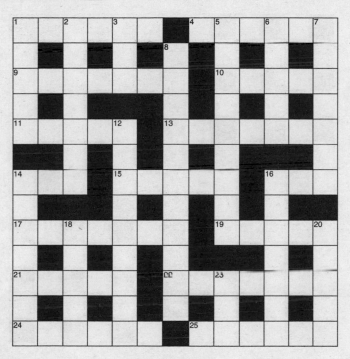

ACROSS

1 Relief road (6)
4 Hateful (6)
9 Prefect; type of lizard (7)
10 Take tiny steps; grind up (5)
11 Covered in creeper (5)
13 Most large (7)
14 A long way (3)
15 Item, object (5)
16 Barley drink (3)
17 Brother, sister (7)
19 Cereal fungus (5)
21 Very fat (5)
22 Put to use; asked (for job) (7)
24 Nakedness (6)
25 Collect together (6)

DOWN

1 Cute animated deer (5)
2 Bike basket (7)
3 (Parliament) was in session (3)
5 Inflammatory speaker (9)
6 Small fluid, dry measure (5)
7 Put (sword) away (7)
8 Land of giants *(Gulliver)* (11)
12 Disadvantage (9)
14 Cover (with bunting) (7)
16 Mental agony (7)
18 Mixture (of e.g. flavours) (5)
20 Royal house of Elizabeth I (5)
23 Ball in whistle (3)

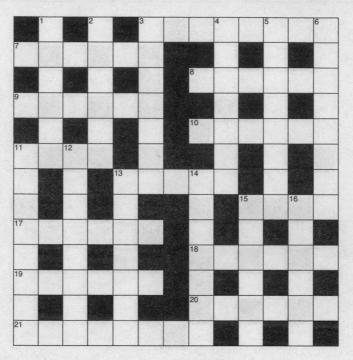

ACROSS

3 Animal with trunk (8)

7 Battle of Hastings tapestry (6)

8 Painful; a beer (6)

9 Nun's headdress (6)

10 Prestige; official seal once (6)

11 Counterfeit (4)

13 Just about manage (3,2)

15 Old Testament book after Hosea (4)

17 Bill of exchange; sounds like *verify* (6)

18 Frightened (6)

19 Lebanon capital (6)

20 Take up again (6)

21 *Hamlet* setting, castle (8)

DOWN

1 Yacht harbour (6)

2 Place of worship; part of head (6)

3 Cost (7)

4 Absence of intrusion (7)

5 Unappealing principal character (8)

6 Prepare to flee (4,4)

11 Violent (8)

12 Dynamics (8)

13 Tahiti painter (7)

14 Amusingly curious (7)

15 A legal expert (6)

16 Mystery (6)

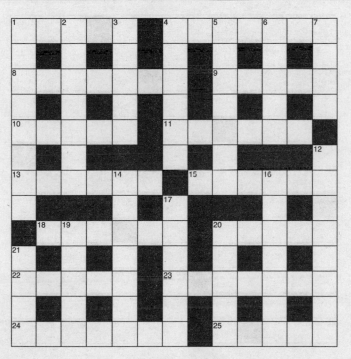

ACROSS

1 Entry recording sum owed (5)
4 Part of Greece; ideal rural country (7)
8 The Waltz King (7)
9 Climb up (5)
10 Be mean with; spell (of work) (5)
11 Annual dog show (6)
13 Strongly encourage (6)
15 Insipid; dry (6)
18 Sick feeling (6)
20 Damaged; penniless (5)
22 (Illicit) love affair (5)
23 The boss *(slang)* (3,4)
24 Be forced back (7)
25 Excavated; seeded with bombs (5)

DOWN

1 Serious misfortune, failure (8)
2 Polish (7)
3 Have confidence in; financial vehicle (5)
4 North-east France region, by Rhine (6)
5 Calculate (7)
6 Intimidate (by difficulty) (5)
7 High male voice (4)
12 Allowed to go free (8)
14 Shyness; spare supply (7)
16 Ideal but impractical (7)
17 Small (often scented) bag (6)
19 Up (e.g. in rigging) (5)
20 Twig broom (5)
21 Just; middling (4)

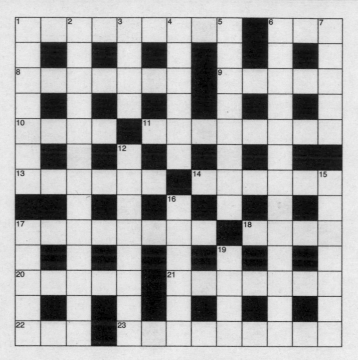

ACROSS

1 Cut short (9)
6 Group of tennis games (3)
8 Authoritatively approve (7)
9 Florida resort (5)
10 "O! for a Muse of –" *(Henry the 17 dn)* (4)
11 Flag; normal (8)
13 Hired assassin *(slang)* (3,3)
14 Robber outlaw (6)
17 Free-form music; Disney 18 *ac* (8)
18 Thin coating layer (4)
20 Hurries; takes a plane (5)
21 Thin flow (7)
22 Ugly old witch (3)
23 Concurrence; 2 *dn* (9)

DOWN

1 See 4 *dn* (7)
2 Intelligence; sympathy (13)
3 Brusquely brief (4)
4 "Come kiss me, sweet and –"(1 *dn Night)* (6)
5 Fiendishly inspired, frantic (8)
6 Amorous activity (4,3,6)
7 See 16 *dn* (5)
12 Asian federation (8)
15 See 19 *dn* (7)
16 "The – of our discontent" *(Richard the 7 dn)* (6)
17 See 10 *ac* (5)
19 "Full fathom –" *(The 15 dn)* (4)

ACROSS

1 *Tempest* magician (8)
7 Listlessness (5)
8 Width between surfaces (9)
9 Expression of disgust (3)
10 Head growth (4)
11 Forcibly apply (6)
13 Hat; car engine cover (6)
14 Having talent (6)
17 Distinct smell; enjoy this (6)
18 Small mountain (4)
20 Capture; cricket practice (3)
22 One successful with women (6,3)
23 Fine, attractive; (especially baby) healthy (5)
24 (Excuse) cease to convince (4,4)

DOWN

1 Small piece, plot (5)
2 Point of view (7)
3 Fish; weapon; (Northern) 18 (4)
4 French coronation city (6)
5 Excessive (5)
6 Seen; able to see (7)
7 Ex-Soviet republic, capital Tallinn (7)
12 With weight (7)
13 Eventually (2,3,2)
15 Great success (7)
16 "Come follow the 13 *ac* of 23 –" *(Scott)* (6)
17 Unfeeling; hard (5)
19 Underclothing (5)
21 Look closely (4)

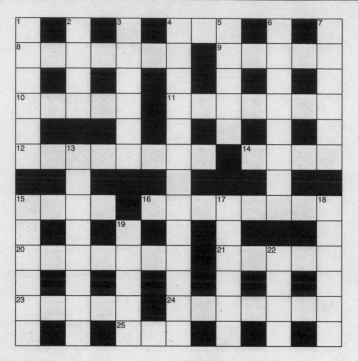

ACROSS

4 Long-life (milk) (1,1,1)
8 Made of baked clay (7)
9 Fight off (attacker) (5)
10 Stratum; a hen (5)
11 Yield easily to (desire) (7)
12 In shy, humble way (8)
14 Floating platform (4)
15 Appearance (4)
16 Naive; several Popes (8)
20 Commit, deliver (7)
21 Method of employment (5)
23 Simple dress; an expedient (5)
24 Bizarre, Dali-esque (7)
25 Word of assent (3)

DOWN

1 Calf-skin parchment (6)
2 A Paris airport (4)
3 Prickles (6)
4 Reluctance (13)
5 Exchange of goods (5)
6 A slopping (ofliquid) (8)
7 Flowing, speaking, easily (6)
13 Spike; *as dead as* it (8)
15 Plague grasshopper (6)
17 Collected works (6)
18 By three times (6)
19 Walter –,Thurber's fantasist (5)
22 Yemen port, once British (4)

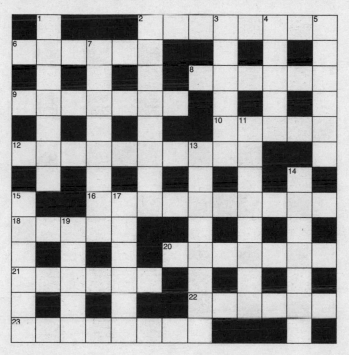

2 Pale yellow-green (3-2-3)

6 Negligent (6)

8 Sacred river; actress/mistress of William IV (6)

9 Contradict (7)

10 Trail dogs follow (5)

12 Seductive (glance) (4-6)

16 Wall anti-moisture layer (4,6)

18 Issue a share (5)

20 Simon –, South American liberator (7)

21 Remove cover (from face, plaque) (6)

22 Corset; sort of scone/cake (6)

23 Go beyond; welfare activism (8)

DOWN

1 Six-sided figure (7)

2 A retreat into fantasy (8)

3 Be half-asleep (6)

4 Poke gently (5)

5 Distance along (6)

7 Sly suggestion (8)

11 Gaming table officiant (8)

13 Diaphragm spasm (8)

14 Attack (7)

15 Enrico –, tenor (died 1921) (6)

17 (Fine) clothes (6)

19 Greenish woollen mixture (5)

ACROSS

1 Macintosh (8)
5 E.g. top-of-pond film (4)
9 Government press-censoring request (1-6)
10 – Keller; – of Troy (5)
11 – Blyton (4)
12 EU food-additive identifier (1,6)
14 New driver's sign (1-5)
16 Part of oyster season (1,5)
19 Batsman's turn (7)
21 June 6, 1944 (1-3)
24 Both *(arch.);* Mark –, author (5)
25 Disease (7)
26 Red gem (4)
27 In adhesive fashion (8)

DOWN

1 Insulting; unpolished (4)
2 New Testament book after II Peter (1,4)
3 Burma resistance fighter (World War 2) (7)
4 Sixth-farmer's exam (1,5)
6 Son of Sycorax *(Tempest)* (7)
7 State with king (8)
8 You *(arch.)* (4)
13 Monastic walk (8)
15 Script Ventris deciphered (6,1)
17 Note between staves (piano score) (6,1)
18 Informal top (1-5)
20 Socially naff (3-1)
22 One from Baku (5)
23 Child's guessing game (1,3)

ACROSS

1 Record; subdue (3,4)
5 Members of scrum (4)
8 Chief conspirator *(Julius Caesar)* (6)
9 Place of bliss (6)
10 Aggressive masculinity (8)
12 Sort of bun, chair, cube (4)
13 Church elder (9)
17 Cheap clearance (4)
18 London station; crushing defeat (8)
20 Forswear (6)
21 Forearm-flexing muscle (6)
23 Hacked out (4)
24 Crusaders' Arab opponent (7)

DOWN

2 Imaginary (6)
3 Speck; Morse signal (3)
4 Aristophanes play; insects (5)
5 Improvise (4,2,3)
6 Bring into existence (6)
7 Selective (6)
11 Lover of Columbine (9)
14 Woodcutter; Twain hero (6)
15 Chatter incoherently (6)
16 Hairpiece (6)
19 Small Indian drum-pair (5)
22 US spy bureau (1,1,1)

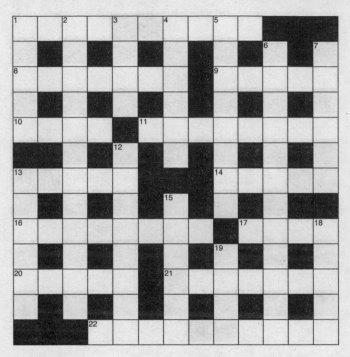

ACROSS

1 Apparent; feigned (10)
8 Very fortunate (7)
9 Cut of pig; brought home by the successful (5)
10 Watery part of clotting milk (4)
11 Lawyers' jargon (8)
13 Art style, especially of ordinary scenes (5)
14 A daisy plant (2-3)
16 Eruption (e.g. of war, disease) (8)
17 South-east Asia country, capital Vientiane (4)
20 A border river; a cloth (5)
21 Element of army division (7)
22 Shiftless type (4-2-4)

DOWN

1 Lake from horseshoe river bend (5)
2 Immediately (5,3,4)
3 Bouquet (of wine) (4)
4 Certainly (6)
5 Type of dog; part of Canada (8)
6 *1001 Nights* storyteller (12)
7 Violent spasm of 3 (6)
12 Resent (8)
13 An increase (6)
15 Curved surface of road (6)
18 Sense associated with 3 (5)
19 Fodder tower; missile hole (4)

ACROSS

1 From Scandinavia (6)
5 Ready for marriage (6)
8 Very keen, desirous (4)
9 Aggressively active (8)
10 Serious, painful (harm, loss) (8)
12 Hoot; make goose sound (4)
13 Offa's kingdom (6)
15 Reach destination (6)
17 Hideous (4)
19 Tempting, alluring (8)
21 Oil-rich water off Britain (5,3)
23 Fruit; a coveted job (4)
24 Taken by thief (6)
25 Stupid talk (6)

DOWN

2 Head-side of coin (7)
3 Move swiftly to avoid (5)
4 Reach maturity (4,2,3)
5 Nothing (3)
6 Meat trader (7)
7 V. I. Ulyanov pseudonym (5)
11 Plastic money, with microchip (5,4)
14 Cut glass; sort of ball, Palace (7)
16 Risky enterprise (7)
18 Tile mortar (5)
20 Bay of Naples island (5)
22 Err morally (3)

ACROSS

1 Little lab vessel (4,4)
5 Discover (4)
8 Party decorations; swells up (8)
9 Fight; nautical pole (4)
11 Usurping military clique (5)
12 Royal household officer (7)
13 Ploy (6)
15 Inelegant helping (of food) (6)
18 Word of identical meaning (7)
19 More than adequate (5)
21 Ceremony (4)
22 Ingenious contrivance (8)
23 Friendly; close to answer (4)
24 Large celebration (8)

DOWN

1 Man-with-hat-shaped mug (4,3)
2 Beauty parlour; art exhibition room (5)
3 Rich/poor gulf *(Disraeli)* (3,7)
4 Golf hazard; underground shelter (6)
6 Put at risk (7)
7 Elizabeth Bennet's match *(Jane Austen)* (5)
10 Dangerously exposed (3,2,1,4)
14 Enormous; deformed thing (7)
16 Go ahead of (7)
17 Mafia code of secrecy (6)
18 Dry stalks; their colour (5)
20 Before; senior monk (5)

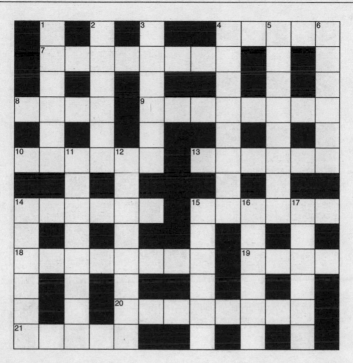

ACROSS

4 Point of fork (5)
7 Twaddle (8)
8 Occur; collapse (4)
9 Glasses without arms (5-3)
10 Loud hooter (6)
13 Engaged man (6)
14 Catcalled (6)
15 Command, requirement *(literary)* (6)
18 Politeness, polite act (8)
19 Space; part of house (4)
20 Discover (technique) again (8)
21 Feudal lord; Belgian city (5)

DOWN

1 Tie up (property); have as consequence (6)
2 Mass arrival (6)
3 Offensive tool (6)
4 Observe (8)
5 Munitions (8)
6 Greedily swallow (e.g. petrol) (6)
11 Sufficient (8)
12 Opera prelude (8)
14 African dog-like scavenger (6)
15 Past; remote places in the back of it (6)
16 Don't stir up its nest (6)
17 Snobbish *(slang)* (6)

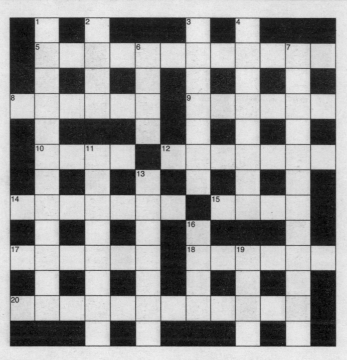

ACROSS

5 Place limits round (12)
8 African country; old coin (6)
9 South American blowpipe poison (6)
10 Player on North's left (4)
12 Schematic drawing (7)
14 A mollusc; a sinister power (7)
15 Assert as untrue (4)
17 Fisherman (6)
18 Association; old distance (6)
20 Tricky quibbling (12)

DOWN

1 Passive agreement (12)
2 Grain husks (4)
3 With e.g. telepathic powers (7)
4 Adjourn (parliament) (8)
6 Salt Lake state (4)
7 Gordon Riots novel *(Dickens)* (7,5)
11 Tobias –, 18th century novelist (8)
13 Go rotten (7)
16 Jam up; footwear (4)
19 Similar, related (4)

ACROSS

1 Drug-affected; (game) slightly off (4)
3 Tending to silence (8)
9 Aromatic flavouring (5)
10 Keep; *dialect (anagram)* (7)
11 Instance; pattern (7)
12 Gloomy darkness (4)
14 Angular unit, app. 57° (6)
16 Have ambition (6)
18 Dispose of (4)
19 Little thorn (7)
22 Colleague, ally (7)
23 Unaccompanied (5)
24 Drama interval; its music (8)
25 Check and correct (text) (4)

DOWN

1 Pub (8)
2 Tolerate what can't be changed (4,3,4,2)
4 Bowman (6)
5 Narrow neck of land (7)
6 Llaregyb play *(Dylan Thomas)* (5,4,4)
7 River of Sudan, Egypt (4)
8 Agency secretary (4)
13 Deeply respectful (8)
15 Site of 1996 Olympics (7)
17 Soul; mood; alcohol (6)
20 Teheran its capital (4)
21 Church recess (4)

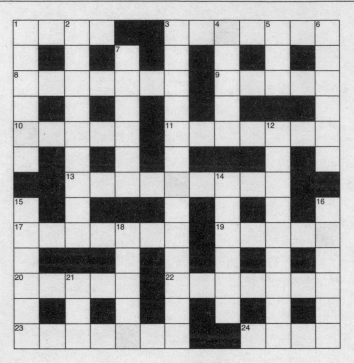

ACROSS

1 Walk through water (4)
3 Played for time (7)
8 Immediate; moment (7)
9 Sequence; command (5)
10 Temptress; aquatic creature (5)
11 Lacking energy, enthusiasm (7)
13 Game; horse-trial site (9)
17 Alas! *(archaic, jocular)* (3,2,2)
19 Assessed (5)
20 Not quite dry (paint) (5)
22 Raging fire (7)
23 Welsh town, castle; *Men of it* (7)
24 Conspiracy; piece of ground (4)

DOWN

1 Caprice; offbeat humour (6)
2 Attractive; worth having (9)
3 TV-reception saucer (9,4)
4 Oak fruit (5)
5 Old money; hallucinogen *(abbr.)* (1,1,1)
6 Mock (6)
7 (Expression) showing distress (6)
12 Artificial (9)
14 List of prices (6)
15 Spasmodic jerk (6)
16 Nimble, quick (6)
18 Distinctive manner (5)
21 Private vehicle (3)

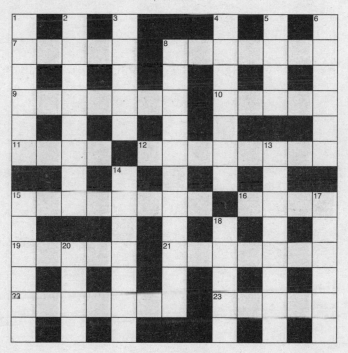

ACROSS

7 Bootleg whiskey (US) (5)
8 Frankness (7)
9 War of the Worlds invader *(Wells)* (7)
10 Compositional idea (5)
11 A mammal; fasten up (4)
12 Intense white lamp (8)
15 Give account of (8)
16 Peruvian Indian (4)
19 Desert waterhole; pop group (5)
21 "Like a – in the sky" *(Carroll)* (3-4)
22 Mounted bullfighter (7)
23 Where Joan of Arc burned (5)

DOWN

1 – Edison, Gainsborough (6)
2 19th century pauper regulations (4,4)
3 Singing group (5)
4 Irregular datum (7)
5 Booty (4)
6 Gain (6)
8 One chipping in (11)
13 Unstinting (8)
14 Study of metre and verse (7)
15 Is limp; sounds like *fruit with stones* (6)
17 Nobody in particular (6)
18 Native New Zealander (5)
20 Footwear item (4)

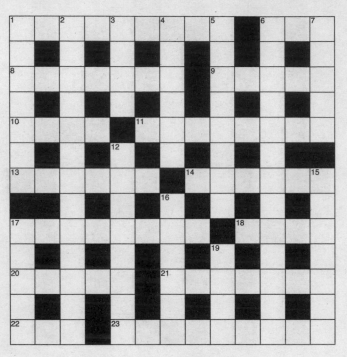

ACROSS

1 Let off (gun, prisoner) (9)
6 Crazy (3)
8 Bracing-point of lever (7)
9 Having come up (5)
10 Back (of neck) (4)
11 Dilemma (8)
13, 14 Speck in Pacific, giant carvings (6,6)
17 Scottish Sabbatarians *(informal)* (3,5)
18 Light-focusing device (4)
20 Suspicious (5)
21 Henry –, English composer (died 1695) (7)
22 Stick; staff of office (3)
23 In over-tolerant fashion (9)

DOWN

1 Self-protection (7)
2 Composed, cool-headed (4-9)
3 Fling (4)
4 Uproar (6)
5 Uncanny state (8)
6 Bad handling (13)
7 Shabby and dirty (5)
12 Treachery (8)
15 To show (7)
16 Make more intense (6)
17 Biscuit with e.g. ice-cream (5)
19 Strongly recommend (4)

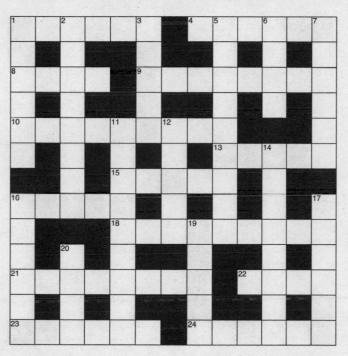

ACROSS

1 Assertion; maxim (6)
4 Self-assurance (6)
8 Glass medicine-holder (4)
9 Suicide (pilot) (8)
10 Purgation of emotions (9)
13 Track down; strap for horse (5)
15 Untrue (5)
16 Be profane; promise (5)
18 Go past (target, destination) (9)
21 Fulfilment (8)
22 Journey; stumble (4)
23 Dwell (6)
24 Obstruct; nearer the back (6)

DOWN

1 Contrivance (6)
2 Severely rebuke, punish (8)
3 Creator (5)
5 Pagan woman officiant (9)
6 By mouth (4)
7 Simple task; light wind (6)
11 Offended, insulted (9)
12 Soothing ointment (5)
14 (Vehicle) fitted with protection (8)
16 Wave-rider (6)
17 Insensible state (6)
19 Cattle-farm (US) (5)
20 Agitation (over trifles) (4)

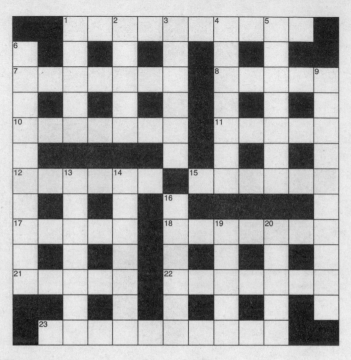

ACROSS

1 Fail to progress (3,7)
7 Viscera (7)
8 Fruit; a disappointment (5)
10 Regal rod (7)
11 Threaded fastener (5)
12 Curly salad plant (6)
15 Humble (oneself) (6)
17 Fire-raising (5)
18 Arthur's, JFK's, court (7)
21 Eagle's nest (5)
22 Scandalous event (7)
23 Five-event athletic contest (10)

DOWN

1 Wish-granting spirit (5)
2 Fortune-telling pack (5)
3 R-month-edible creature (6)
4 Bishopric of Rome (4,3)
5 Regret for wrong (7)
6 *Taming of Shrew* musical (4,2,4)
9 From time to time (3,3,4)
13 Merit, earn (7)
14 – Van Gogh (7)
16 Approach (to confront) (6)
19 Substance as e.g. gold, iron (5)
20 Acquire knowledge (5)

ACROSS

1 Laid with flags (5)
7 Anointing with oil; suave charm (7)
8 St Francis's espoused *Lady* (7)
9 City of oranges, of Barber (7)
11 Runner-up's place (6)
13 Try anyway (4,2,1,2)
15 Wrinkles by eyes (5,4)
19 Animal that gnaws (6)
21 Acrobat's garment (7)
23 Intuitive sympathy (7)
24 Portable rocket-launcher (7)
25 Girls' toys (5)

DOWN

1 Samuel –, diarist (5)
2 Briskly *(music)* (6)
3 Boldness (6)
4 Ropes; London hospital (4)
5 Rigorous (6)
6 Patchwork artform (7)
10 English city, sounds like *one leaving* (6)
12 Disagree (6)
14 A club; a weapon-store (7)
16 Moist-timber disease (3,3)
17 Sluggish, dormant (6)
18 Flinch, start back (6)
20 New Testament book; Roman emperor (5)
22 Haul; a bore (4)

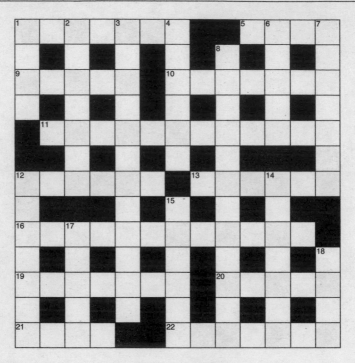

ACROSS

1 Cut, shared (7)
5 Self-righteous moralist (4)
9 Map book (5)
10 Cavalryman; to coerce (7)
11 Demagogue (6-6)
12 Unclear (weather, liquid) (6)
13 Playful enjoyment (6)
16 Unemotional, plain (6-2-4)
19 Nightclub steward (7)
20 Musical drama (5)
21 Flood-containing wall (4)
22 How hope springs *(Pope)* (7)

DOWN

1 Dingy; dull brown (4)
2 Natural eruptor (7)
3 "Of Man's first –," *(Paradise Lost)* (12)
4 Midlands town; Robert –, Elizabeth I's Earl of Leicester (6)
6 Digs with snout; origins (5)
7 Not branded (drug) (7)
8 Unpaid chore (6,2,4)
12 On which to sleep in tent (4,3)
14 Bible stand (7)
15 Musical evening (6)
17 Vehicle; dealings (5)
18 Place of confinement (4)

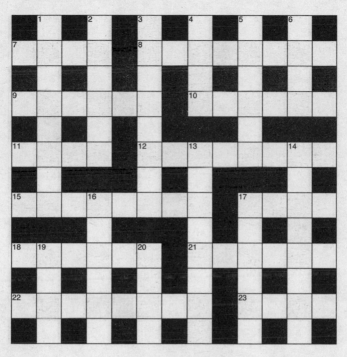

ACROSS

7 An adhesive (4)
8 Of armorial science (8)
9 One on foot (6)
10 (Especially Cornish) fairies (6)
11 Satellite (4)
12 Nietzsche's top person (8)
15 Memento (8)
17 Sin; substitute (4)
18 Unfree persons (6)
21 Mental health (6)
22 Fabled treasure city (2,6)
23 Nipple (4)

DOWN

1 Prohibition-era gangster (2,6)
2 Indicate to approach (6)
3 Personal magnetism (8)
4 Let fall (4)
5 Magical remedy (6)
6 Rasp; dossier (4)
13 Journalists' enclosure (5,3)
14 California prison, had Birdman (8)
16 Conditioned-reflex researcher (6)
17 Conceit; pointlessness (6)
19 Wonderful thing; Berg opera (4)
20 G. B. –, *Man and 12* author (4)

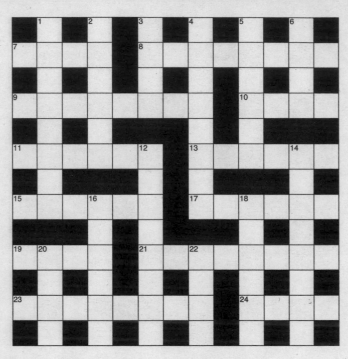

ACROSS

7 Become limp; lose energy (4)
8 Chaotic; lawless (8)
9 Short, serious publication (8)
10 Without sensation (4)
11 Efficacious, forceful (6)
13 Take possession of (6)
15 Longest World War 1 battle, on Meuse (6)
17 Spotted block for game (6)
19 Cot; steal (one's ideas) (4)
21 Majestic; system of measures (8)
23 Determined (8)
24 Unwell (4)

DOWN

1 Oral exam (4,4)
2 Most important; wire fastener (6)
3 Cease to interest (4)
4 Conclusive remark; newest fashion (in) (4,4)
5 Attractive (view) (6)
6 Unyielding (4)
12 Ringing in ears (8)
14 Town of *P. Cezanne (anagram)* (8)
16 One owing money (6)
18 Swampy area (6)
20 Submerged ridge (4)
22 (Remove) rind (4)

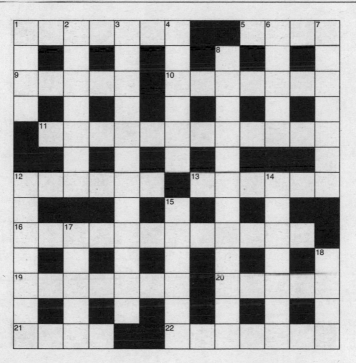

ACROSS

1 Discharge of random bullet (3-4)
5 Repair (4)
9 Nervous agitation (5)
10 Solo ballet dance (3,4)
11 Laudable (12)
12 Thinly scattered (6)
13 Scurrilous (6)
16 Occasionally (4,2,1,5)
19 Pouched-bill bird (7)
20 *Gerontius* composer (5)
21 Dip (e.g. biscuit in tea) (4)
22 Meet (7)

DOWN

1 Breathe hard; light cake (4)
2 Greek restaurant (7)
3 Tendency to group together (4,8)
4 Intermittent-motion part (6)
6 Bring to bear (5)
7 Held up (7)
8 Great surprise (12)
12 Bent, lowered oneself (7)
14 Declares, makes out (7)
15 Riviera resort, has film festival (6)
17 Two-dot mark; part of body (5)
18 Nondescript colour (4)

ACROSS

6 "Cotton-wool" cloud (7)
7 Equipped with weapon (5)
9 An extremist (5)
10 Whole number (7)
11 One of pack of 52 (7,4)
14 Property seller (6,5)
17 Walk awkwardly (7)
19 Puccini's opera-singer heroine (5)
21 Furnishing etc. scheme (5)
22 Rhombus; precious stone (7)

DOWN

1 Soot flake; dirty jokes (4)
2 Agreeable (8)
3 Birthplace of St Francis (6)
4 Stupid, crazy (4)
5 One leaving to settle abroad (8)
6 Weapon; association (4)
8 Tyrolean dress, skirt (6)
11 Italian poet, loved Laura (8)
12 1914-18 world conflict (5,3)
13 Skilled (in); sounds like *Russian distance* (6)
15 Item list for meeting (6)
16 (Celtic) poet (4)
18 Reveal; unadorned (4)
20 Hole for coin (4)

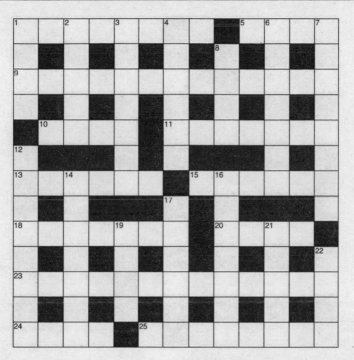

ACROSS

1 Seriousness; avoiding excess (8)
5 Cask-stopper (4)
9 Vegetable plot (7,6)
10 A fish; singe (4)
11 Opponent of (mechanised) progress (7)
13 Louisa May –, US author (6)
15 Subject of Genghis Khan (6)
18 Support (7)
20 Summit (4)
23 Boxing division; triviality (13)
24 Third Gospel (4)
25 Taken to task (8)

DOWN

1 Turbaned Indian (4)
2 Set of e.g. loaves (5)
3 Come into (7)
4 Complicated mess (6)
6 (One's) ruin (7)
7 Tentative (8)
8 Magician's stick (4)
12 Grail-winning knight *(Wagner)* (8)
14 Don warrior (7)
16 Tyrannise over (7)
17 Right of admission; a dish (6)
19 Dull pain (4)
21 Rage (5)
22 Collar fastener (4)

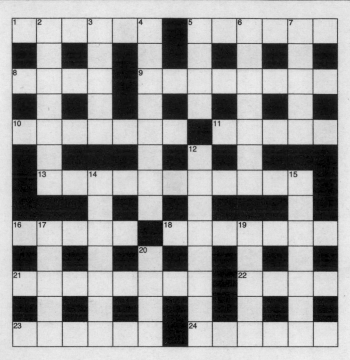

ACROSS

1 Impaled; (news story) scrapped (6)
5 Deprived (6)
8 Chess man; hock (4)
9 Arrangement within set (8)
10 Sarcastic; corrosive (7)
11 Foolish; very close (fielder) (5)
13 (Comic act) flop (3,3,5)
16 School of fish (5)
18 Religious saviour (7)
21 Spring flower; pale yellow (8)
22 Hello there (*nautical*) (4)
23 Area round Dorset (*Hardy*) (6)
24 Be characteristic of (6)

DOWN

2 Printed poster (7)
3 Chess pieces; two books of Bible (5)
4 Aerial combat (8)
5 Inky mess (4)
6 Exact copy (7)
7 Ultimate (5)
12 Supporter, hanger-on (8)
14 Old humanist; *masseur (anagram)* (7)
15 Prevent, intercept/divert (4,3)
17 Mob; sounds like *store* (5)
19 Overwhelm; bog (5)
20 Wheedle (4)

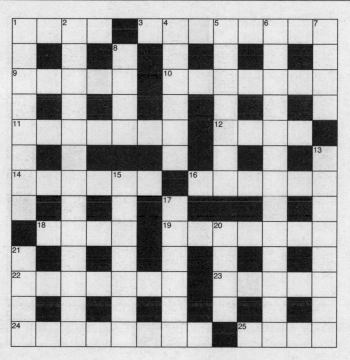

ACROSS

1 Parched; tedious (study) (4)
3 Ludicrous (8)
9 Desert plants (5)
10 Fishing vessel (7)
11 Current-measuring device (7)
12 Implement (4)
14 Unintelligent (6)
16 Seductive appeal (6)
18 Heel over; set of items (4)
19 Not listened to (7)
22 As 8 is of 18 (7)
23 Caribbean *voodoo* island (5)
24 Twilight *(Scottish)* (8)
25 Complacent (4)

DOWN

1 Word not in current use (8)
2 (Held) in solitary (13)
4 Blood-circulating tube (6)
5 Personal possession (7)
6 Word in informal use (13)
7 Traditional wisdom (4)
8 River sediment (4)
13 Selling (small items, drugs) (8)
15 Meantime (7)
17 Armed criminal (6)
20 Sunken boundary (2-2)
21 Group of workmen, criminals (4)

ACROSS

1 Hurl; disconcert (5)
4 Noble lady; *My Last – (Browning)* (7)
8 Light-blue university (9)
9 Anger (3)
10 Seize; a recording sequence (4)
11 Debilitate (8)
13 South American cloak, hole for head (6)
14 Supervisor, (e.g. college) head (6)
17 Free of charge (8)
19 Bunch of bananas (4)
22 Ordinance (3)
23 Law (9)
24 Conjugal (7)
25 Timer; observe (5)

DOWN

1 Unspoken, understood (5)
2 Savoury cheese dish (7)
3 Do a job; perform properly (4)
4 Real tennis gallery; *sanded (anagram)* (6)
5 Road, no stopping allowed (8)
6 – Doolittle *(Pygmalion)* (5)
7 Illicit hooch den (7)
12 Gradually cease to use (5,3)
13 Food for thought (7)
15 Pond-searching equipment; police hunt (7)
16 Of mediaeval society; of quarrel (6)
18 Shrink in fear (5)
20 "Go, and he goeth ... Do this, and he – it" *(Matt. 8)* (5)
21 Be aware of (4)

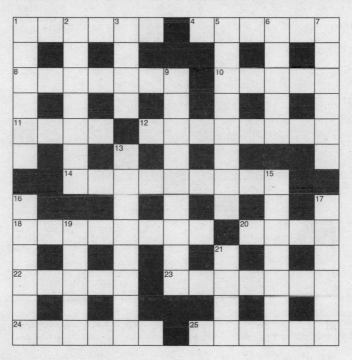

ACROSS

1 Take casual interest (in) (6)
4 Satirise (4,2)
8 Rowdy party (7)
10 Inquiry; search (5)
11 Leap; rubbish-bin (4)
12 Raider (8)
14 Abandoned baby (9)
18 Test (of e.g. actor for job) (8)
20 Cross-dressed panto role (4)
22 Energy; phase of water (5)
23 Citizen army (7)
24 Modest; coy (6)
25 Coloured pencil (6)

DOWN

1 Cease (from) (6)
2 Landowner's steward (7)
3 Simple board game (4)
5 Stress (8)
6 Edwin – *(Dickens)* (5)
7 What "gets lost in translation" *(Frost)* (6)
9 Where soldier may be under arrest (9)
13 Patron (of shop) (8)
15 Frightful; pallid (7)
16 Serried (ranks) (6)
17 Vichy Marshal (6)
19 Night-time fantasy (5)
21 Indistinct view (4)

ACROSS

1 Jug; baseball-player (7)
5 Important person; ski mound (5)
8 Change (5)
9 W. E. Johns' flying hero (7)
10 We shall see eventually (4,4,4)
12 Latin verbal noun; on the back (6)
14 (Sailor) on land (6)
17 Remain imperturbable (3,4,1,4)
21 Yellowstone Park state (7)
22 Feast; children's comic (5)
23 One from Salonika (5)
24 Highest peerage rank (7)

DOWN

1 Rehearse (8)
2 Symbolic animal (5)
3 Got with difficulty (4-3)
4 Rough stone pieces (6)
5 Power (5)
6 Inquisition-victim physicist (7)
7 Luxuriant; alcoholic (4)
11 Valuable piece handed down (8)
13 Cause to happen; annoy (7)
15 South African rhino whip (7)
16 Emotionally cold (6)
18 Use brain; sort of tank (5)
19 (Give) prize (5)
20 Tiny branchlet (4)

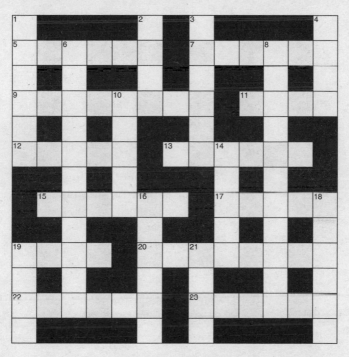

ACROSS

5 Cricket, football, side (6)
7 Incompetent (6)
9 Rebound (bullet) (8)
11 Breathe fast, shallowly (4)
12 Horse dealer (5)
13 Tell off (6)
15 French cafe (6)
17 (Dog) sound menacing (5)
19 Take meal (4)
20 "Nor all, that –, gold" *(Gray)* (8)
22 Of superior quality (2,4)
23 Gateman; type of ale (6)

DOWN

1 Of our new system of measures ... (6)
2 ... short distance in the old (4)
3 Acute; elusive; hard to grasp (6)
4 Dispatched (4)
6 Out of the ordinary (11)
8 German region, has *gateau* (5,6)
10 Jean Baptiste –, landscapist (5)
14 Counterfeit (5)
16 Rue (6)
18 Non-trick-winning cards (6)
19 Caucus-race organiser *(Alice)* (4)
21 Zulu regiment (4)

ACROSS

1 Free, emotional composition (8)
5 Rebounding sound (4)
8 Raised structure; thick sole (8)
9 Upright support post (4)
11 Gangway (5)
12 Financial supporter (7)
13 Of the lips (6)
15 One that vets (6)
18 All-powerful cure (7)
19 Lowest deck (5)
21 Colleague, supporter (4)
22 Unstable (8)
23 (Plane) run along ground (4)
24 A taking apart for examination (8)

DOWN

1 Archangel; Renaissance artist (7)
2 Collect in a heap (5)
3 Toleration; tacit consent (10)
4 Compulsion (6)
6 Frame (of car) (7)
7 Remote from centre (5)
10 Show obedience (4,2,4)
14 Three original EC members (7)
16 Subjugate; banish (thoughts) (7)
17 Heavy gun; billiard stroke (6)
18 Intertwined hair (5)
20 – Pasteur, Armstrong (5)

ACROSS

1 Non-deciduous trees (10)
8 Lamentational (poem) (7)
9 Quickly prepare; incur (3,2)
10 Slender (4)
11 Spanish Jew (8)
13 Church teaching (5)
14 Arrest; treat (new car) gently (3,2)
16 Sherlock Holmes's antagonist (8)
17 Tube; wind instrument (4)
20 Of the nose (5)
21 Roman town, buried by Vesuvius (7)
22 Blowfly; policeman *(slang)* (10)

DOWN

1 Occurrence (5)
2 Formal dinner wear (7,5)
3 Stone particles; courage (4)
4 5 town; type of cake (6)
5 "I am constant as the – star" *(Julius Caesar)* (8)
6 Stubborn (12)
7 Possible choice (6)
12 Following similar course (8)
13 Require, insist on (6)
15 Treeless plain (6)
18 Banish (5)
19 Projectiles for weapons *(abbr.)* (4)

ACROSS

4 Monastic head (5)

7 What those in trouble get into (3,5)

8 Cut into cubes (4)

9 Dismiss as unimportant (5,3)

10 Disrupt (speaker) (6)

13 Container for boiling (6)

14 Importance; brief time (6)

15 Recording-room (6)

18 Give confidence; confirm (8)

19 Fizzy water (4)

20 Anglican afternoon service (8)

21 Passenger ship (5)

DOWN

1 Prosper (6)

2 Thin irregular line; run fast (6)

3 Prolonged trouble *(slang)* (6)

4 Reasoned debate; heated debate (8)

5 Obsessed (8)

6 A sweet; a nothing (6)

11 Coordinated course of action (8)

12 Sir Edwin –, animal painter (8)

14 Tidbit (6)

15 Laurence –, *Tristram Shandy* author (6)

16 Outcome (6)

17 Deep blue colour, dye (6)

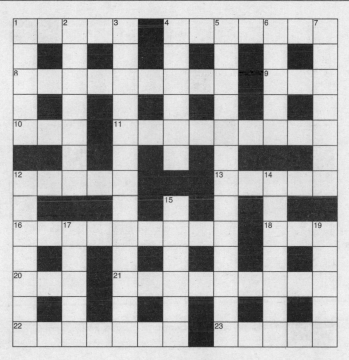

ACROSS

1 Impose (the unwanted on) (5)
4 Waterfall (7)
8 Untouchable (9)
9 Lubricate (3)
10 Hair-preparation; a semi solid (3)
11 An explosive; a Plot (9)
12 Fold, tuck (in garment) (5)
13 Touch of colour (5)
16 Get too big, old for (4,3,2)
18 Synagogue cupboard; place of shelter (3)
20 Boy child (3)
21 Lifeless (9)
22 Performer of operations (7)
23 Precise (5)

DOWN

1 Hurl; dance; love affair (5)
2 Include; implicate (7)
3 *1984* orthodoxy enforcers (*Orwell*) (7,6)
4 Chink (6)
5 Fail to conform (4,3,2,4)
6 Keep away from (5)
7 Make bigger (7)
12 Mythical winged horse (7)
14 US/Canada 4 *ac* (7)
15 Melody; exert severely (6)
17 Possessor (5)
19 Got down (e.g. to pray) (5)

ACROSS

1 Psychological battle (3,2,6)
8 W. H. –, poet (5)
9 Mass slaughter (7)
10 Crease; animal pen (4)
11 Painstaking (8)
13 Fuss; trivial objection (6)
14 Star group, may be spiral (6)
17 Odds-against competitor (8)
19 To spring (4)
22 Pungent gas, NH3 (7)
23 Of the same value (5)
24 A vegetable casserole (11)

DOWN

1 Quay (5)
2 Danger, revolution emblem (3,4)
3 Cravenly avoid (4)
4 Greek geometer (6)
5 Perpendicular (8)
6 Quench (thirst) (5)
7 Priest's robing-room (6)
12 Single-reed instrument (8)
13 Chewy sweet (6)
15 In normal way (2,5)
16 Composer of e.g. 12 Quintet, Concerto (6)
18 Show reluctance (5)
20 Regular rhythmic beat (5)
21 Girl's admirer; dandy (4)

ACROSS

1 Put a number to (8)
5 Knock (toe); portion of ticket (4)
9 Burning (5)
10 Having bad manners (3-4)
11 Drown; succumb (2,5)
12 Sift (5)
13 Really enjoy oneself (4,1,4)
18 Improvised (2,3)
20 (Especially government) income (7)
22 Projecting fortification; defence (7)
23 Instrument; flower (5)
24 Arduous journey (4)
25 Trend; inclination (8)

DOWN

1 Unelected administrative body (6)
2 Horizontal bearing (of e.g. star) (7)
3 Heavy step (5)
4 He married Juliet *(Shakespeare)* (5,8)
6 Curt, brief (5)
7 An animal; to harass (6)
8 Largest US state (6)
14 One suffering accident, crime (6)
15 US president; shade of green (7)
16 Poor batsman; chatter (6)
17 Gift in will (6)
19 Hurry (5)
21 Strongly coloured; graphic (5)

ACROSS

6 (Fight) furiously (5,3,4)
7 A sweet dish; a jolly outing (6)
8 Call into question (6)
9 Informal note (4)
10 Protruding stomach (3,5)
12 Hostile, harmful (8)
16 Flexible pipe (4)
18 Quaker; supporter (6)
20 (E.g. fin) on the back (6)
21 *Man's first disobedience* poem (8,4)

DOWN

1 Avid reader; destructive larva (8)
2 Imprison; be quiet (4,2)
3 Ceremonially oil (6)
4 Break; card game (4)
5 Gaelic hero, has Cave (6)
6 Armistice (5)
11 Outside (8)
13 Fortinbras its Prince *(Hamlet)* (6)
14 Golfer's assistant (6)
15 Climbing frame (6)
17 Shock of explosion (5)
19 Formal test (4)

ACROSS

2 Ruskin-libelled painter (8)
6 Savoury tart (6)
8 Thick, muddy (liquid) (6)
9 London cathedral (2,5)
10 South American mammal (5)
12 Weird pattern in wheat (4,6)
16 (Army) non-officers (5,5)
18 Large type of steak (1-4)
20 Easily influenced, altered (7)
21 Thundercloud; saintly aura (6)
22 Element I, its tincture an antiseptic (6)
23 Alchemical; tightly sealed (8)

DOWN

1 Breach; sever (7)
2 Very nearly (4-4)
3 Violent gust; scream (6)
4 Land to Egypt's west (5)
5 Spreading from centre (6)
7 Tournament winner (8)
11 Public money for defendants (5,3)
13 Russian (alphabet) (8)
14 Horizon; buildings seen against it (7)
15 Appalling smell (6)
17 Right to keep job (6)
19 A mollusc, the sea-ear (5)

ACROSS

1 Exchange; some false hair (6)
5 Gulp (4)
9 Swathe (7)
10 Stockholm its capital (6)
11 Emphatic, vigorous (8)
12 Landsman *(derog.)* (6)
15 Adjective modifier (6)
18 Pre-retirement performance (4,4)
20 *Way down upon* this river (S. C. *Foster)* (6)
22 Coarsely behaved (7)
23 Dominion; totter (4)
24 Flights of bees (6)

DOWN

2 Cricket annual (6)
3 Get across (8)
4 Barrier; protect risk (5)
6 Diminish (light, power) (4)
7 Mourn (6)
8 Grinding tool (6)
13 Cabbage, turnip etc. plant (8)
14 Preoccupy (6)
16 Prospects for water (6)
17 Motet (6)
19 Awry (5)
21 Exploding star (4)

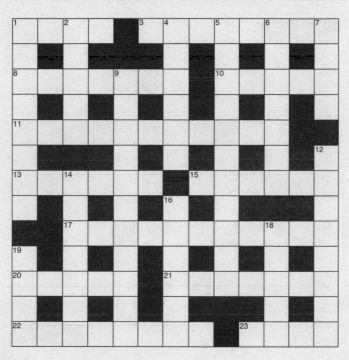

ACROSS

1 Pond plant; run to attack (4)
3 Contiguous (8)
8 Soft roll (7)
10 Something to write on, to sleep on (5)
11 Its grin stayed longest (*Carroll*) (8,3)
13 Kind; science journal (6)
15 Uncivilised; fierce (6)
17 Polite, obliging (11)
20 One from outer space (5)
21 (View) that can be held (7)
22 – Swinburne; _ Moncrieff (*Wilde –
  Importance*) (8)
23 Leave out (4)

DOWN

1 Ruddy (8)
2 Work slackly (*slang*) (5)
4 Depressingly dull (6)
5 Club; friendship (11)
6 Daughter of Agamemnon (7)
7 Ballet skirt (4)
9 *Moonlight Sonata* key (1,5,5)
12 Having perceptions (8)
14 Mattress fabric; making clock noise
  (7)
16 Very drunk (*slang*) (6)
18 Cuttings book (5)
19 Icelandic family story (4)

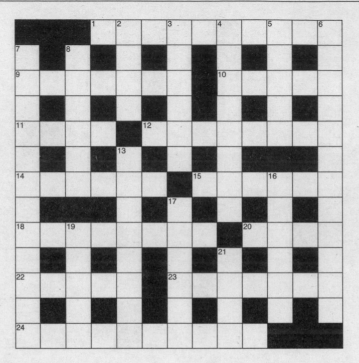

ACROSS

1 Narrow squeak (5,5)
9 Generally; a garment (7)
10 Up, on map (5)
11 Unit of molecule (4)
12 In no way; don't mention it (3,2,3)
14 Conspiracy of producers (6)
15 Brief rainfall; demonstrator? (6)
18 Of Iberian origin (8)
20 Small clue (4)
22 Go; permission (5)
23 Bird; game of dare (7)
24 (Drug) withdrawal symptoms (4,6)

DOWN

2 Accidental escape (4)
3 Not often (6)
4 Bask in natural rays (8)
5 Principal artery (5)
6 Raising the spirits (12)
7 Soft (drink) (3-9)
8 Greedily swallow (6)
13 Showing cultural decline (8)
16 Scotch (but not Irish) (6)
17 (Military) surrounding (movement) (6)
19 Little (5)
21 Contemptible, cheap (4)

ACROSS

1 Idle chat (6)
5 Male deer; try to throw rider (4)
8 Boggy ground (4)
9 Departing from norm (8)
10 Roy Plomley interviewee once (8)
11 Baghdad its capital (4)
12 One out of place (6)
14 Catalyst protein in cell (6)
16 Dressed (in) (4)
18 Unwhipped division (4,4)
20 Stephane –, French symbolist (8)
21 Orchestra; ring (4)
22 Norse thunder god (4)
23 Wiping cloth (6)

DOWN

2 Japanese paper-folding (7)
3 Old wheat; made (a word) (5)
4 Take dangerous risks (4,4,4)
5 Hector –, French composer (7)
6 Long-line dance (5)
7 Title of Dean (4,8)
13 Violinist; type of crab (7)
15 Afternoon performance (7)
17 Dog lead (5)
19 Atmosphere, feelings (*slang abbr.*) (5)

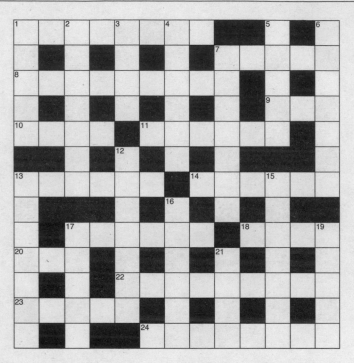

ACROSS

1 Confirm by ticking list (5,3)
7 Cattily belittling (5)
8 Manage in unplanned way (9)
9 Record; block of wood (3)
10 Ship's base structure (4)
11 Fruit; – –ripe *(Herrick)* (6)
13 Nurse; nun (6)
14 Parchment curled up (6)
17 A 4; sounds like *gazes* (6)
18 (Clouds) move swiftly (4)
20 Vehicle; the front (3)
22 Hearten (9)
23 Gnash; wear down (5)
24 Inner and Outer Scottish islands (8)

DOWN

1 Fissure; weakness, in armour (5)
2 Put into words (7)
3 Round handle (4)
4 Air journey (6)
5 Oz kettle; may be Silly, Puffing (5)
6 Shore bird (7)
7 Stealth, concealment (7)
12 Transmitted along (7)
13 Rescue (from shipwreck) (7)
15 Field of fruit (7)
16 Obscure prophecy (6)
17 Proverbially slow creature (5)
19 Clothing; align (5)
21 German industry area, river (4)

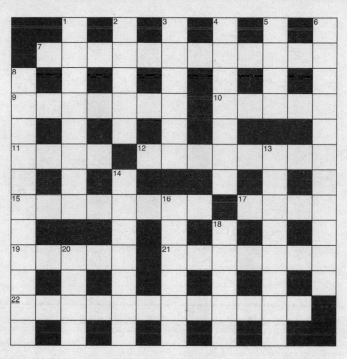

ACROSS

7 The –, Peachum/ Macheath piece *(Gay)* (7,5)

9 Minor illness (7)

10 Hard-skin fruit; has *bottle* variety (5)

11 Vigorous stylishness (4)

12 Rotation (8)

15 Taking no notice (8)

17 Fake; a pudding (4)

19 Manservant, steward (5)

21 French pilgrimage town (7)

22 -,wear it! (2,3,3,4)

DOWN

1 Give-away (4-4)

2 As best laid schemes aft gang *(Burns)* (5)

3 To some extent; attractive (6)

4 Jell; start to set (7)

5 Home of Incas, Paddington Bear (4)

6 Inflexible (rule) (4-3-4)

8 Become a nun (4,3,4)

13 Overwhelm with water (8)

14 Be nervous; a bet (7)

16 Deep bow (6)

18 Prominent up-brushed tuft (5)

20 One from Riga (4)

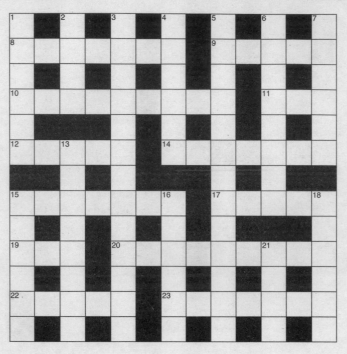

ACROSS

8 Fish exhibitions (7)
9 English county; Devereux earldom (5)
10 Murderer; a razor (9)
11 Son-in-law of the Prophet (3)
12 Involuntary, convulsive, movement (5)
14 Foot lever (7)
15 Astronomical calendar (7)
17 Trial panellist (5)
19 Trick; study (3)
20 Unwilling (9)
22 Inserted map, page; teacher training day (5)
23 Frozen block in drink (3,4)

DOWN

1 Faction; sort of race *(Alice)* (6)
2 Upset, wound (4)
3 Greek abbot; *radiance, mirth (anagram)* (13)
4 A seasoned stew (6)
5 Biker's accessory (7,6); fish, larva (13)
6 One from e.g. Man (8)
7 Cease to be valid (6)
13 Rebuke (8)
15 North polar region (6)
16 Town *lying in* Mary I's *heart* (6)
18 For preference (6)
21 Shivering fit (4)

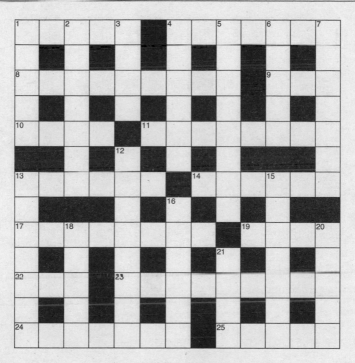

ACROSS

1 Odyssey author (5)
4 Ulysses – Grant; Wallis – (7)
8 Decorations (9)
9 Tea-brewing vessel (3)
10 Consume by fire (4)
11 Have one leg either side of (8)
13 Comfort in distress (6)
14 Tough outside (as bread) (6)
17 Seaweed gelatin (4-4)
19 Soothing ointment (4)
22 First note of scale; sounds like *flour/water* (3)
23 Janitor; interim (office holder) (9)
24 Rich (7)
25 A rustic; Dr. Johnson's cat (5)

DOWN

1 Thermonuclear weapon (1-4)
2 Uncertain-parentage dog (7)
3 Play boisterously (4)
4 Upper House (6)
5 Slaughter (8)
6 Measure (sea) depth; valid (5)
7 Convent (7)
12 Short-tempered; poor-quality (LP) (8)
13 Fame, as entertainer (7)
15 Piled neatly (7)
16 Loathing (6)
18 Very pale (shocked face) (5)
20 Verge *(poet.);* butter substitute (5)
21 Restless desire (4)

ACROSS

1 River-race festival (7)
5 Theme (5)
8 Keep firm hold of (5)
9 Well behaved; 5 *dn* (7)
10 One from the capital (8)
11 Spurn (lover) (4)
13 Police etc. entry authority (6,7)
16 Peak; horn of moon (4)
17 Asphyxiate (8)
20 Restrict, imprison (7)
21 Public, open (5)
22 Ghana capital (5)
23 Relaxation of tension (7)

DOWN

1 Punic War general; Leo star (7)
2 Particle of sand (5)
3 First-rate (3-5)
4 With all ideas exhausted (2,4,4,3)
5 Neat (4)
6 "Lost" girl *(Winter Tale)* (7)
7 Room under church (5)
12 Erupt; escape (prison) (5,3)
14 A poison; *can rise (anagram)* (7)
15 Playhouse (7)
16 (Often at bedtime) drink (5)
18 Gather (odd bits) (5)
19 Travel permit (4)

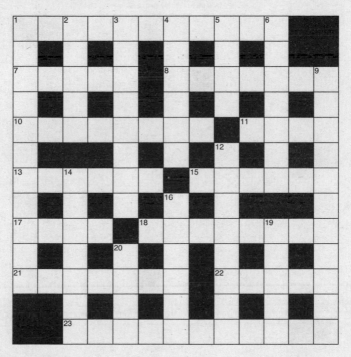

ACROSS

1 French 16th century astrologer, prophet (11)
7 Stoppers; advertisements (5)
8 Not deep (7)
10 Aristocrats (8)
11 Motion-transmitting mechanism (4)
13 Physical well-being (6)
15 Praying insect (6)
17 Bundle of e.g. straw (4)
18 Plain (especially cloth) (8)
21 Beloved (7)
22 Steam bath (5)
23 Fish, shocks prey (8,3)

DOWN

1 Prevent in early stages (3,2,3,3)
2 A firework; lampoon (5)
3 Family including Dante, Christina (8)
4 Scatter, banish (6)
5 Honey wine; lea (4)
6 Conspicuous; jutting defensive line (7)
9 Despite any imperfections (5,3,3)
12 Glide behind motorboat (5-3)
14 Uncaptured (2,5)
16 Fail to remember (6)
19 One excessively modest (5)
20 Go on long walk (4)

ACROSS

1 Neat keyboarded copies (11)
8 Sordid (5)
9 Lazarus's home town (7)
10 And the rest *(Latin, abbr.)* (2,2)
11 Rural labourer (8)
13 Tree, provides mace (6)
14 Fights with lances (6)
17 Cambridge mathematician once (8)
19 A fish; a singer (4)
22 Language-learner's book (7)
23 Sound (bell); be consistent (5)
24 March girls book *(Alcott)* (6,5)

DOWN

1 A sense; a small sample (5)
2 Behave insincerely (4-3)
3 A bean, makes meat substitute (4)
4 Walter Scott novel (3,3)
5 An (alcoholic) drink *(literary)* (8)
6 Informal expressions (5)
7 Greektrurkish island (6)
12 A pear; a citrus, gives perfume (8)
13 Post-Christian "religion" (3,3)
15 Sports ground (7)
16 Sea bird, sounds like *fuel* (6)
18 Be of use (5)
20 Surface lustre (5)
21 Barge; (US) yacht (4)

ACROSS

1 Disorientation after flight (3,3)
5 Gesturing; curving (6)
8 Tartan skirt (4)
9 "The – of America is –" *(Coolidge)* (8)
10 Lay up (for disuse) (8)
12 Underworld river (4)
13 Fanatic (6)
15 High point of heavens (6)
17 Panel game (4)
19 Refutation (8)
21 Nagging old woman (8)
23 Jacob stole his birthright (4)
24 An island; a pullover (6)
25 Asphyxiate; suppress (6)

DOWN

2 One programme of series (7)
3 Door fastener (5)
4 The Rock (9)
5 Used to be; looked *(reversed)* (3)
6 Deer meat (7)
7 Unpleasant (5)
11 Idle person (9)
14 Beggar Dives spurned; one resurrected (7)
16 Hard labour (7)
18 Tsarist edict (5)
20 Rome coin-throwing fountain (5)
22 Barren; tedious (3)

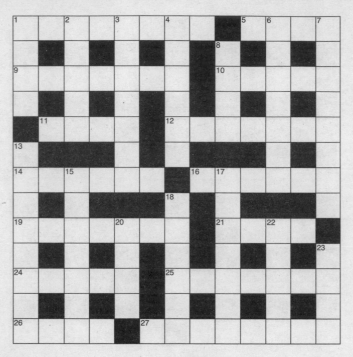

ACROSS

1 Exhibition tent; summerhouse (8)
5 Mammals; crazy (4)
9 Throw away (7)
10 Prisoner restraints; domestic appliances (5)
11 Surety for prisoner (4)
12 Not exceptional (7)
14 Catch fire (6)
16 (Supply) be exhausted (3,3)
19 Tiredness (7)
21 Grand dance (4)
24 Felled tree remains (5)
25 Sewer's finger guard (7)
26 Twisted fibres; set of e.g. pearls (4)
27 Limit, edge (8)

DOWN

1 Absorbent felt pieces; walks quietly (4)
2 Prospect, e.g. down avenue (5)
3 Publicity sheet (7)
4 Severe trial (6)
6 Dull green; a "pear" (7)
7 Has an idea; possible criminals (8)
8 Extensive (4)
13 Anti-glare light fitting (8)
15 All-suits-equal (contract) (2,5)
17 Central Italian; school of Raphael (7)
18 Type of penguin; *got one? (anagram)* (6)
20 Stare with mouth open (4)
22 Astrological sign, September/October (5)
23 Depend (on) (4)

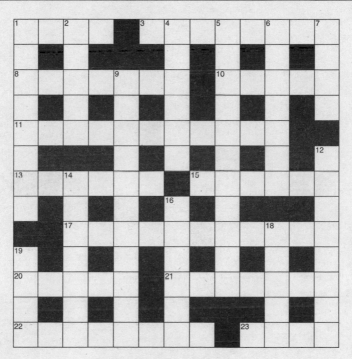

ACROSS

1 Draw off lees; driven cloud (4)
3 Carvings collectively (8)
8 One from Lhasa (7)
10 Police rank *(abbr.); jolly* good (5)
11 Occurring together (11)
13 1645 Parliament victory (6)
15 Cleave (to) (6)
17 Hardly any *(colloq.)* (8,3)
20 Ladle; unrivalled news story (5)
21 Less cloudy (7)
22 Ghostlike (8)
23 Walk slowly, painfully (4)

DOWN

1 Taciturn (8)
2 Wooden house; crew room (5)
4 Lawn game (6)
5 Sleep fitfully (4,3,4)
6 One with limb removed (7)
7 Mongolian tent (4)
9 Regularly-afflicted place (7,4)
12 America (3,5)
14 Imagine, assume (7)
16 Noxious vapour (6)
18 Ornamental strip; ruff (5)
19 In its existing state (2,2)

ACROSS

1 Exhausted (4,4); useless person (8)
5 Without strength (4)
9 Out of order, ruined (5)
10 Screw up; collapse (7)
11 Word formed of initials (7)
12 (Sudden) swelling (5)
13 Unwanted scraps (9)
18 Jumped (5)
20 Cattle disease, may infect man (7)
22 Victoria Falls river (7)
23 Green snooker fabric (5)
24 Magical (Nordic) character (4)
25 Ignored (8)

DOWN

1 Decree imposed (6)
2 Clothing *(archaic)* (7)
3 Relay runners' stick (5)
4 Housing; settlement (13)
6 Drive out (5)
7 Zoo, museum, worker (6)
8 Soap-film ball; risky investment (6)
14 In better condition; gasman (6)
15 Close-pressed (ranks) (7)
16 (School, club) jacket (6)
17 Lengthen (6)
19 Capital of Jordan (5)
21 Item of furniture; list of data (5)

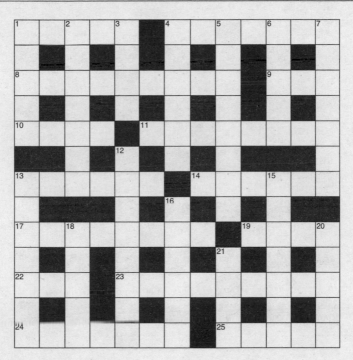

ACROSS

1 "'*Twas the* – ..." (5)
4 Generous (supply) (7)
8 "... *before* –,*when* ..." (9)
9 A meal; a drink (3)
10 Way out (4)
11 Rebel aboard (8)
13 Fighting team (originally Roman) (6)
14 (Horse) in the first three (6)
17 Fellow-feeling (8)
19 Solid; tricky (4)
22 Note of debt (1,1,1)
23 Indifference (9)
24 Minotaur killer (7)
25 "... *all through the* – ..." (5)

DOWN

1 Mother-of-pearl (5)
2 Decorate (food) (7)
3 Duty (4)
4 University site (6)
5 Feasible (8)
6 Eccentric, improper (5)
7 Shadow-boxed; argued (7)
12 "... *not a* – *was stirring,* ..." (8)
13 Sophist (7)
15 French country house (7)
16 Shells (peas); oh dear! (US) (6)
18 "... *not even a* –" (C. C. *Moore*) (5)
20 Slow learner (5)
21 Egyptian looped cross (4)

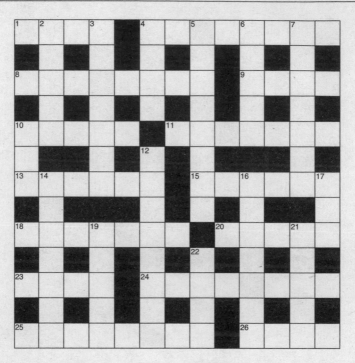

ACROSS

1 South American "ostrich" (4)
4 Analysis of poetic metre (8)
8 Earn degree (8)
9 Widespread (4)
10 Ignominy (5)
11 Post from admirers (3,4)
13 Jump (on prey) (6)
15 One avoiding; Dickens's was *Artful* (6)
18 Substantial, important (7)
20 Love feast; open mouthed (5)
23 Work for, group of, three (4)
24 Of music theatre (8)
25 Public computer link (8)
26 Hastened (4)

DOWN

2 Severe (5)
3 Insect's rear section (7)
4 Skin mark; craggy outcrop (4)
5 William IV's queen (8)
6 Blood fluid (5)
7 In illegal position (football) (7)
10 Tiny taste of liquid (3)
12 Disastrous failure, especially nuclear (8)
14 Swamp; hurry too far (7)
16 Hot, inactive period (3,4)
17 Part of fish; type of deer (3)
19 Small wood; music dictionary (5)
21 Winner's reward (5)
22 Immediately following (4)

ACROSS

6 Lady's private room (7)
7 Alternative name (5)
9 Place for books, old maids (5)
10 Multi-clawed anchor (7)
11 (Living) rurally remote (2,3,6)
14 In cahoots (4,2,5)
17 Huge (7)
19 Tradesman; Sherlock Holmes's street (5)
21 Nairobi its capital (5)
22 Harmony (7)

DOWN

1 Stratagem (4)
2 Bits thrown at happy couple (8)
3 Shoe; accent (6)
4 Maori, All-Black war dance (4)
5 Highest point; e.g. spire on tower (8)
6 Part-statue; broken (4)
8 Send water over (6)
11 State of shame (8)
12 Instrument, has slide (8)
13 Cower; psychiatrist (*colloq.*) (6)
15 "The glory that was –" (*Poe*) (6)
16 Lattice (4)
18 Close; mean (4)
20 John –, Presbyterian founder; sounds like *raps* (4)

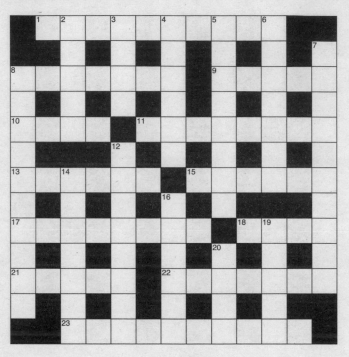

ACROSS

1 *Three Bears* girl (10)
8 Most important; a US election (7)
9 Doctor-repelling fruit (5)
10 Unspeaking (4)
11 Most soon (8)
13 Drink in (6)
15 Passionate enthusiasm (6)
17 Tangential (8)
18 (In) place (of) (4)
21 More advanced in years (5)
22 Lord High Everything Else *(Mikado)* (4-3)
23 Seized (goods for debt) (10)

DOWN

2 Drug; China wars over it (5)
3 Bargain; wood (4)
4 Non-expert (6)
5 Slow movers; obsequious people (8)
6 Overlord (7)
7 Transparent (3-7)
8 London terminus (10)
12 Covers, hides (8)
14 Having facial hair (7)
16 Gunman in ambush (6)
19 Inspire; permeate (5)
20 Hindu meditator (4)

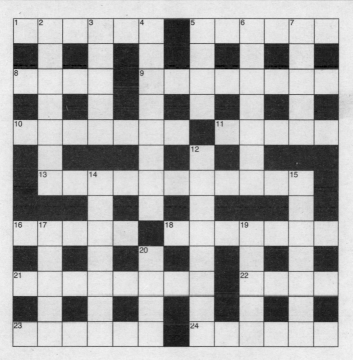

ACROSS

1 Plumber's ringlet (6)
5 Little case on neck-chain (6)
8 High (meat) (4)
9 (Scottish) smallholders (8)
10 Mass-for-one's-soul chapel (7)
11 Agitate (especially milk) (5)
13 Stained, tarnished (11)
16 Kills (fly) (5)
18 Busy (2,3,2)
21 Hint; close (8)
22 Fruit; appointment (4)
23 Andy –, US pop artist (6)
24 Plural of Mr (6)

DOWN

2 Embarrassed (7)
3 He composed 104 symphonies (5)
4 Black v white disturbance (4,4)
5 Crossed-curve figure (4)
6 Baseball fielder; – in the Rye, *Salinger* (7)
7 Mistake (5)
12 Shaft of satellite light (8)
14 Too fond of drink (7)
15 Sirius (3,4)
17 Girl's name; sounds like *roam* (5)
19 Classical underworld (5)
20 Bird; train track (4)

ACROSS

1 Latin, Greek (civilisation) (9)
6 Kanga's child *(Pooh)* (3)
8 Enormous; it sank (7)
9 Cultivated soil (5)
10 Trim, peel (4)
11 Shocking; unpleasant (8)
13 Borne on breeze (6)
14 Moral philosophy (6)
17 Uphill stone-roller (Greek myth) (8)
18 Epiphany visitors (4)
20 Bring into coordinated order (5)
21 Smiled widely, nastily (7)
22 Enclosure; mate of cob (3)
23 Finally result (in) (9)

DOWN

1 A dupe; breeze on water (4-3)
2 Roughly speaking (5,1,7)
3 George –, Chopin's lover (4)
4 Bird (in wrong nest) (6)
5 Able to read and write (8)
6 Arne patriotic song (4,9)
7 Brownish-yellow earth (5)
12 Answer (8)
15 Rod holding e.g. bobbin (7)
16 Blunder (6)
17 Top of head; trophy (5)
19 Closed hand (4)

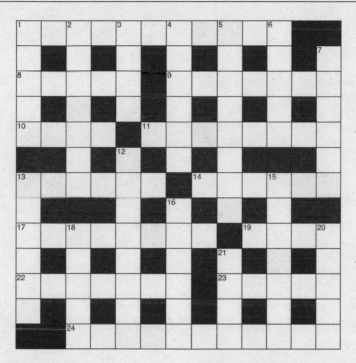

ACROSS

1 (Body) taken apart (11)
8 High-pitched alarm sound (5)
9 Mogadishu its capital (7)
10 Four legs were (*Animal Farm*) (4)
11 Flute, oboe, etc. (8)
13 (Wood) jointed; wearing 4's hat (6)
14 Tooth decay (6)
17 One-sided; resistance fighter (8)
19 Depressed; grassland (4)
22 Dishevelled (7)
23 Edible bulb; Russian dome (5)
24 In mad(ly happy) way (11)

DOWN

1 Remove trousers (as joke) (5)
2 Walk faster (4,3)
3 Catch sight of (4)
4 Diagonal-path piece (6)
5 Curative (8)
6 Indian city; sounds like *cooked meat shop* (5)
7 Doctor Who time machine (6)
12 Mild epilepsy (5,3)
13 Clears away (spillage, last resisters) (4,2)
15 Tusks; piano keys (*slang*) (7)
16 Lose momentum (6)
18 On slope; smoothed (5)
20 French city; sailor's girl (5)
21 Performance by one person (4)

ACROSS

1 Fissure, chink (4)
3 One rejected (7)
8 In attendance; this moment (7)
9 Let in; confess (5)
10 Ladies' garment (5)
11 Lift up (7)
13 Of old age, the old (9)
17 Ribboned post, danced round (7)
19 Having tendency (to) (5)
20 Corner; old tribesman (5)
22 Shamefully secretive (7)
23 Competitor (7)
24 Strengthened seam; leather strip on shoe (4)

DOWN

1 State of rest (6)
2 With emotion (9)
3 Superficially (2,3,4,2,2)
4 Poke gentle fun at (5)
5 Purpose (3)
6 (Animal's) rope (6)
7 Improved; punter (6)
12 Hermit (9)
14 Bang; written account (6)
15 To skewer (6)
16 Throw back (6)
18 Last Greek letter (5)
21 Obtain (3)

ACROSS

1 Measure of air moisture (8)
5 Long, heroic poem (4)
9 Darling girl *(Peter Pan)* (5)
10 Singing to backing tape (pub) (7)
11 Distinguished (7)
12 Bottomless pit (5)
13 Unlike (9)
18 Projecting roof edge (5)
20 Milan opera house (2,5)
22 Speak briefly of (7)
23 Experienced, skilful (5)
24 Bonds; neckwear (4)
25 Improvident (8)

DOWN

1 Nautical cable (6)
2 People as a whole (7)
3 Sir Arthur Conan – (5)
4 Commit oneself (to risk) (4,3,6)
6 A delegated vote (5)
7 A food; very 13 from chalk (6)
8 Suave (6)
14 Relic (of long-ago animal) (6)
15 Acrobat's swinging bar (7)
16 Allow; entry document (6)
17 Aniseed aperitif (6)
19 Meeting-place (5)
21 Slap; fishing boat (5)

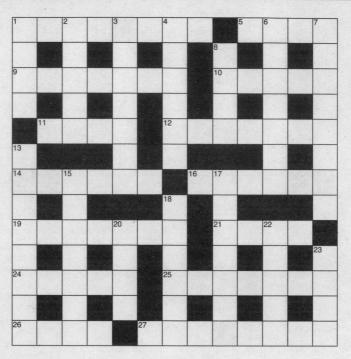

1 Queer, strange (8)

5 Quit; halt (4)

9 Quake, shiver (7)

10 Quid note (5)

11 Quiz, examination (4)

12 Quips; sudden charges (7)

14 Quid pro quo (6)

16 Qualification, proviso (6)

19 Quota, share (7)

21 Quieten (4)

24 Quick (5)

25 Quisling (7)

26 Queue (4)

27 Quarter, mercy (8)

DOWN

1 Play across green (4)

2 El Greco birthplace (5)

3 Crustacean, had Quadrille (7)

4 Opposed, lath (6)

6 Of the sense of touch (7)

7 One living off another (8)

8 Prevent; stooge (4)

13 Suggestion, plan (8)

15 Act of twisting; state of being twisted (7)

17 Warm public praise (7)

18 Gradually introduce (idea) (6)

20 Tiny bit; Greek *I* (4)

22 Language of Horace (5)

23 Quarry (4)

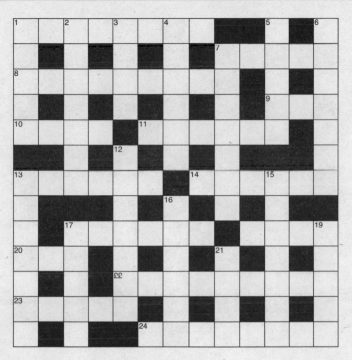

ACROSS

1 Mouth cosmetic (8)
7 Previous; a religious (5)
8 A butterfly; sulphur (once) (9)
9 Meadow (3)
10 Went; socialist (4)
11 Boy's name; was wicked *(reversed)* (6)
13 SI temperature unit (6)
14 Renter of property (6)
17 Ceramic worker; vaguely fill time (6)
18 Comfily ensconced (4)
20 Hatchet (3)
22 Investigator (9)
23 Varlet; jack (5)
24 (Girl) receiving patronage (8)

DOWN

1 Defamatory publication (5)
2 Agonising (7)
3 Assigned job (4)
4 Anger; sounds like *part of jacket* (6)
5 Housman's were *blue remembered* (5)
6 Syrup; cloying flattery (7)
7 Small coins (7)
12 Turbulent current (7)
13 In pub, 15 to tape (7)
15 Art of the voice (7)
16 Trusted (older) adviser (6)
17 Part of flower; "now sleeps the crimson –" *(Tennyson)* (5)
19 Incumbent's plot of land (5)
21 North Briton (4)

ACROSS

1 Frank, honest (6)

5 Piecing-together puzzle (6)

8 Door-frame side (4)

9 Horse-equipment business (8)

10 Climbing-plant frame (7)

11 Insipid (5)

13 Disturb (settled situation) (4,3,4)

16 Chuck; supporting strap (5)

18 Dim; puzzling (7)

21 Wrist ornament (8)

22 Useless; conceited (4)

23 Charlie –, *Lord Jim* narrator *(Conrad)* (6)

24 Jacob –, Scrooge's partner *(Dickens)* (6)

DOWN

2 Non-professional (7)

3 Fix (computer program) (5)

4 Uninhabited; friendless (8)

5 New Testament epistle; – the 18, *Hardy* (4)

6 Italian astronomer, Inquisition victim (7)

7 Brother of Moses (5)

12 Word for word (8)

14 Sneering; suspecting worst motives (7)

15 Coarse pate (7)

17 Immature insect form (5)

19 Protect; deal with (5)

20 Bird's nail (4)

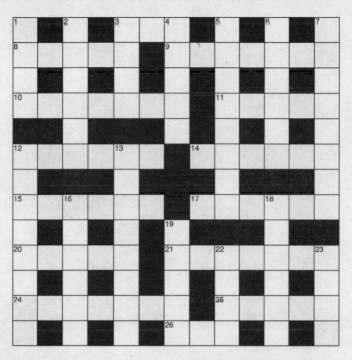

ACROSS

3 Enormous bird *(Sinbad)* (3)
8 Jewelled headdress (5)
9 Stir up, make anxious (7)
10 Loss of wits (7)
11 Increased (5)
12 Capital of Germany (6)
14 Lowest parts (of e.g. sea) (6)
15 Cite (as example) (6)
17 Parentless child (6)
20 Jeans cloth (5)
21 Got thinner towards end (7)
24 Academic class (7)
25 Forearm joint (5)
26 Act as crew of (3)

DOWN

1 Restrain; word root (4)
2 Be indulgent, accommodating (to weakness) (6)
3 Speed contest; rapid current (4)
4 Motive; lawsuit (5)
5 Shakespearian tragedy (4,4)
6 Go to restaurant; etch (3,3)
7 *Idylls of the King* poet (8)
12 Wave threateningly (8)
13 Arriving; new (e.g. government) (8)
16 Generator; energetic person (6)
18 Helena's rival *(MND)* (6)
19 Tempest (5)
22 Chessman; dupe (4)
23 Responsibility; tax (4)

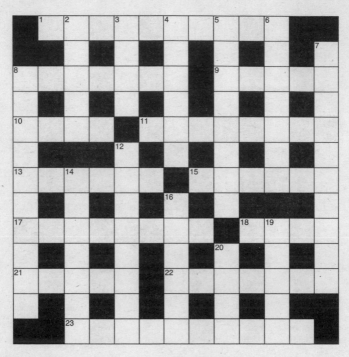

ACROSS

1 Put into other words (10)
8 Staying power (7)
9 Freight boat; shove (in) (5)
10 Cooker (4)
11 More powerful (8)
13 Utter snarl-up (6)
15 Start (fire) (6)
17 Tiny sea organisms (8)
18 Oh dear! (4)
21 Wagner *Ring* river (5)
22 Rumour (7)
23 Fine writing; sales brochures (10)

DOWN

2 Astound (5)
3 Surrounded by (4)
4 Warm, friendly; big (meal) (6)
5 Food of the gods (8)
6 Made very angry (7)
7 With bold courage (10)
8 Wet blanket (10)
12 Unfair charge by landlord (4-4)
14 Icy (7)
16 Ritually eatable *(Jewish)* (6)
19 CD-reading beam (5)
20 Excrescence, may be charmed away (4)

ACROSS

1 Uneasy feeling (7)
5 At this place (4)
8 Officer's servant (6)
9 Prolong (6)
10 An order to attend court (8)
12 Secluded corner (4)
13 *Gondoliers* Duke (5,4)
17 Dismiss; enthuse (4)
18 France/Spain mountains (8)
20 Regular earnings (6)
21 Evening-dress neckwear (3,3)
23 (Tree) trunk (4)
24 Raging 17 (7)

DOWN

2 Counting frame (6)
3 Purpose; direct (at target) (3)
4 Burn slightly (5)
5 Non-stop accident (3-3-3)
6 Haphazard (6)
7 Occupant of premises (6)
11 Proceeds of petty theft (9)
14 Light breeze (6)
15 Violent woman (6)
16 Well-intentioned; unthreatening (6)
19 Cock bird, killed by Sparrow (5)
22 Misery (3)

ACROSS

6 Account dishonestly (4,3,5)
7 Ill will (6)
8 Number of fluid ounces in pint (6)
9 Spring; fit (4)
10 Laughably small (8)
12 Britain's highest mountain (3,5)
16 Charge per unit; to deserve (4)
18 A streaming in (of crowd) (6)
20 Unparalleled (6)
21 Progress of material success (4,2,6)

DOWN

1 Plain broth (8)
2 Be present at; wait upon (6)
3 Drink of the gods (6)
4 Observe; scribbled comment (4)
5 One moving on ice (6)
6 Bird; lifting device (5)
11 Unbending; honest (8)
13 Group of nine (6)
14 Street interview (3,3)
15 Artist's workroom (6)
17 Fasten; tomato cluster (5)
19 Be deprived of (4)

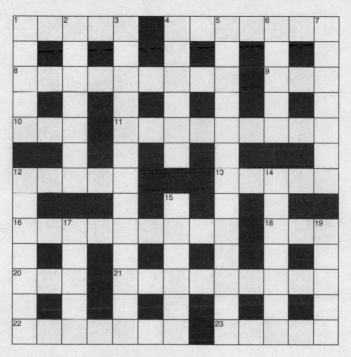

ACROSS

1 Husks; banter (5)
4 With unfounded hope (7)
8 Failure to follow correct line (9)
9 Wave; a wit (3)
10 Hurry; a cricket score (3)
11 See (9)
12 (Played) without a score (2,3)
13 Be evasive; (engine) cut out (5)
16 Really enjoy oneself (4,1,4)
18 A share; slight wound (3)
20 Song; appearance (3)
21 Month of Robespierre's fall (9)
22 When Solomon Grundy was christened (7)
23 Welsh town; below (5)

DOWN

1 A pine, sweet-smelling wood (5)
2 Progress; lend (7)
3 Bowled over (13)
4 Caprice; fanciful humour (6)
5 Bible love-poem book (4,2,7)
6 Not so many (5)
7 Rational (7)
12 (Recited) without book (2,5)
14 Rural paradise (7)
15 Up till just now (6)
17 Section of e.g. hymn (5)
19 Portable light (5)

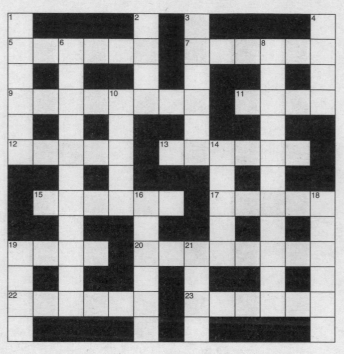

ACROSS

5 Ill-advised (6)
7 Irrational fear (6)
9 Shore region; sounds like *prosaic* (8)
11 Look for (4)
12 Gift voucher; nominal (5)
13 The next day *(poet.)* (6)
15 Misery (6)
17 Defend; it had *Yeomen* (G. & S.) (5)
19 Garden water pipe (4)
20 Of the throat (8)
22 River, proverbially *Blue* (6)
23 Pamper (6)

DOWN

1 Item of ammo (6)
2 Scorch, brand (4)
3 Greek sun god ... (6)
4 ... lie in his rays (4)
6 (The same to you) only more so (4,5,2)
8 Capital of Argentina (6,5)
10 Possessor (5)
14 "All's – with the world!" *(Pippa Passes)* (5)
16 Wild parties (6)
18 Remove (from sequence) (6)
19 Animal skin; with 11, a game (4)
21 Horse equipment; a sailing course (4)

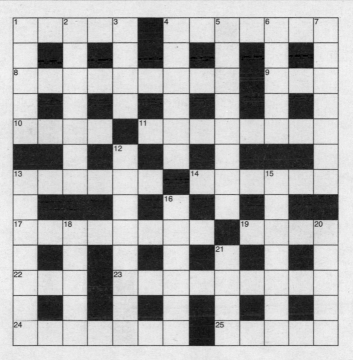

ACROSS

1 Bogus doctor (5)
4 Drum; embroidery frame (7)
8 Water-ski board; (driver) lose control in wet (9)
9 (Tide) recede (3)
10 State of pique; blow hard (4)
11 Paraffin oil (8)
13 Of the flesh (6)
14 (E.g. face) spotty (6)
17 An emperor; a pig (*Orwell*) (8)
19 Responsibility (4)
22 Mother of Cain (3)
23 Hustling for success (2,3,4)
24 Football teams (7)
25 Utterly untypical (5)

DOWN

1 Annul (verdict) (5)
2 Rock as water source (7)
3 French military cap (4)
4 England's longest river (6)
5 Memory aid (8)
6 Grossly fat (5)
7 Elastic; toughly flexible (7)
12 Poetry muse; a steam organ (8)
13 Call (meeting) (7)
15 Emergency (landing); a byword for flatness (7)
16 Spanish Assembly; a Conquistador (6)
18 Irritate (5)
20 (E.g. dust) particle (5)
21 Hard of hearing (4)

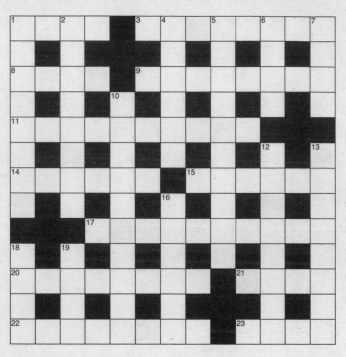

ACROSS

1 Avoid; military command (4)
3 Shameless (wrongdoing) (8)
8 True statement (4)
9 One from Kingston (8)
11 Obscenely defamatory (10)
14 Astute insight (6)
15 Foil, butt (6)
17 Barred liftable gate (10)
20 Fragrant (plant) (8)
21 Pottery oven (4)
22 *Ode to Joy* poet (8)
23 Curtain (4)

DOWN

1 Large-majority constituency (4,4)
2 Oily, ingratiating (8)
4 Answerable (6)
5 Unprovoked (10)
6 Expert (4-); roguish (4)
7 Sound quality; musical interval (4)
10 General melee (4-3-3)
12 Hot compress (8)
13 Occurring at certain times of year (8)
16 Conflict; *none worth* Landor's (6)
18 Bulk; a service (4)
19 Scottish lake, sea arm (4)

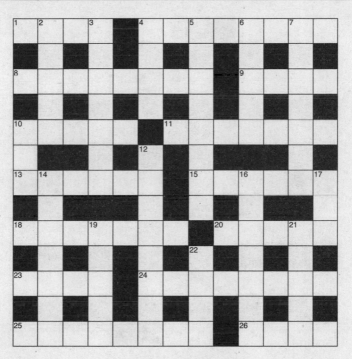

ACROSS

1 Sell *(slang);* thrash (4)
4 Intimidate (8)
8 Send, pass on (8)
9 Spout out (4)
10 Improvised (2,3)
11 Diocese of Rome (4,3)
13 Glossy coating, especially of teeth (6)
15 A dog; creator of exam (6)
18 When Heaven lies about us *(Wordsworth)* (7)
20 Cheerful; a marine *(slang)* (5)
23 Garden pest; pellet (4)
24 Sea pollution trail (3,5)
25 Old fire-retardant (8)
26 Window frame; cloth strip (4)

DOWN

2 Vivid, shocking (5)
3 Enticed (7)
4 Collide with; a swelling (4)
5 A building in yard (8)
6 Pushchair; infested (5)
7 Spartan (7)
10 Tailless primate (3)
12 Faint; sudden darkness (8)
14 Take aback; negation of 22? (7)
16 Lover of Cressida (7)
17 Light-beam (3)
19 Develop point of view (5)
21 Place *(legal);* set of points *(maths)* (5)
22 In addition (4)

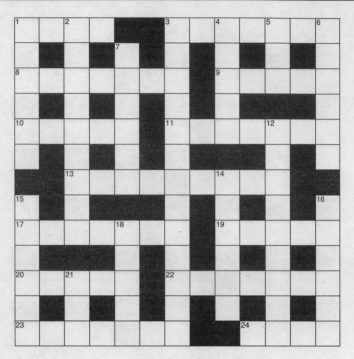

ACROSS

1 Elder and Younger PMs (4)
3 Driving force (7)
8 Caustically sharp (wit) (7)
9 Tripoli its capital (5)
10 Secret hoard (5)
11 Type of victory, as costly as defeat (7)
13 Link; colleague (9)
17 Short piece from e.g. book (7)
19 More private, secret (5)
20 Move mazily, as smoke (5)
22 Nicotine plant (7)
23 Riled (7)
24 Apollo's instrument (4)

DOWN

1 Fish; sounds like *site* (6)
2 Forceful, incisive (9)
3 Disabled (13)
4 Of the northernmost regions (5)
5 Bath; slow boat (3)
6 Small cloth sample (6)
7 Haunt; dominate mind of (6)
12 Commotion (after absconder) (3,3,3)
14 With hands on hips (6)
15 Japanese hostess (6)
16 Guiding channel (6)
18 Calm (suspicion) (5)
21 Atom with extra/missing electron (3)

ACROSS

1 Letters; people in play (10)
8 Feat; make use of (7)
9 Force (on one) (5)
10 Cooperative group (4)
11 Big eater (8)
13 Curl lip (5)
14 Passion; bright orange/ red (5)
16 Radio user; old BBC magazine (8)
17 Water creature; strengthening plate (4)
20 Cheated; hurt by wasp (5)
21 Niceties, to be minded (2,3,2)
22 El Alamein victor (10)

DOWN

1 Storage box (5)
2 First course with letters in (8,4)
3 Unit of matter (4); first half of alphabet? (1,2,1)
4 Indelible skin decoration (6)
5 The rabble (4-4)
6 Bursting with health (3,2,1,6)
7 Heavy pudding (6)
12 Broken chord (8)
13 Publicity display; a little soda water (6)
15 Tyrant (6)
18 A dog; hoarse (5)
19 Ring oflight (4)

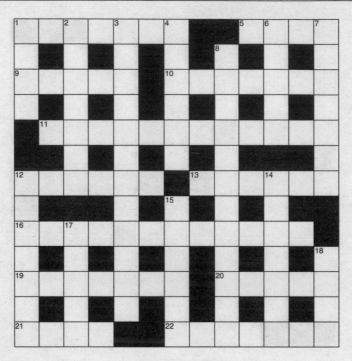

ACROSS

1 Scottish oatmeal cake (7)
5 Feel passion; char (4)
9 French workman's cap (5)
10 Italian port, two post World War 1 treaties (7)
11 Trained for man's use, for home life (12)
12 Thrown plate (6)
13 (Gone) off course (6)
16 Adverse, ominous (12)
19 On the other hand (7)
20 Sort of whiskey, bull, stew (5)
21 John, Beau, Ogden – (4)
22 Later this evening (7)

DOWN

1 Newborn, tiny (4)
2 Apprehensive (7)
3 Alert, watchful (2,3,3,4)
4 Unarmed combat (Japan) (6)
6 Not illuminated (5)
7 Twelve; highest (sun) (4-3)
8 Astronauts' base (5,7)
12 French king's eldest son (7)
14 Rich *(slang);* group of Stones (7)
15 Tower in e.g. castle wall (6)
17 Young deer; is obsequious (5)
18 Tiniest amount; a Sunday (4)

ACROSS

7 Tibetan priest (4)
8 Will administrator (8)
9 Greater (6)
10 Henry –, author; tradesman (e.g. of Dee) (6)
11 Body of water; red dye (4)
12 A shrub; *red alone (anagram)* (8)
15 Unwanted remnants (8)
17 Head covering (4)
18 Disreputable, shifty (6)
21 Wise old Greek *(Iliad)* (6)
22 One hanging about idly (8)
23 Scowl, be menacing (4)

DOWN

1 Computer info store (8)
2 Hang; hold out enticingly (6)
3 End-of-affair (letter) (4,4)
4 Consider, judge (4)
5 Irish capital (6)
6 Lavish foolish love (on) (4)
13 Setting of *Hamlet* (8)
14 Closedown programme (8)
16 Abandon occupancy of (6)
17 Shove; be aggressive salesman (6)
19 Instrument, has *d'amore* version (4)
20 Charlotte Bronte's Jane (4)

ACROSS

1 Small; Dickens's *Dorrit* (6)
4 Roman emperor title (6)
9 Top-people guide (4,3)
10 Milk can; butter-maker (5)
11 Profit; give in (5)
13 Cautious, attentive (7)
14 Second person pronoun (3)
15 Soiled (5)
16 Rodent; Pied Piper victim (3)
17 River 4 crucially crossed (7)
19 Impatient, keen (5)
21 Take as one's own (5)
22 Egg white (7)
24 Talk under one's breath (6)
25 James –,US gangster film actor (6)

DOWN

1 L. S. –, industrial painter (5)
2 Henry –,US *Walden* author (7)
3 Moo (3)
5 Original model; unconscious image *(Jung)* (9)
6 Extinguish; some tobacco (5)
7 Curl of hair (7)
8 Partner's parent; her tongue a plant (6-2-3)
12 To whom e.g. book is inscribed (9)
14 Can drink, when sun over it *(nautical)* (4-3)
16 Course of diet (7)
18 Encourage, lift (5)
20 Long-, loose-limbed (5)
23 Snake; feather scarf (3)

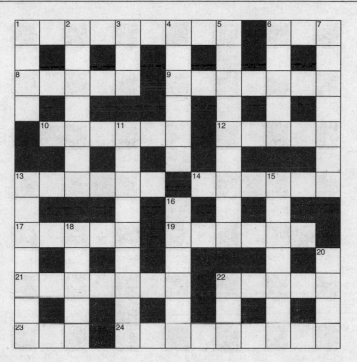

ACROSS

1 Deceptive lightening (5,4)
6 Tiny taste from glass (3)
8 Workforce; surveying rod (5)
9 Rostrum; popular leader (7)
10 Stolid calmness (6)
12 Pivot joint; (philatelic) mount (5)
13 Grow strongly; prosper (6)
14 Forcibly persuade (6)
17 (Ear) anvil bone (5)
19 Staunch; take into custody (6)
21 Roman soldiers' god (7)
22 10% tax (5)
23 Tear (3); farewell (1,1,1)
24 Unexciting chef (5,4)

DOWN

1 Quick; unable to move (4)
2 Tanned skin (7)
3 Mischievous spirit (3)
4 Breathing disorder (6)
5 Man next door (9)
6 Reject with contempt (5)
7 Go before (7)
11 Listen at window (9)
13 Cutter; a Vicar of Bray (7)
15 Rice/stock dish (7)
16 Sickness; revulsion (6)
18 Dissected; upset (3,2)
20 Gesture *(poetic);* mountain stream (4)
22 Can; element Sn (3)

ACROSS

7 (Horse) coat sprinkled with white (4)
8 Fit of anger; a stroke (8)
9 Vague, misty state (8)
10 Summit (4)
11 Peeping Tom (6)
13 Start golf round (3,3)
15 Horrified (6)
17 Require; state firmly (6)
19 Photo; guess; injection (4)
21 All-embracing (8)
23 Hat maker (8)
24 Uninteresting (colour) (4)

DOWN

1 (Going) very cheaply (3,1,4)
2 Complete (6)
3 Bringer of destruction (4)
4 Dante Gabriel –, Pre-Raphaelite (8)
5 Missing quantity of liquid (6)
6 Wheelshaft (4)
12 Saying little (8)
14 Celebration; Britain's, in 1951 (8)
16 Hun king (6)
18 Poor quality (material) (6)
20 Greeting; bad weather (4)
22 Go off; change colour; reach (an age) (4)

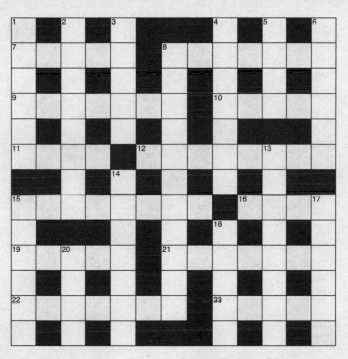

ACROSS

7 An eccentric; starting handle (5)
8 Fish; *a few lie* about (7)
9 Outstanding performance (7)
10 Bird; Irish dean, satirist (5)
11 Assistance (4)
12 Pocket cutter (8)
15 Catastrophe (8)
16 Mark; place; observe (4)
19 Shaver (5)
21 Ralph Waldo –, US poet (7)
22 Seek, request earnestly (7)
23 Uttered; part of wheel (5)

DOWN

1 Frustrate; sort of egg, fir, mist (6)
2 Rod-shaped pathogen (8)
3 Do (task) carelessly fast (5)
4 Japanese ivory toggle (7)
5 Flightless bird; a fruit (4)
6 Insect; Stalky's friend *(Kipling)* (6)
8 Success in task; an escutcheon (11)
13 False person; 9 and 15 *ac*, for Kipling (8)
14 Flightless bird; one refusing to face facts (7)
15 Compulsion (6)
17 Offer; sore (6)
18 – Owens, James; David's father (5)
20 Emile –, wrote *J'accuse* (4)

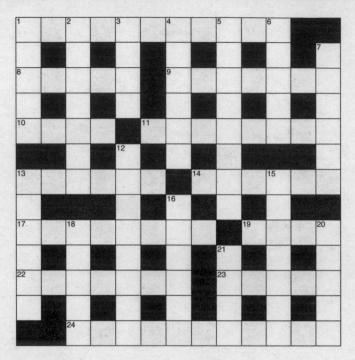

ACROSS

1 Timer, has two notes (6,5)
8 An accent; four-minim note (5)
9 Nauseous; irritable (7)
10 Lie in wait (4)
11 New European republic, 1993 (8)
13 Pierre Auguste –, Impressionist (6)
14 A seeming automaton (6)
17 Outdoor cooked meal (8)
19 Feudal land (4)
22 Easily broken (7)
23 Bestow (5)
24 Fantasy, pretence (4-7)

DOWN

1 Political plotters' group (5)
2 NCO's stripe shape (7)
3 Cattle (4)
4 Make shoes; a road stone (6)
5 Forgetfulness; Time's *alms for* it
   (Troilus) (8)
6 Sales booth (5)
7 Run away (6)
12 Companion, helper (8)
13 Snub (6)
15 Group of battalions (7)
16 Excellent, grand (6)
18 Sphere, kingdom (5)
20 Evade, misrepresent (issue); a sweet
   (5)
21 Become boring; shroud (4)

ACROSS

1 Speed, urgency (5)
4 Partner; use thriftily (7)
8 Spanish treasure ship (7)
9 Sydney beach (5)
10 Pier, dock (5)
11 Protection; scutcheon (6)
13 A Gorgon; a jellyfish (6)
15 Las Vegas state (6)
18 Regular, even (6)
20 Aver; condition (5)
22 Tawny nestling (5)
23 Chemical element variant (7)
24 To merit (7)
25 Card-game rule-book compiler (5)

DOWN

1 Athletics event; the naughty for it (4,4)
2 Acknowledged officer (7)
3 Foe (5)
4 Frank, trustworthy (6)
5 (Flood, tumult) go down (7)
6 Make void (5)
7 Irish assembly (4)
12 Unaided vision (5,3)
14 Disperse (7)
16 Comparison drawing similarity (7)
17 Journalist's name on column (2-4)
19 Stories; emergency jury (5)
20 A sin; an animal (5)
21 Precious metal (4)

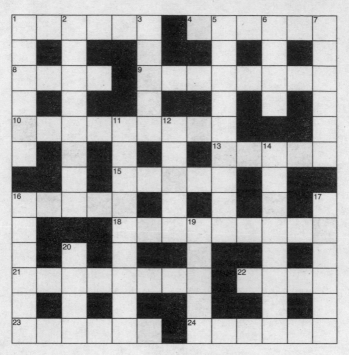

ACROSS

1 Dispatch; sudden bang (6)
4 A French pastry (6)
8 Destiny (4)
9 Become cordial with (8)
10 Food shopping (9)
13 Dumas musketeer; a monastic Mount (5)
15 Incantation; work period (5)
16 Fop (5)
18 Magnifying tube (9)
21 Appreciation of one deceased (8)
22 Side of pitch; wound (game bird) (4)
23 Prize; victory memorial (6)
24 Formidable adversary; deposit on teeth (6)

DOWN

1 Place of safety (6)
2 Disease-causing organism (8)
3 Dahlia root; potato stem (5)
5 Encased pupa (9)
6 Yemen port (4)
7 Centre/circumference line (6)
11 One receptive to beggar (4,5)
12 Model of perfection (5)
14 One living for pleasure (8)
16 Godly, prayerful (6)
17 Radioactivity counter inventor (6)
19 Country Exodus was out of (5)
20 Open-air pool (4)

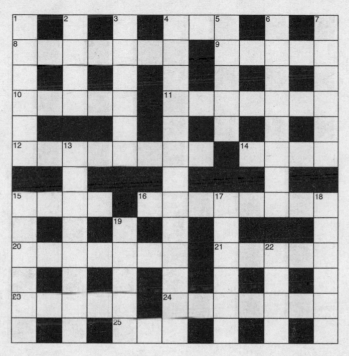

ACROSS

4 Driver's compartment (3)
8 A wrench (7)
9 Coordinate; straighten (5)
10 Bonus; more (5)
11 Poise (7)
12 Decisive gunfight (5-3); suddenly extend (5,3)
14 English saint, historian (4)
15 Verdi Egyptian opera (4)
16 Weight, intensity (8)
20 One messing up task (7)
21 Darling girl *(Peter Pan)* (5)
23 Play (instrument) idly (5)
24 Tomb inscription (7)
25 Block (action; of soap) (3)

DOWN

1 Evaluate (6)
2 With dull surface (4)
3 Unopened, unharmed (6)
4 Scream in alarm *(slang)* (3,4,6)
5 Snooker-table line, area (5)
6 Swedish botanist, naming-system inventor (8)
7 In celebratory mode (2,4)
13 Humdrum; unvarying parts of Mass (8)
15 Head nun (6)
17 US non-mainland state (6)
18 Mower's implement (6)
19 Ascend (5)
22 Trim; undiluted (4)

ACROSS

3 One still alive (8)

7 Place of pilgrimage (6)

8 Village; a play (6)

9 Projecting rim (6)

10 Compassionate (6)

11 Part of leg, sounds like *cure* (4)

13 Show malicious glee (5)

15 First wife of Jacob (4)

17 Belittle (6)

18 (Small) share (6)

19 Glory; ten or higher *(bridge)* (6)

20 Cup rest (6)

21 Fraught with danger (8)

DOWN

1 Slope gently; put off (6)

2 Gesture; important (6)

3 More than one (7)

4 Road, rail bridge (7)

5 French satirist, *Candide* author (8)

6 Economise (8)

11 Poverty, distress (8)

12 One setting test (8)

13 Slow and steady (7)

14 Attend to; where one lives (7)

15 (Chemical) test, paper (6)

16 Portuguese Atlantic islands (6)

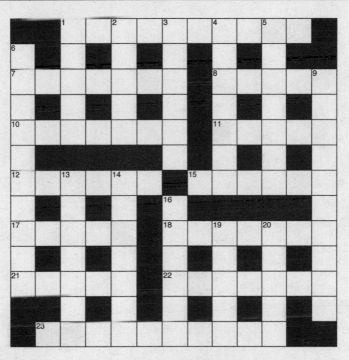

ACROSS

1 Work fast, carelessly (3,7)
7 Menial; liveried servant (7)
8 Firm, hard (5)
10 Result (7)
11 Horseman; addendum (5)
12 Herald's jacket (6)
15 Toboggan (6)
17 Supply with kit (5)
18 Prepare to fence! (2,5)
21 Move furtively, crabwise (5)
22 St. Thomas –, theologian (7)
23 De Gaulle's group, 1940 (4,6)

DOWN

1 Woo; royal household (5)
2 Capital of Japan (5)
3 Element O (6)
4 Non-artificial; uncultivated (state) (7)
5 (Cape) passed; (number) with fraction ignored (7)
6 Simple; without exertion (10)
9 Practical intelligence (5,5)
13 Bad mistake (7)
14 Full (of food) (7)
16 Mend; go (to) (6)
19 Quark-joining particle (5)
20 (US) cattle farm (5)

ACROSS

1 Bumpy skin from cold, fright (5-5)
9 Accept share (of) (7)
10 Sharp, pungent (e.g. smell) (5)
11 Loud (crowd) noise (4)
12 Lay out (cash) (8)
14 Georg –, mathematician; church singer (6)
15 Unimportant facts (6)
18 Of sound; unamplified (guitar) (8)
20 – of Cleves, of Green Gables (4)
22 Gandhi's country (5)
23 On horseback; went up (7)
24 Hopeless idea; one scratching (3-7)

DOWN

2 Ellipse; a cricket ground (4)
3 Money in coin (6)
4 Gustave –, *Bovary* author **(8)**
5 Mistake (5)
6 Ulterior motive (6,6)
7 Gain (of value); thanks (12)
8 Command; make priest (6)
13 Unvarying, faithful (8)
16 Conceit; a case, a Fair (6)
17 Cook gently; be about to rage (6)
19 (In) ancient (days) *(archaic)* (5)
21 Lovably sweet (4)

ACROSS

1 Brightly coloured; graphic (5)

4 Atone for (7)

8 Inheritance, endowment (9)

9 Fish eggs; a deer (3)

10 Black; secret (4)

11 Showing elation (8)

13 Flinched (with pain) (6)

14 (E.g. quiz contestant's) signalling device (6)

17 Gilbert's partner (8)

19 Pollution haze (4)

22 Jack Sprat's wife ate it (3)

23 Craven behaviour (9)

24 Portable light (7)

25 Lost force, declined (5)

DOWN

1 Insipid; lacking content (5)

2 Old soldier (7)

3 Leak slowly; 1*dn* person (4)

4 Mass departure (6)

5 Size, shape of body (8)

6 Main blood-vessel (5)

7 Voter; Hanover ruler (7)

12 Disappointingly average (8)

13 Pensive, sad (7)

15 One from Lusaka (7)

16 *Origin of Species* author (6)

18 Blurt out; pretend (3,2)

20 Excess appetite (5)

21 Front of vessel (4)

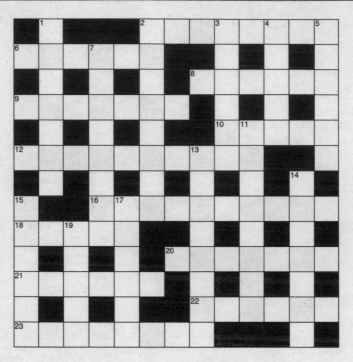

ACROSS

2 More likely than not (8)
6 African expedition (6)
8 Hurtling; going by air (6)
9 Specially made (suit) (7)
10 Thieves' slang (5)
12 Rashness (10)
16 Neek and neck *(especially US)* (3,3,4)
18 Leaves; even (5)
20 Escape; go on holiday (3,4)
21 Attack, criticise, violently (6)
22 Older, more important (6)
23 Fine weather (8)

DOWN

1 Capital of Sicily (7)
2 Taken into hand; gained (speed) (6,2)
3 *Comedie humaine* author (6)
4 Fetch (5)
5 The last Kings Henry, Edward (6)
7 Obvious; type of heir (8)
11 Hold back (8)
13 Gibberish (8)
14 Eight-sided figure (7)
15 Wives of braves (6)
17 Major Old Testament prophet (6)
19 Henrik –, dramatist (5)

ACROSS

1 Old Labourite (9)
6 Rudiments of reading (1,1,1)
8 Spilt; emotionally hurt (5)
9 Tendency to resist motion (7)
10 (Watchman) make rounds (6)
12 A bedtime drink (5)
13 Foul smell (6)
14 Deviously achieve, obtain (6)
17 Leisurely walk (5)
19 Milne's gloomy donkey (6)
21 Idle chatter (7)
22 Greek *th* (5)
23 Teachers union *(abbr.);* one with *bolt* (3)
24 Turned up (nose) (9)

DOWN

1 Speck of soot (4)
2 Waterfall (7)
3 Paintings, etc. (3)
4 Frozen drips (6)
5 Rule by priestly caste (9)
6 Loft room (5)
7 Travesty; parlour-game episode (7)
11 Reader, I *(Jane Eyre)* married him (9)
13 Whet (7)
15 Works outdoors; the salley –, *Yeats* (7)
16 Flaw; go over to enemy (6)
18 Wild animal (5)
20 Green stone; a nag (4)
22 Excessively; also (3)

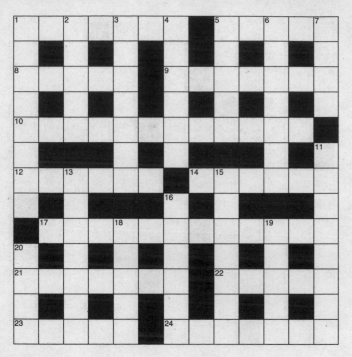

ACROSS

1 Natural environment (7)
5 Footwear; hotel employee once (5)
8 Be king (5)
9 Unvarying; placid (7)
10 Desperately vital (matter) (4-3-5)
12 Withdraw (from political union) (6)
14 Johannes –, laws-of- motion discoverer (6)
17 Disassemble (4,2,6)
21 Short axe (7)
22 Paperwork (5)
23 Stains; notices (5)
24 Type of jacket; Sir Winston – Churchill (7)

DOWN

1 Innocuous (8)
2 Short; advise (5)
3 Beer mug (7)
4 With-it (6)
5 Robert the –: Lenny –, US comedian (5)
6 Electron's path (7)
7 A canal; 1956 debacle (4)
11 One in confinement (8)
13 Division of book (7)
15 Type of Muslim country (7)
16 Developed embryo (6)
18 Characteristic spirit (5)
19 Funny man (5)
20 Feigned (4)

ACROSS

1 Himalayan guide (6)
5 Exasperated sound (4)
8 Boast; a card-game (4)
9 Hostile (8)
10 Less enthusiastic second thoughts (4,4)
11 Pith, argument (4)
12 Bequest (6)
14 Burroughs' Lord of the Jungle (6)
16 US Mormon state (4)
18 Bullfighter (8)
20 Soil, sully (8)
21 Spanish portraitist (4)
22 Slide out of control (4)
23 Negotiation under truce (6)

DOWN

2 Endocrine-gland product (7)
3 Unyielding (5)
4 You're lying! (1,6,5)
5 Dirty laugh (7)
6 It's greener, beyond the hill (5)
7 Absolute rule (12)
13 Mortified (7)
15 Pain-relieving (7)
17 Finely adjust; pinch (e.g. ear) (5)
19 Rage (5)

ACROSS

1 Rather fat (5)
4 Milk/cornflour sauce (7)
8 Wrestled (7)
9 American elk (5)
10 A flower; an instrument (5)
11 Voice-box (6)
13 Itinerant mender (6)
15 A seafood; prise (out) (6)
18 Portuguese port, on Douro (6)
20 Up and active (5)
22 Indian language (5)
23 Able to read minds (7)
24 Scots purse (7)
25 Church assembly (5)

DOWN

1 Smarten oneself up (8)
2 Instrument; Wedding Guest heard it *(Coleridge)* (7)
3 Crimean town, 1945 conference (5)
4 Nice to hug (6)
5 Japanese warrior caste (7)
6 Oak fruit (5)
7 Piece for two (4)
12 In stepped layers (8)
14 Before (7)
16 Chef's domain (7)
17 Detachable ticket (6)
19 Christmas show *(abbr.)* (5)
20 Bottomless pit (5)
21 In such a way (4)

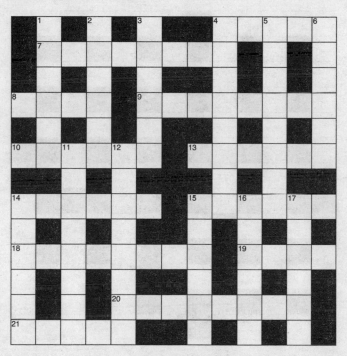

ACROSS

4 Road up to house (5)

7 Roof-reeder (8)

8 Barrie's pirate; boxer's punch (4)

9 Jean Jacques –, *Confessions* author (8)

10 Quick look (6)

13 Desperate food shortage (6)

14 Have for choice (6)

15 Home *(symbol.);* bottom of furnace (6)

18 Most astounding, beautiful (8)

19 Haul; influence (4)

20 Final (8)

21 Use broom; old chimney climber (5)

DOWN

1 Gentle walk (6)

2 Philip –, poet, was Hull librarian (6)

3 Accumulate (e.g. interest) (6)

4 Horse obedience training (8)

5 Lower; worse (8)

6 Pardon; reason (6)

11 Sufficient (8)

12 Mops; scoops the pool (6,2)

14 Fish star-sign (6)

15 Scots offal dish (6)

16 Attraction; request to umpire (6)

17 Bank cashier (6)

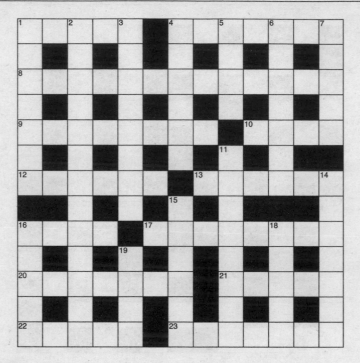

ACROSS

1 Think darkly; set of offspring (5)
4 Tiniest discrete amount; a theory (7)
8 Indefensibly unfair (13)
9 Squinting; awry (8)
10 Limbs; bingo "eleven" (4)
12 Dried grape (6)
13 Alcohol; water (for beer-making) (6)
16 Cousin's mum (4)
17 Not equally balanced (8)
20 Israeli farm commune (7)
21 In the vicinity; a pub (5)
22 Damage beyond repair (5)
23 Ireland such an isle (7)

DOWN

1 Doorman; head-high ball (7)
2 Arousing complaint (13)
3 Reading disorder (8)
4 Arrow holder (6)
5 Greedy (4)
6 Dramatic scene; frozen stage action (7)
7 Satisfies; is introduced to (5)
11 Mix into water (8)
14 Coloured red; unkempt (7)
15 Spout on hose (6)
16 Out of true (5)
18 Russian country cottage (5)
19 Chinese boat; lumber (4)

ACROSS

1 Parvenu (7)
5 Gentlewoman (4)
8 Stout stick (6)
9 Non-transparent (6)
10 Henry VI's queen (8)
12 Entry-room; sounds like *pull (4)*
13 Without precedent (7-2)
17 Back of head; counting of votes (4)
18 One supplying (provisions) (8)
20 Hot season (6)
21 Defame, malign (6)
23 Blood vessel; sounds like *conceited* (4)
24 Field where James IV died, 1513 (7)

DOWN

2 More than one *(grammar)* (6)
3 Label; child's game (3)
4 Stationery item; king (5)
5 Hateful (9)
6 Twice as much (6)
7 The Grossmiths' *Nobody* (6)
11 Smugglers; they prefer blondes (9)
14 The sun never set on ours (6)
15 Capacity; a book (6)
16 Cushion as seat (6)
19 Fellow-competitor (5)
22 (Box) top (3)

ACROSS

1 Truthfulness (8)
5 Swiss mountains (4)
9 Alcohol-processing organ (5)
10 Return to bad ways (7)
11 Imply (7)
12 Bell-shaped spring flower (5)
13 Interplanetary vehicle (9)
18 Tender, hold out (5)
20 Insult (7)
22 Biassed; attracted (to) (7)
23 Gather (little bits) (5)
24 Hazardous ridge; shorten sail (4)
25 Putting together; a meeting (8)

DOWN

1 Overnight bag (6)
2 Ruinous actions, effects (7)
3 Bendy line (5)
4 Reverse a (losing) situation (4,3,6)
6 Folded-back part of jacket (5)
7 Somnolent (6)
8 Hold tight; part of car (6)
14 Skilful, deft (6)
15 Saw, saying (7)
16 Barrel-maker; James Fenimore – (6)
17 Parsimonious (6)
19 Counterfeit; smithy (5)
21 Organ piece, often preceded by toccata (5)

ACROSS

1 Bus-to-city-centre scheme (4,3,4)
7 Examination bed (5)
8 Swaggering courage (7)
10 Wave up and down (8)
11 Sound of geese, unhappy audience (4)
13 Symbolic object (6)
15 Lambert –, royal impostor; type of cake (6)
17 Wharf (4)
18 Imagines, theorises (8)
21 A wearing away (7)
22 Train of followers (5)
23 Undergo conversion (3,3,5)

DOWN

1 Vividly pretty (e.g. view) (11)
2 Circular; delivery route (5)
3 Sulky Trojan War hero (8)
4 Formal discussion (6)
5 Terrible czar (4)
6 Dishonest avoidance (7)
9 Becoming out of date (11)
12 Getting rid of; right to use (8)
14 Signal fires; Brecon has some (7)
16 Slake (thirst) (6)
19 Child's toy; be hanged (5)
20 Rub clean (4)

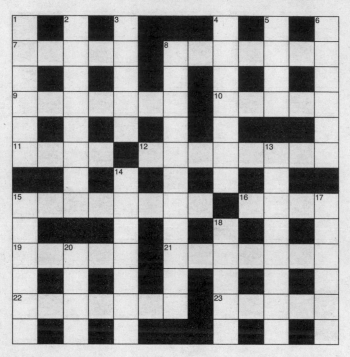

ACROSS

7 Big cat; small weight (5)
8 Range of colours (7)
9 Spot of condensation (7)
10 Making knot (5)
11 Fringe benefit; cheer (up) (4)
12 Tooth-strengthening water additive (8)
15 Definite; utter (8)
16 Arduous journey (4)
19 Devon/Cornwall boundary river (5)
21 Playhouse (7)
22 Batsman's turn (7)
23 Saltpetre (5)

DOWN

1 Display; delay (4,2)
2 Unconsciously (8)
3 (Art) category (5)
4 Food addict (7)
5 Ornamental needlecase (4)
6 West Indian music style (6)
8 Lands ruled from Vatican once (5,6)
13 Vex (8)
14 Looking daggers; obvious (error) (7)
15 First Irish county (alphabetically) (6)
17 Guardian, especially of museum collection (6)
18 Creature (5)
20 (Especially food) option list (4)

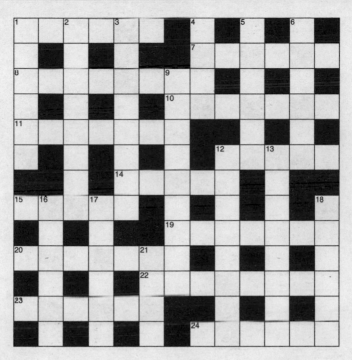

ACROSS

1 Chide (6)
7 Occur (6)
8 Little sketch, view (8)
10 Results; belongings (7)
11 SE Asia country, 1960s war with US (7)
12 Old Scots noble (5)
14 Vertical; very fine (5)
15 Mate its object (5)
19 Curative herb (7)
20 Cook up (7)
22 Oxygenating exercises (8)
23 Arthurian wizard (6)
24 Sounds like *feebly;* sort of magazine (6)

DOWN

1 Breathe new life into (6)
2 French stick (8)
3 Enthusiasm (8)
4 Professional cook (4)
5 Oration (6)
6 Church caretaker (6)
9 Unextreme (climate) (9)
12 The chronicler of Barset (8)
13 Printer's star (8)
16 Car horn; nose *(slang)* (6)
17 Island off Italy toe (6)
18 Shiny; sort of magazine (6)
21 Insincere, empty, talk (4)

ACROSS

1 Dull, disappointing episode *(joc.)* (8)
5 Fetter; James –, 007 (4)
8 In frail, insubstantial way (8)
9 Winged creature; prison *(slang)* (4)
11 Iron/carbon alloy; sounds like *pinch* (5)
12 Arise, flow (from) (7)
13 Mediaeval friar, pilgrim (6)
15 Apostate Roman emperor; type of calendar (6)
18 Element found in sand, computers (7)
19 Companion of Gog (5)
21 Giselle composer; water his ale (4)
22 Of the Great Flood (8)
23 Tax-deduction-at-source system (1,1,1,1)
24 Carer for flock (8)

DOWN

1 Elevates (5,2)
2 Patrick –, Australian Nobel author (5)
3 Bankrupt condition (10)
4 Latest winner of title (6)
6 Japanese paper modelling (7)
7 Jump out of way of (5)
10 Air-expelling machine (6,4)
14 Baby-soothing song (7)
16 Mildly, persistently, irritated (7)
17 Make wealthy (6)
18 On the dot (time); out of tune (5)
20 (False) appearance (5)

ACROSS

1 Academic, unwordly retreat (5,5)
8 Helps to rise; robbers' cry? (5,2)
9 The first disciple; – Bolivar (5)
10 Fighting tooth (4)
11 Enjoyable (8)
13 Strong loathing (6)
15 One ordained (6)
17 One eating all sorts of food (8)
18 Hasty; impetuous (4)
21 Seat; professorship (5)
22 Emphatic type (7)
23 Putting on best clothes; disguising (8,2)

DOWN

2 Goddess, planet (5)
3 Ploy (4)
4 Regular little drink (6)
5 Cleverclogs (8)
6 Disorderly search (7)
7 Laughing uncontrollably (2,8)
8 Jumble of items (10)
12 Wayward, contrary (8)
14 Isle of Man parliament (7)
16 Ancient Celtic 15s (6)
19 Farewell (5)
20 Principal; high seas *(poet.)* (4)

ACROSS

1 Happen together (8)
5 Of that nature (4)
8 Small (Scottish) farm (5)
9 Titivates; composes (5,2)
11 – Johnson, aviatrix; youngest of *Little Women* (3)
12 Old Harare; a Plain (9)
13 Go on board (6)
15 Rim, edge (6)
18 Recycleable-metal store (9)
19 Seed; *Great Expectations* hero (3)
20 Waves; paint spreaders (7)
21 2nd and 6th US presidents (5)
22 Tell of danger (4)
23 Install as king (8)

DOWN

1 Badge in hat (7)
2 Incongruity; mild sarcasm (5)
3 Calamitous reverse (11)
4 Little crease in chin (6)
6 Not reliable, not rigorous (7)
7 Joyful (5)
10 Friendly but fatal gesture (4,2,5)
14 Housebreaker (?)
16 Quick retort (7)
17 Plumlike tree (6)
18 Fastener; warder *(slang)* (5)
19 Socratic-dialogue author (5)

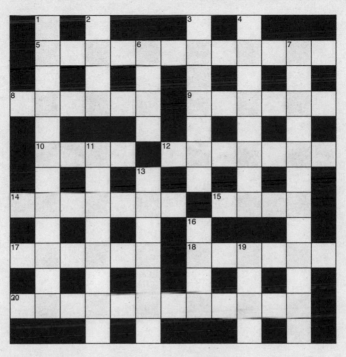

ACROSS

5 Main office (12)
8 Swiss breakfast "little mush" (6)
9 Devon grazing land; type of pony (6)
10 The 14 in *Othello* (4)
12 Soothe, hush (7)
14 Wicked man; criminal (7)
15 Greek *B* (4)
17 Industrial "action"; hit (6)
18 Bowman (6)
20 Disease; *far cleverest (anagram)* (7,5)

DOWN

1 Complacently superior; jingoistic (12)
2 Howls (at moon); coves (4)
3 Unsleeping (7)
4 Mad rush (8)
6 Little joke (4)
7 Brazil chief port (3,2,7)
11 Old lively dance (8)
13 Old and shrivelled (7)
16 Fifty percent (4)
19 Underground hollow; look out! (4)

ACROSS

1 Self respect *(French)* (5,6)

8 Cambridge college; two Bible books (5)

9 In angry way (7)

10 (Archbishop of) York; a handicap race (4)

11 1815 victory (8)

13 Background, locale (6)

14 Killed (by mob); high on pot (6)

17 Melbourne state (8)

19 Stone particles; courage (4)

22 Pornography (7)

23 Rental agreement (5)

24 The Dominicans (5,6)

DOWN

1 Leg/foot joint (5)

2 Damaging blunder (3,4)

3 Hazard (4)

4 Of human types (6)

5 Character; possession (8)

6 Artist's stand (5)

7 Famous representative, example (6)

12 Speedwell; a cloth, a pass (8)

13 The films (US) (6)

15 Buddhist nothingness (7)

16 Act of air piracy (6)

18 (Southern) valley, hollow (5)

20 Lock of hair (5)

21 Indistinct sight (4)

ACROSS

1 Philosopher, killed with hemlock (8)
5 Cock's crest; some honey (4)
9 Race for 1000, 2000 of them (7)
10 Linger (5)
11 Linger (4)
12 With pinkish plumage (7)
14 French white-wine region (6)
16 Counterbalance (6)
19 Remove deep dirt (7)
21 Offered; conceded (4)
24 Scottish landowner (5)
25 Wraith (7)
26 Out of danger (4)
27 Foot traveller (8)

DOWN

1 Indication, gesture (4)
2 Porcelain; mate *(slang)* (5)
3 Free of germs (7)
4 Make certain (6)
6 Joan of Arc its Maid (7)
7 Wagner festival town (8)
8 Probability; may go with *ends* (4)
13 Maths with infinitesimals (8)
15 Wild West policeman (7)
17 Cover for Adam and Eve (3,4)
18 Former Iran (6)
20 Naked; painting of one such (4)
22 Elector (5)
23 Try; listen to (4)

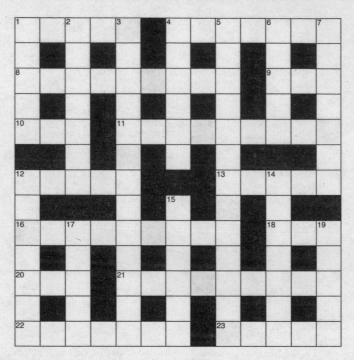

ACROSS

1 Shinbone (5)
4 Confused, slightly drunk (7)
8 *Cogito ergo sum* thinker (9)
9 Dull-coloured; press for payment (3)
10 Do winter sports (3)
11 Washerwoman (9)
12 Struggle, contest (5)
13 Soothe, put at rest (5)
16 Bow the knee (9)
18 Business end of pen (3)
20 Personality, selfishness (3)
21 A butterfly; *operating (anagram)* (6-3)
22 Foot lever (7)
23 Wood nymph (5)

DOWN

1 Daily sea movements (5)
2 Moistening (roast); sewing loosely (7)
3 No help at all *(sarcastic)* (1,3,3,2,4)
4 Irregular, patchy (6)
5 Handicapped (13)
6 Little house, especially for beavers (5)
7 Line of kings (7)
12 Invention (of the imagination) (7)
14 Protracted (7)
15 People in household (6)
17 Running knot (5)
19 Two-legged creature (5)

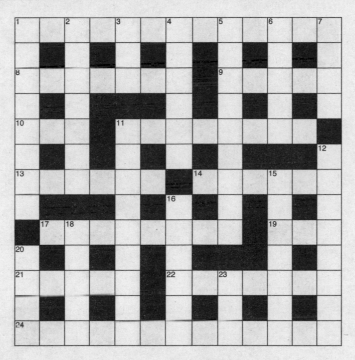

ACROSS

1 Oddments (4,3,6)
8 Handicraft with hooks (7)
9 Compel; violence (5)
10 Floor-cleaner; shock of hair (3)
11 Hostile reaction (8)
13 Regular, undeviant (6)
14 Difficulty; graze (6)
17 Special representative (8)
19 A cat; the piper's son (3)
21 South American "camel" (5)
22 Reading desk (7)
24 Becomes attached to place (4,4,5)

DOWN

1 Attractive; turning into (8)
2 Cavalryman (7)
3 Tree; burnt residue (3)
4 To separate (6)
5 (Hunt) hot on trail (2,4,3)
6 (Especially military) functional unit (5)
7 Tool store (4)
11 E.g. colliery musicians (5,4)
12 End of the line (8)
15 30s movement; *redcoat (anagram)* (3,4)
16 Left uncultivated (6)
18 Intended (5)
20 Undergarment; error (4)
23 Mangy dog (3)

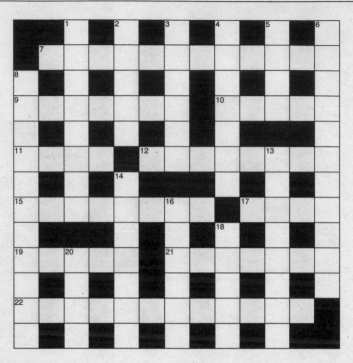

ACROSS

7 Friendly (12)
9 Lady's room (7)
10 Concentrated fire (5)
11 Bird; bar (4)
12 Indebted (to) (8)
15 Trilby's master *(du Maurier)* (8)
17 Muslim mystic (4)
19 Turn, rotate; one that does (5)
21 Traveller; US space probe (7)
22 Force to cooperate (5,4,3)

DOWN

1 Gushingly emotional (8)
2 Greek fabulist (5)
3 Die of hunger (6)
4 *War and Peace* author (7)
5 Nobleman (4)
6 Scout around (11)
8 Mid-Welsh university town, resort (11)
13 Chores (8)
14 Nimbleness (7)
16 Source of (especially vicar's) income (6)
18 Romany (5)
20 Send forth (4)

ACROSS

1 Preserve in brine· naughty child (6),

4 Explosive-carrying plane (6)

9 A blend; (especially dentist's) alloy (7)

10 Drink (one's) health (5)

11 Gurkha knife (5)

13 (Shady) share of profit (4-3)

14 Headgear; stopper (3)

15 Different, alternative (5)

16 Pulse seed; a *sweet* flower (3)

17 A god; a liquid metal (7)

19 Change, move; spell of work (5)

21 *Balance* star-sign (5)

22 Connector plug (7)

24 Silly laugh (6)

25 Fraud, cheating (6)

DOWN

1 Sawn length (5)

2 Break down; extol (5,2)

3 Carry awkwardly; sort of sail, of worm (3)

5 Fringes (of town) (9)

6 Well done! (5)

7 A liqueur; almond biscuit (7)

8 *Rubáiyát* author (4,7)

12 Give protective jab (9)

14 King Arthur's court (7)

16 Love potion; sounds like *strainer* (7)

18 Automaton (5)

20 Fortune-telling cards (5)

23 Reverent fear (3)

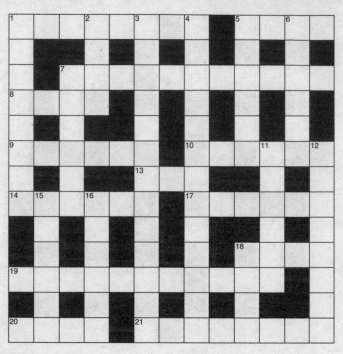

ACROSS

1 Think over (8)
5 (Skin) flake off; fruit skin (4)
7 Rodent, losing out to grey cousin (3,8)
8 Ambush; snare (4)
9 Olympic city, 2004 (6)
10 Proficient people (6)
13 Play on words (3)
14 Rotatory force (6)
17 Game tile with spots (6)
18 Gave temporarily (4)
19 Jewish linked-triangle motif (4,2,5)
20 Brawl; start to wear (4)
21 Idle type (8)

DOWN

1 Compare unlike features (8)
2 (Liquid) ooze out (4)
3 Cheeky (13)
4 Crude but adequate (5-3-5)
5 Conditional early release (6)
6 All leave *(stage direction)* (6)
7 Somewhat; for preference (6)
11 Self-possessed; balanced (6)
12 Quick way (5-3)
15 Ejection; *sure to (anagram)* (6)
16 Excavation pit; one hunted (6)
18 E.g. wing, flipper, leg (4)

ACROSS

1 Totally unused (5,3)
7 Cover (with cloth) (5)
8 A Franciscan monk (4,5)
9 A spread; a nasty position (3)
10 Use voice; confess (4)
11 Bad luck; its bringer (6)
13 Hindu god, with Brahma, Shiva (6)
14 Moderate; a maggot (6)
17 Fruit in Chekhov's Orchard (6)
18 Animal; centre of target (4)
20 Conflict (3)
22 Of hairdressing (9)
23 Requirements (5)
24 Horrible-looking; (US) thug (4-4)

DOWN

1 Counterfeit (5)
2 Roman lake, underworld entrance; *van user (anagram)* (7)
3 A pudding; faulty (4)
4 Magazine head (6)
5 Concert-party instrument (5)
6 Mound-building insect (7)
7 Bed-clearing vessel (7)
12 Puts inside (7)
13 Watching (e.g. TV) (7)
15 Driving round (7)
16 Clifton Bridge designer (6)
17 Pitiless (5)
19 Sweet on stick; money *(slang)* (5)
21 Dinner signal; award *(slang)* (4)

ACROSS

6 One leaving work on the dot (5,7)
7 Unspeaking (6)
8 Dark and sad (6)
9 A fruit, sounds like *dim-witted* (4)
10 Unpaid (officer) (8)
12 One-cell tiny organisms (8)
16 Poor dwelling (4)
18 Old thing to pack up troubles in (6)
20 Peak (6)
21 By chance (12)

DOWN

1 Change of position; campaign (8)
2 Quick drawing (6)
3 Strongman shorn by Delilah (6)
4 A swindle (4)
5 Panic; a *Reign* of it, 1794 (6)
6 A cold; to cool (5)
11 Be like (8)
13 (Allotted) for each person (6)
14 Teased; unjustified (margin) (6)
15 Advantages (6)
17 Concord; the number one (5)
19 Runny French cheese (4)

ACROSS

1 Hurl; indulgent spell (5)
7 Documented; formally but not practically (2,5)
8 Distinction; bullet diameter (7)
9 Doncaster classic (2,5)
11 Twain hero; sounds like *type of bean* (6)
13 Annual admission of income (3,6)
15 Non-government warship (9)
19 Aptitude; ancient money (6)
21 Rifle-fixed stabber (7)
23 Clumsy (7)
24 Defer to another time (7)
25 Come in; write down (5)

DOWN

1 Concentrate (on) (5)
2 Partner's family (2-4)
3 Gallows (6)
4 Carries out; some deer (4)
5 Dormant; potentially there (6)
6 Boisterous partying (7)
10 At which to aim (6)
12 Baby's toy; loose component noise (6)
14 V.Woolf novel; – Furioso *(Ariosto)* (7)
16 Haitian animism (6)
17 Fester (6)
18 Meal, food (6)
20 Royal house of Henry VII (5)
22 Armoured vehicle; fuel holder (4)

ACROSS

1 London entertainment district (4)
3 Absorbed; wholly underwater (8)
9 Push on, forward (5)
10 – Monroe (7)
11 Hamlet died in his arms (7)
12 Wide-mouth pitcher (4)
14 Sudden (6)
16 Slowly simmered (6)
18 Well-known actor (4)
19 Determine, declare (7)
22 Three kings, one "wicked" (7)
23 Russian buckwheat pancake (5)
24 Noise-reducer (in car, gun) (8)
25 Shivering fit (4)

DOWN

1 Shaven yob (8)
2 Too ready to complain (13)
4 Wealth (as a god) (6)
5 A pledge; serious (7)
6 Couple's twenty-fifth anniversary (6,7)
7 Take formal meal (4)
8 Dull; a place to live (4)
13 Sticky substance (8)
15 Be relevant (7)
17 Deal with; touch (6)
20 Employment; may be for the boys (4)
21 Rainbow goddess; part of eye (4)

ACROSS

1 Mock; supply (to hotel room) (4,2)
5 Fruit; Peter –, mechanical *(MND)* (6)
8 Piece of computer; wood shaving (4)
9 Dampness (8)
10 Referee (6)
12 Smell strongly (4)
15 Crossing-place to execution (Venice) (6,2,5)
16 March tiredly; hit wildly (4)
17 Not illegal (6)
19 Height (8)
21 Fibre; old invading German (4)
22 One from Nairobi (6)
23 Long, angry speech (6)

DOWN

2 Short-lived (9)
3 Drop; pickpocket (3)
4 Treated luxuriously (8)
5 Question and answer game (4)
6 Meeting for job applicant (9)
7 Motor vehicle (3)
11 Minor humiliation (9)
13 Tired out; spent (9)
14 Well off (8)
18 Disaster; bankruptcy (4)
20 Fib; relax (3)
21 Judder; container (3)

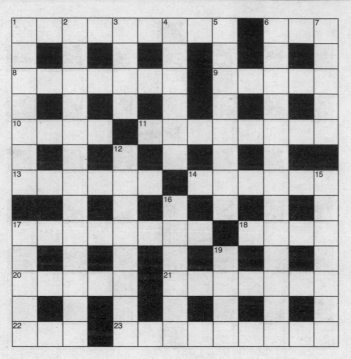

ACROSS

1 Inconsiderate (9)
6 Swan; horse; loaf; pipe (3)
8 Shop surface; measurer (7)
9 Suite; conveyance (5)
10 Piece of news; likewise (4)
11 Pristine; unhackneyed (8)
13 Ribbon of 17 *dn* (6)
14 Fisherman with line (6)
17 Overfussy (8)
18 Pound; chewing tobacco (4)
20 Thin; have mercy on (5)
21 Foreign; unusual (7)
22 Expert; a card (3)
23 Rapidly grows (9)

DOWN

1 Ointment; soothing suavity (7)
2 Very famous person (9,4)
3 Behind; dead (4)
4 Uproar (6)
5 One suing (8)
6 England/France connection (7,6)
7 Hackneyed (5)
12 World War 1 poppy site; Anne of Cleves its mare (8)
15 Richard –, *Oklahoma!* composer (7)
16 Humiliating disaster (6)
17 Italian dough (5)
19 Crustacean; an apple (4)

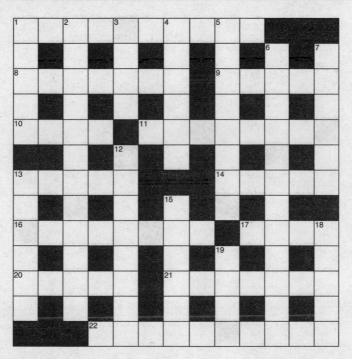

ACROSS

1 Supervise exam (10)
8 Word such as *NATO, laser* (7)
9 Cutting tool (5)
10 Hit; pare; film extract (4)
11 Vacuous waffle (8)
13 Hotel lobby (5)
14 Jape; edible-bud shrub (5)
16 Informal interview programme (4,4)
17 Fruit fibre; essence (4)
20 Making good sense (5)
21 Rope; artist (7)
22 Final battle *(Revelation)* (10)

DOWN

1 Son of Abraham (5)
2 Oxbridge contest (7,5)
3 Heredity unit (4)
4 Unwanted furniture (6)
5 Withdraw, recover (4,4)
6 Frustrated, let down (12)
7 Shooting star (6)
12 Fighter for cause (8)
13 Capricious (6)
15 Fairground game (4-2)
18 Grey/white wader (5)
19 Penalty; clear, dry (4)

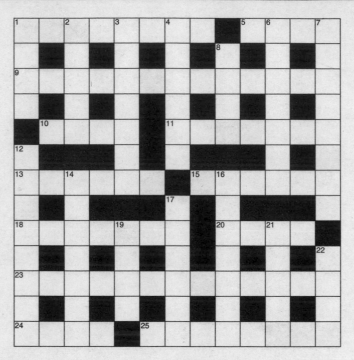

ACROSS

1 Always in same role (8)
5 Light-focusing device (4)
9 Huxley future-hell novel (5,3,5)
10 Stronghold; retain (4)
11 Eye protectors (7)
13 Agreement; harmony (6)
15 Disfigure; old squeezer (6)
18 Supplement to will (7)
20 Lavish, succulent (growth); alcoholic (4)
23 Be dishonoured (4,4,5)
24 Burden (4)
25 (E.g. clock's) oscillator (8)

DOWN

1 Mr Punch's dog (4)
2 Chatter idly (5)
3 Soft-soled shoe; plant like ivy (7)
4 Conveyance; sounds like *kill* (6)
6 Personal sound-stopper (7)
7 Move to avoid (4-4)
8 Gulp (4)
12 Imaginary; whimsical (8)
14 C-softening mark *(French)* (7)
16 Declared without evidence (7)
17 Niche (6)
19 Hit with hand; part of shirt (4)
21 Threatening look, growl; tangle (5)
22 Ray; timber support (4)

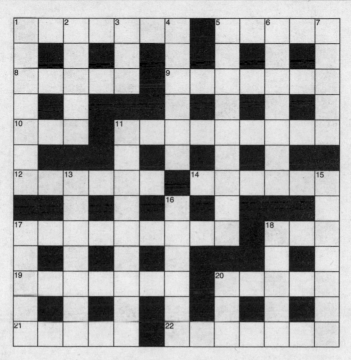

ACROSS

1 Afternoon meal (4,3)
5 A fish; (bird) sit (5)
8 Little wood (5)
9 Fired clay (article) (7)
10 Poisonous snake (3)
11 *Oedipus Rex* playwright (9)
12 Depressing; economics such a science *(Carlyle)* (6)
14 Half an island; one man in a boat *(Jerome)* (6)
17 Briefly return for contact (5,4)
18 Peat-growing area (3)
19 Post-mortem (7)
20 (Sheep) feed; abrasion (5)
21 Poem of lament (5)
22 Overlook; disregard (7)

DOWN

1 Drawn; Rider –, author (7)
2 Band, collection (5)
3 Fasten; cup game (3)
4 Receive (6)
5 Slowly strain through (9)
6 A walker; a rose (7)
7 Pawns; horse's ankles (5)
11 Cheerfully careless (4-5)
13 Run (away); sink (ship) (7)
15 Portion; part of line *(maths)* (7)
16 (US) ravine (6)
17 Make gentle fun of (5)
18 Mark on horse; burn (5)
20 Joke; silence (3)

ACROSS

1 Ideal world (6)
5 In footwear (4)
9 Utterly unoriginal (copy) (7)
10 Radio antenna (6)
11 Instinctive (reaction) (4-4)
12 Be tangible expression of (6)
15 Barred grid, screen (6)
18 Speaking little (8)
20 Animal shed; solidly based (6)
22 Rider's foot support (7)
23 Broken in; boring (4)
24 Expel from country (6)

DOWN

2 Herbal infusion (6)
3 Calm, undisturbed (8)
4 Similar (5)
6 One due to succeed (4)
7 Require, insist (6)
8 Cocktail mixer; US sectarian (6)
13 To flatter (6,2)
14 Loathe (6)
16 Glass vessel; witty answer (6)
17 Appropriate, correct (6)
19 Youngster (5)
21 Edge; to be very full (4)

ACROSS

1 Serious setback (4-4)
5 Stout string (4)
8 Financially ruined (8)
9 Refuse (authority) (4)
11 Glaring, sensational (5)
12 Mechanism-damaging imp (7)
13 Render ineffective (6)
15 Urge forward (6)
18 Very light, eggy dish (7)
19 French currency (5)
21 (Official) gown (4)
22 The ordinary bloke (8)
23 A river; sounds like *drinks* (4)
24 A stiffened muslin (8)

DOWN

1 Hanging Gardens city (7)
2 Kind giver (5)
3 Idle and fed up (5,5)
4 Attack, question (in argument) (6)
6 Partly coincide (7)
7 Senior member (of corps) (5)
10 Solid land (5,5)
14 Mutter complaints (7)
16 Unbridled freedom; a permit (7)
17 River creature; apprentice Scout (6)
18 Strengthening bar; walk proudly (5)
20 Carrying weapon (5)

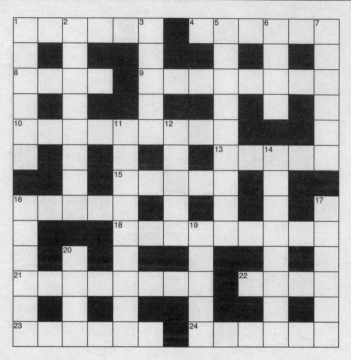

ACROSS

1 Fortuitous; offhand (6)
4 Part of e.g. cauliflower head (6)
8 Horrid, contemptible (4)
9 Left-handed fighter (8)
10 In free, romantic effusion; *drip chaos (anagram)* (9)
13 In strange way (5)
15 (Woman) well-built (5)
16 Ground, founding principle (5)
18 Permission (to land); type of sale (9)
21 Wary (8)
22 A drink; a naval town (4)
23 Inter-state agreement (6)
24 Not far off (6)

DOWN

1 Prance around (6)
2 Content of (school) course (8)
3 Rope with noose (5)
5 One not on time (9)
6 Absorbed, carried away (4)
7 Vulgar, trashy (6)
11 Below the line (character) (9)
12 Southern US; cooking pot (5)
14 Heavy shower (8)
16 Animal as lion, tiger (3,3)
17 Vicar's robing-room (6)
19 Malicious ignition (5)
20 Smoke, e.g. with anger (4)

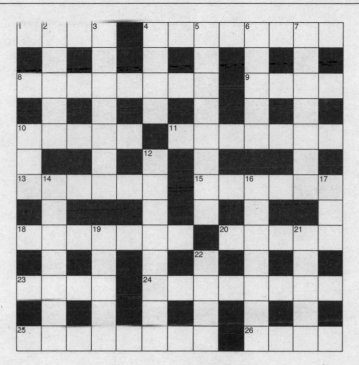

ACROSS

1 West Indian citrus fruit (4)
4 Leonid –, 70s USSR chief (8)
8 Endurance; G. & S. operetta (8)
9 Drink too much (4)
10 Relax; area of authority (5)
11 Of the stars (7)
13 Responsible (for crime) (6)
15 Way of speaking; mark over letter (6)
18 Sailors' spear (7)
20 Antipodean soldier (5)
23 Yugoslav dictator (4)
24 Rain protector (8)
25 Tobias –, *Random, Pickle* author (8)
26 Two-master; a jolly-boat (4)

DOWN

2 Fruit; type of shot (5)
3 First (letter) (7)
4 Rely; riverside (4)
5 Occurring in due course (8)
6 Commercial lodging (5)
7 Make clear (7)
10 Apparatus; equip (vessel) (3)
12 The focus of all eyes (8)
14 Element U (7)
16 Tinned-goods factory (7)
17 Nervous twitch (3)
19 Move around looking for prey (5)
21 Give permission for (5)
22 Be right next to (4)

144

ACROSS

1 Yellow-skin disease (8)
5 Lapdog *(abbr.);* sounds like *summit* (4)
9 Blunder (5)
10 Edible plant; nonsense (7)
11 Hermione's husband *(Winter's Tale)* (7)
12 Irritable; Mole's friend *(Grahame)* (5)
13 Dostoevsky's Brothers (9)
18 Of the same value (5)
20 Sheet with cut pattern (7)
22 Old hospital welfare officer (7)
23 Vex (5)
24 Longer forearm bone (4)
25 Towards the sunset (8)

DOWN

1 Keep balls in air (6)
2 Degrade (priest) (7)
3 Lived (in); lingered (on) (5)
4 Seasonal fir (9,4)
6 Forcibly obtain; precise (5)
7 Post-conception stage (6)
8 Sort of glass, of watch (6)
14 Charlemagne knight, Oliver rival (6)
15 Italian home of Palladio (7)
16 Sense of reliving a scene (4,2)
17 Took part in game, drama (6)
19 Deprive (chap) of courage (5)
21 Glorify (5)

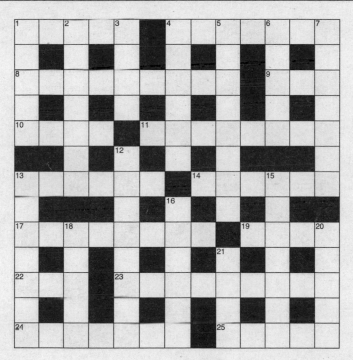

ACROSS

1 Fulcrum (5)
4 Fetched (7)
8 Kerry town, near lakes (9)
9 Period, epoch (3)
10 Actual (4)
11 Courtly dances (8)
13 Chain for animal (6)
14 Drenched (6)
17 Consummate skill (8)
19 Twin of Jacob *(Genesis)* (4)
22 Oz bird; EU project (3)
23 E.g. house paint; specious excuses (9)
24 Improve appeal of (7)
25 Albrecht –, engraver (5)

DOWN

1 A rod; a betting game (5)
2 Doughty (7)
3 Jewel-in-head creature (4)
4 *Pilgrim's Progress* author (6)
5 Conjunction-of-opposites device *(rhetoric)* (8)
6 Huge man (5)
7 Betrayal (7)
12 *I got Rhythm* composer (8)
13 Swinging bar (7)
15 Hopelessness (7)
16 Mark of blow (6)
18 Verity (5)
20 Deferentially escort (5)
21 Notice (paid) (4)

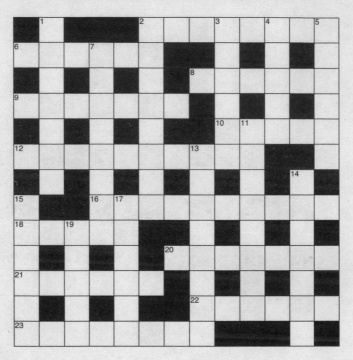

ACROSS

2 Bridgetown its capital (8)
6 Bargain over price (6)
8 Area of authority, of expertise (6)
9 One raised *(John)*; a beggar *(Luke)* (7)
10 Aroma trail (5)
12 Merchant sailing ship (10)
16 (Chair) padding (10)
18 Conscious (of) (5)
20 Throb, oscillate (7)
21 Water down (6)
22 Land for crops (6)
23 Confusion; ailment (8)

DOWN

1 First man into space (7)
2 Leave (in will) (8)
3 Lady's top (6)
4 First Englishman round world (5)
5 An upper house (6)
7 Majesty; God's – *(Hopkins)* (8)
11 Judgment yardsticks (8)
13 Unit of air pressure (8)
14 Liable to snap (7)
15 Came down; sort of gentry (6)
17 Annoy, bother (6)
19 African range; sort of book (5)

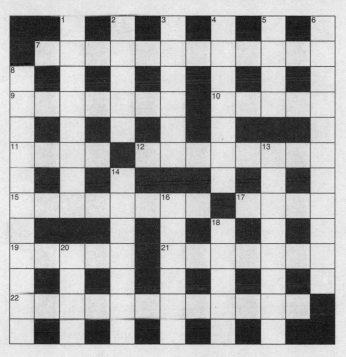

ACROSS

7 Earnest prayer (12)
9 Macbeth told to *beware* him (7)
10 Steal; cook slowly (5)
11 Ship, its frame (4)
12 Belonging to C. of E. (8)
15 Painting of clouds (8)
17 Aspersion (4)
19 Wall under pitched roof (5)
21 Adjudications (7)
22 Huge (like interstellar distance) (12)

DOWN

1 A trade; carnage (8)
2 Poppy drug (5)
3 Light (Indian) meal (6)
4 Young frog (7)
5 Capital of Peru (4)
6 Witch (11)
8 American Indian message; *Mike's slogan (anagram)* (5,6)
13 Dated event list (8)
14 Level, rank; staggered formation (7)
16 Length of time (6)
18 Elderly person *(slang)* (5)
20 (Fish) take bait (4)

ACROSS

1 Special assault unit (8)
5 Complacent (4)
9 Spiral of disaster (7,6)
10 Horseback game (4)
11 Mariners' star-angle measurer (7)
13 One dying for cause (6)
15 Conceal; front of TV (6)
18 Giant David killed (7)
20 Before (4-); a stake (4)
23 Shaw play; *madman – he rants (anagram)* (4,3,3,3)
24 Use keyboard (4)
25 Natation (8)

DOWN

1 South American guinea pig (4)
2 Aggressively masculine (5)
3 Expression of regret (7)
4 Cease (from) (6)
6 Ornamental cord knotting (7)
7 Saying hello to (8)
8 Hoodoo (4)
12 One going to live abroad (8)
14 Pickled herring fillet (7)
16 Kent port; Pitt its Earl (7)
17 Follow closely, secretly (6)
19 Not quite closed (4)
21 Musical speeds (5)
22 Catch (clothes); minor hiccup (4)

ACROSS

7 Grain husks (4)
8 From the East (8)
9 Feelers (8)
10 Uriah –, Dickens's cringer (4)
11 Jean-Paul –, French existentialist (6)
13 A hat; a cricketer (6)
15 Slow (movement) (6)
17 Car repair shop (6)
19 Textile frame; impend (4)
21 Charge on house (8)
23 Peaceful (8)
24 Wound-dressing fabric (4)

DOWN

1 An inebriate (8)
2 Put money (into) (6)
3 Planted (4)
4 An assortment (5,3)
5 In no special way (6)
6 Be indolent (4)
12 Gigantic (8)
14 Taking on; attractive (8)
16 Playing at casino (6)
18 Ply, entertain well (6)
20 Monster (4)
22 Irk (4)

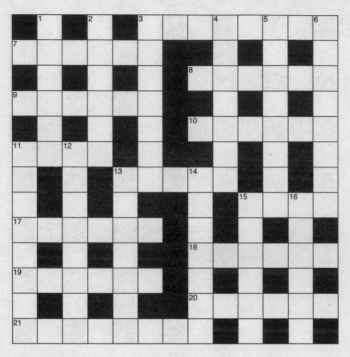

ACROSS

3 Town where Jesus grew up (8)
7 Adjust; sounds like *a melody* (6)
8 A sweet; nonsense (6)
9 Sharply stylish (clothes) *(slang)* (6)
10 Overwhelm with light (6)
11 Stare steadily (4)
13 Instant, flash (5)
15 Harmful insect (4)
17 Sharp double bend (6)
18 Showy type of rhododendron (6)
19 Food store (6)
20 Rub gently with nose (6)
21 Set off (bomb) (8)

DOWN

1 Verse of poem (6)
2 Eat like pig (6)
3 January 1 (3,4)
4 To hero-worship (7)
5 Steal employer's funds (8)
6 French Protestant (8)
11 Greying; cried fretfully (8)
12 (Babylonian) stepped pyramid (8)
13 Exchange (old for new) (5,2)
14 Paul –, Post Impressionist (7)
15 Italian square (6)
16 Fitting, proper (6)

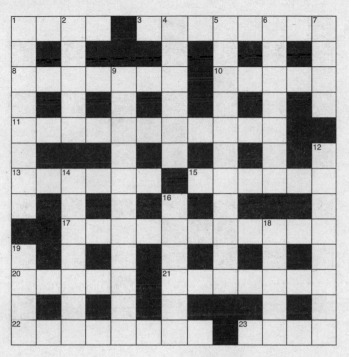

ACROSS

1 Shipshape (4)
3 Blameworthy (8)
8 Abu Simbel pharaoh; *mere ass? (anagram)* (7)
10 A daisy plant (2-3)
11 Pop-music-writing district (3,3,5)
13 German art songs (6)
15 Entertained (6)
17 Travelling (teacher) (11)
20 Lean veal-neck (end); to 1*dn* (5)
21 Appearing before judge (2,5)
22 17th century Protestant sect (8)
23 Catcall (4)

DOWN

1 Strangle; sort of valve (8)
2 Evil spirit (5)
4 Remove (rider, MP) (6)
5 Causing difficulties (11)
6 Farewells; (baby's) sleep (3-4)
7 At any time (4)
9 Pre-performance panic (5,6)
12 Teacher (8)
14 Ruler; Beethoven's fifth piano concerto (7)
16 Possible choice (6)
18 Temporary cease-fire agreement (5)
19 At earliest convenience *(abbr.)* (4)

ACROSS

1 Curve; sort of galaxy, of staircase (6)
5 Type of ink, club; an ocean (6)
8 Nasty smell *(slang)* (4)
9 Answer impertinently (4,4)
10 Lower (6)
12 Strange; very *(Scots.)* (4)
15 Be utterly ruthless (4,2,7)
16 Anonymous; Lady Jane – (4)
17 Fairy king *(MND)* (6)
19 Deep-freezing-the-dead science (8)
21 Ominous; disastrous (4)
22 Mediterranean island, south of Turkey (6)
23 (Hair) shaped; (person) titled (6)

DOWN

2 Film-playing device (9)
3 Scrap (of cloth); piece of syncopated music (3)
4 Able to read (8)
5 Lazy, unemployed (4)
6 One of dissipated life (9)
7 Part of circle (3)
11 Cheap-drink time (5,4)
13 Crowd; open space for gathering (9)
14 Giant statue (8)
18 Student lodgings; barbed remarks (4)
20 A fish; a beam (3)
21 Forget one's lines (3)

ACROSS

1 Release (prisoner); fire (gun) (9)
6 Tricked; owned (3)
8 Break in line of verse (7)
9 Augustus –, Victorian Gothic architect (5)
10 Someone tricked (4)
11 Only-one-wife/husband system (8)
13 Plan, system; plot (6)
14 Bring to conclusion; tease *(slang)* (4,2)
17 Ill-defined; vague (8)
18 Small (skirt, computer) (4)
20 Set of steps (5)
21 Inspired predictor (7)
22 Induced; was in front (3)
23 One tearing down; a warship (9)

DOWN

1 Makes mind up (7)
2 Win everything (5,3,5)
3 Lug; booty (4)
4 Excuse; logic (6)
5 Wild joy (8)
6 Arrogant (4-3-6)
7 Dark and dirty (5)
12 Earnestly pleaded (8)
15 Lecturer's stick; gun dog (7)
16 A brawl (6)
17 Of the nose (5)
19 Grimly obstinate (4)

ACROSS

1 In advance (10)
7 Annul (7)
8 Demand (one's rights) (5)
10 French novelist, wrote *Gigi* (7)
11 Be of benefit (5)
12 Season Keats addressed (6)
15 Prevent from leaving (6)
17 German World War 2 submarine (1-4)
18 Drug from hemp (7)
21 Aristocrat; old coin (5)
22 Heartfelt, expressive (7)
23 The old days (10)

DOWN

1 Herb in Keats's pot (5)
2 Welsh town; a stone (5)
3 Save; buy back (6)
4 Foreign measure, over two acres (7)
5 US/Canada Falls (7)
6 Keats's Attic pot (7,3)
9 Sad state Keats addressed (10)
13 Problem; to worry (7)
14 Annual car inspection (3,4)
16 Engraver; another (different) drink (6)
19 Froth (5)
20 Make deduction (5)

ACROSS

1 Easy skill; (US) plant (8)
5 Washtub; a city (4)
9 Counterproductive consoler (4,9)
10 Andean country (4)
11 Unenthusiastic, feeble (7)
13 Respond (6)
15 One living from robbery (6)
18 Notion (7)
20 John –, composer; barred enclosure (4)
23 Hamlet's question (2,2,2,3,2,2)
24 Labyrinth (4)
25 He does one's dirty work (8)

DOWN

1 Pacific ex-British republic (4)
2 Hawser; electricity wire (5)
3 Academic talk; scolding (7)
4 Disorderly din (6)
6 Amaze (7)
7 Genetic transmission from parents (8)
8 Benefit; close (companion) (4)
12 Man of all work (8)
14 Entertainment industry (7)
16 One severely self denying (7)
17 Attitude (mental, physical) (6)
19 Sailors' diluted rum (4)
21 Darkness, misery (5)
22 Depend (on); spare (4)

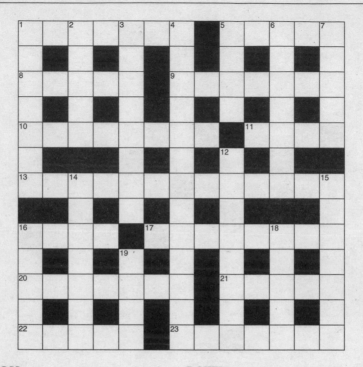

ACROSS

1 Emblems of royalty (7)
5 Mad (dog) (5)
8 Sudden spurt; exploded (5)
9 Advantage (7)
10 Deep crack in ice (8)
11 Part of eye; to hit; to fasten (4)
13 Signature album (9,4)
16 Applaud (4)
17 Block before house; close, on one's (8)
20 *Manon Lescaut* composer (7)
21 Indian police stick (5)
22 Coarse mineral used for polishing (5)
23 Saying *th* for s (7)

DOWN

1 Manderley book *(du Maurier)* (7)
2 Furze (5)
3 Lassitude (8)
4 Relating to envoys (13)
5 Official position; smelling off (4)
6 An ox; a bison (7)
7 To dump; a channel (5)
12 Laughs delightedly (8)
14 Instalment (of e.g. loan) (7)
15 *Mandalay* poet (7)
16 Spinney (5)
18 All play *(music)* (5)
19 Thin but strong (person) (4)

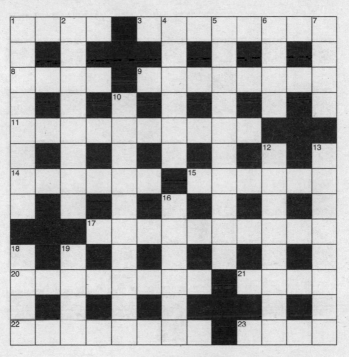

ACROSS

1 Brood, be sullen (4)
3 Rough comic verses (8)
8 Land force (4)
9 Wheedle a loan (8)
11 The wrong crowd to mix with (3,7)
14 Say from memory (6)
15 Corrupt behaviour (6)
17 Within reach; easy to understand (10)
20 Feeble person (8)
21 Therefore; monster *(reversed)* (4)
22 Physically real (8)
23 Contradict (4)

DOWN

1 Sword sheath (8)
2 One wounded, ineffective (4,4)
4 Take possession of, fill (6)
5 Without basis (10)
6 Tirade (4)
7 Edible bulb; sounds like *liquid escape* (4)
10 *Primavera* artist (10)
12 Scout gathering (8)
13 Ritual (8)
16 Edible part of nut (6)
18 Squash (fly) (4)
19 Win; profit (4)

ACROSS

1 German emperor title (6)
5 Giving off reek (6)
8 Part of guitar; worry (4)
9 Window-cleaner's scraper (8)
10 Overall chief (7)
11 Grind (teeth) (5)
13 In malcontented mood (11)
16 Certificate; wallet *(archaic)* (5)
18 Temporary expedient (7)
21 Diffuse through (8)
22 Statue worshipped (4)
23 Salvage (6)
24 Circular; plump (6)

DOWN

2 Unable to float off (7)
3 Indian stringed instrument (5)
4 Remembrance herb (8)
5 Retained portion of ticket (4)
6 Never-ending; Rome this city (7)
7 Fertile, wind-deposited dust (5)
12 Woolly clothing (8)
14 Of earthquakes (7)
15 Cavalryman; to coerce (7)
17 Crinkly fabric; pancake (5)
19 Produce hard copy (5)
20 Bag; set of arguments (4)

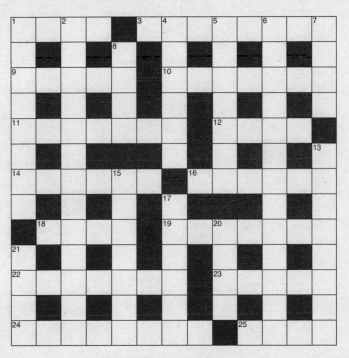

ACROSS

1 Tack; prompt payment, on it (4)
3 Administrative assistant officer (8)
9 Essential (5)
10 Shoe repairer; an iced drink (7)
11 To a large extent (7)
12 An instant; give eye signal (4)
14 Hypnotised state (6)
16 Hateful (6)
18 An animal; put up with (4)
19 Bullfight horseman (7)
22 Arousing strong feeling (7)
23 *Goodbye, Mr –; – with Everything* (5)
24 Earnest plea (8)
25 A crony of Falstaff (4)

DOWN

1 Find the route (8)
2 Suffering together (2,3,4,4)
4 Metrical foot, *tum-ti-ti* (6)
5 (Head bloodied but) erect (7)
6 In due course (3,2,4,4)
7 Mountain pool (4)
8 Strip (in e.g. blind) (4)
13 Strong-coffee method (8)
15 Joined-up (writing) (7)
17 Optimistic (6)
20 Bird; set (gun) ready to fire (4)
21 Charity event; to entertain lavishly (4)

ACROSS

1 Silent waterbird (4,4)
5 Food in shell; crazy (4)
9 One calved from e.g. Antarctic (7)
10 River mammal (5)
11 A fish; singe (4)
12 More strong and healthy (7)
14 Send to custody before trial (6)
16 Correct (manuscript) again (6)
19 School bag (7)
21 Agitate (4)
24 Of less importance (5)
25 Deathly drinks (7)
26 Protest march (4)
27 Lets go (8)

DOWN

1 To cripple (4)
2 Parts of body, of gear wheel (5)
3 (E.g. candle) fat; *nastier (anagram)* (7)
4 South-west African country (6)
6 Never tested; still on 14? (7)
7 Women's club *(especially US)* (8)
8 Throw up (coin, pancake) (4)
13 Took for granted; took liberties (8)
15 Part for whole, as *rod* for *angler* (7)
17 (Bath) attached to bedroom (2,5)
18 (Time) pass (6)
20 Five-year-old male deer (4)
22 Presses; fetters (5)
23 Wife/sister of Osiris (4)

ACROSS

1 Knocks off (e.g. pedestal) (7)
5 Royal golfcourse near Ayr (5)
8 (Mountain) crest (5)
9 Member of periodic table (7)
10 A game; horse-trials venue (9)
12 Debtor's note (1,1,1)
13 Sang under breath; (place) was busy (6)
14 Outskirts; short hair over brow (6)
17 Boy child (3)
18 Cleanshaven (9)
20 Volcanic (rock) (7)
21 Viper (5)
23 Horse (*poet.*) (5)
24 A fertiliser; sounds like *off-peak charge* (7)

DOWN

1 Pulsate (5)
2 Doctorate (*abbr.*) (2,1)
3 Sheltered half (of ship) (3,4)
4 Half rains half snows (6)
5 Coordinate (e.g. book with TV series) (3,2)
6 Compliance (9)
7 Japanese carved ivory (7)
11 Exercise of ascendancy (9)
13 Important person's jocular title (3,4)
15 Wholly change (document) (7)
16 Relay; die (4,2)
18 Fairhaired (man) (5)
19 Loose-stone slope (5)
22 Genetic-info molecule (*abbr.*) (1,1,1)

ACROSS

1 Abstemious, sparing (6)
5 Pig flesh (4)
8 Container; sounds like *wan* (4)
9 Unbalanced (3-5)
10 Individual; extraordinary (8)
11 Colleague (4)
12 To slow (development) (6)
14 (Old LP) needle (6)
16 Enormous (4)
18 Touring performance (especially pop) (8)
20 Irish town; type of verse (8)
21 Irregular reading; spot on screen (4)
22 Non-permanent secretary (4)
23 Royal seat (6)

DOWN

2 Bring to fruition (7)
3 Soviet labour camp system (5)
4 Dickens's eponymous Amy (6,6)
5 (Session) of all members (7)
6 Competitor; be as good as (5)
7 Man's (tweed) coat (6,6)
13 Belgian province, Scheldt port (7)
15 Impractically ideal (7)
17 Nimble (5)
19 Dull; sedate; unflamboyant (5)

ACROSS

1 Supporter (6)

4 Of no effect (4)

9 Plant life; Miles's sister (*The Turn of The Screw*) (5)

10 Lowest-form-of-wit practitioner (7)

11 (E.g. bishop) nominal (7)

12 *Prisoner of Chillon* poet (5)

13 Jester's insignia (3,3,5)

17 Photo, stamp book (5)

19 Plotted secretly (7)

22 Spanish red wine/fruit drink (7)

23 Druid priestess (*Bellini opera*) (5)

24 Feel absence of (4)

25 Poach (trout); amuse (6)

DOWN

1 Be appropriate to (5)

2 Zagreb its capital (7)

3 Computer-sent messages (1-4)

5 Say; complete (5)

6 Enticing (6)

7 Love potion (11)

8 Make possible (6)

14 Look up to (6)

15 Inheritance-of-acquired-traits theorist (7)

16 Kidnapper's demand (6)

18 Marriage announcements (5)

20 Vietnam capital (5)

21 Put (cloth) over (5)

ACROSS

7 US alliance, once v USSR (*abbr.*) (4)
8 Judgment court (8)
9 Regional dialect (6)
10 Servile dependant (6)
11 Lose intensity; (moon) decline from full (4)
12 Missionary efforts (8)
15 Albert —, Nobel physicist (8)
17 Embittered; infertile (land) (4)
18 Shortage (6)
21 Lag behind (6)
22 Husband of Minnehaha (*Longfellow*) (8)
23 A headland; a Loch (4)

DOWN

1 Dancer, World War 1 German spy (4,4)
2 Very serious matter (2,4)
3 Ear-viewing implement (8)
4 Tablet (4)
5 Savoury tart (6)
6 A smoother; his progress, *Hogarth* (4)
13 Baffled by music (4-4)
14 Ungracious (8)
16 Canny (6)
17 Seeding; sounds like *needlework* (6)
19 — Morecambe, comedian (4)
20 Loathe (4)

ACROSS

1 Ability to float (8)

5 Sound of laughter, of thunder (4)

9 Programme of character assassination (5,8)

10 Hock; one manipulated (4)

11 Frank; authentic (7)

13 Salad plant; a firework (6)

15 Of milk (6)

18 Wine merchant (7)

20 Storage shelf; broken blown cloud (4)

23 Perfunctory (*ironic*) (5,3,5)

24 Paved enclosure; a distance (4)

25 Missionary keenness (8)

DOWN

1 Bankrupt; a sculpture (4)

2 Work as *Lulu, Aida* (5)

3 Classify (7)

4 Odd coins; reorganise (6)

6 Belonging to a top group (7)

7 Forbearance, mercy (8)

8 Interval of space, time (4)

12 Farcical mockery (8)

14 Points-of-equal-height line (7)

16 Air spray (7)

17 A fruit; a royal house (6)

19 One quickly jotted (4)

21 Deceive (5)

22 Restrain; support; wait (4)

ACROSS

1 Deep puzzle (7)
5 Travel round (4)
8 Irritable; (make it) quick (6)
9 Unrefined (6)
10 Herman —, *Moby-Dick* author (8)
12 Offensive vehicle; large container (4)
13 Bad dream (9)
17 Suspend; execute (4)
18 Exercise rooms (8)
20 Move to lower rank (6)
21 Small beer cask (6)
23 Infant (4)
24 Session (7)

DOWN

2 An American; a multiple bet (6)
3 Summit; child's toy (3)
4 Of the sovereign (5)
5 Italian restaurant (9)
6 Bearlike (6)
7 Howl; something very funny (6)
11 Boastful ostentation (9)
14 Thomas —, *Tom Brown* author (6)
15 Picture taker (6)
16 Immobilise (arms); little cogwheel (6)
19 Civvies; Islamic jurist (5)
22 Deep wheel track (3)

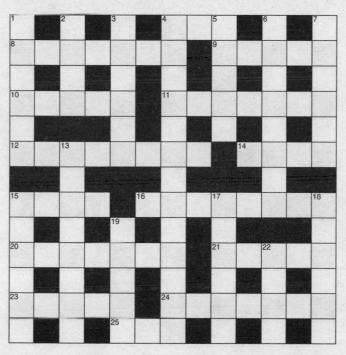

ACROSS

4 Plant's pouch-like cavity (3)
8 Increase, add to (7)
9 (Games, show) ring (5)
10 Ventilated (5)
11 Frame with V-shaped legs (7)
12 Moon-loving shepherd; Keats's subject (8)
14 A service; a quantity (4)
14, 15 Wholesale slaughter (8)
15 1/640th square mile (4)
16 Impurity remover (8)
20 (Special) clothing (7)
21 Disprove; force back (5)
23 Put ball in play; do spell of duty (5)
24 French, Italian Mediterranean coast (7)
25 Add (up); child (3)

DOWN

1 Cope; run (6)
2 Seaweed product (4)
3 Not often (6)
4 Technologically advanced (5-2-3-3)
5 Small role, relief carving (5)
6 Hold back (8)
7 Stands for canvases (6)
13 Laughably inadequate (8)
15 The right to see, get to (6)
17 Reach destination (6)
18 Form of ceremony (6)
19 Peaceful; at low volume (5)
22 Some meat; a complaint (4)

ACROSS

1 Panda food (6)
5 South American animal, its wool (6)
8 Contends (4)
9 More lethal (8)
10 Cut-letter sheet (7)
11 Earth tremor (5)
13 Dickens's David (11)
16 Test (metal) purity (5)
18 Dog-end bowl (7)
21 "Hard pounding" battle (8)
22 Othello's malignant enemy (4)
23 Powerful (6)
24 Imitation (article) (6)

DOWN

2 To do with the largest continent (7)
3 North American ox (5)
4 Commanded; made priest (8)
5 Two Trojan War warriors (4)
6 Befoul (7)
7 Make sure; call at chess (5)
12 (Funds) out of taxman's reach (8)
14 Inert pill (7)
15 Potion; board-game piece (7)
17 Hardly sufficient; to stint (5)
19 Ends of branches; cottons on (5)
20 Advertise; stopper (4)

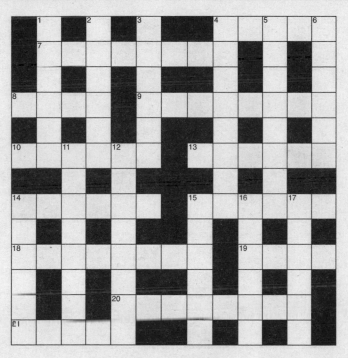

ACROSS

4 Empty-headed (5)
7 Praiseworthy (8)
8 Run fast; one thrown from oche (4)
9 Latest completion time (8)
10 Impertinent (6)
13 Different people (6)
14 Window-screens; dazzles (6)
15 Teacher; become expert in (6)
18 Making twice as big (8)
19 Offer; elasticity (4)
20 Confirm genuineness of (8)
21 A sense; a sample (5)

DOWN

1 Chemically whiten (6)
2 Busy activity; pad under skirt (6)
3 Virtually not; not at all (6)
4 Feud (8)
5 Gable on e.g. Parthenon (8)
6 Compulsion (6)
11 Refined diners (8)
12 Soft hand-cover; delicate (treatment) (3,5)
14 (Plan within) money limit (6)
15 *One for sorrow* bird (6)
16 Gesture, indication (6)
17 Was jealous of (6)

ACROSS

1 *Terrible beauty born* poet (5)
7 (Make) progress (7)
8 A unit of heat (7)
9 Feebleness, infirmity (7)
11 Gullet (6)
13 Cursory, half-hearted (effort) (9)
15 One going on all fours (9)
19 Lion's den man (6)
21 Red bits of US flag (7)
23 Widely liked (7)
24 A flower; *fair, see (anagram)* (7)
25 Large (especially US) farm (5)

DOWN

1 Pleasure craft (5)
2 Glamorous appeal (6)
3 Extend; a risk of middle-age (6)
4 Head of kitchen (4)
5 At mercy of wind and waves (6)
6 Power source; an artillery unit (7)
10 Woken up (6)
12 Right to keep job (6)
14 Food store, (college) shop; tasting of dairy produce (7)
16 Chauffeur; a club (6)
17 Neatly dressed (6)
18 The fiddle (6)
20 Stagger; the abandoned left in it (5)
22 Box; a mineral (4)

ACROSS

1 Race; elan (4)
4 Source of newsprint (4,4)
8 One rung by visitor (8)
9 Greek *I* (4)
10 Ben —, our highest mountain (5)
11 Beethoven opera (7)
13 A slight shaking (6)
15 Secured (good job); having estates (6)
18 Thin, glued board (7)
20 School group; put up (5)
23 — Austen, novelist (4)
24 Green gems (8)
25 Under pressure; accentuated (8)
26 Looked at (4)

DOWN

2 Place of residence (5)
3 Outstanding bravery (7)
4 Work in garden; feeble person (4)
5 Source of "black gold" (8)
6 Value, cost (5)
7 Criss-cross screen (7)
10 Trap; after tax (3)
12 Superior nun (8)
14 Dependent (7)
16 New baby; *no, a teen (anagram)* (7)
17 Female rabbit (3)
19 In what place? (5)
21 Edge furtively along (5)
22 Curve (4)

ACROSS

1, 7 Richard III's final defeat (8,5)
8 Unrefined (bread) (9)
9 Total (3)
10 Well off (4)
11 Passionate (6)
13 Lombardy tree (6)
14 Render in stone (6)
17 Seats; hoists in triumph (6)
18 So be it (prayer) (4)
20 Fuss (3)
22 Quasimodo's condition (9)
23 Richard's *kingdom for* it at 1 *ac* (5)
24 Yorkshire town; Henry Tudor earldom (8)

DOWN

1 Shelter; boudoir; an anchor (5)
2 White top of e.g. Mount Fuji (7)
3 Some 5s of the 7 *ac* (4)
4 Speculative idea (6)
5 Wild animal (5)
6 Unyielding (substance) (7)
7 Full competence (in foreign language) (7)
12 Stylish confidence (7)
13 Voracious tropical fish (7)
15 Lower back pain (7)
16 Borneo sultanate (6)
17 Woo; king's retinue (5)
19 Unclothed (5)
21 Iran monarch title once (4)

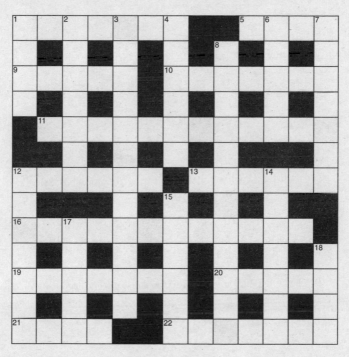

ACROSS

1 File of papers (7)
5 Take water exercise (4)
9 Old gold coin; e.g. Shylock's (5)
10 Aroma; posy (7)
11 Completely mature (bird) (5,7)
12 Thomas —, *Leviathan* author (6)
13 Shock absorber; old fool (6)
16 Where fruitless efforts, storm water, go (4,3,5)
19 Casual, rude (7)
20 Circular painting in relief (5)
21 Sea swell, foam (4)
22 Alpine-plant setting (7)

DOWN

1 Extinct Mauritius bird (4)
2 Give in (to) (7)
3 Egghead (12)
4 Snub (6)
6 Squeezed (5)
7 Bullfighter (7)
8 Involving red tape (12)
12 Very ugly (7)
14 Glazed earthenware (7)
15 Melt down; hand over (6)
17 Thin crisp biscuit (5)
18 Inquisitive (4)

ACROSS

1 Christopher —, discoverer of 6 (8)
5 Go by boat (4)
9 Supernatural (7)
10 Wide expanse of water (5)
11 Univ. athlete; sad (4)
12 A flower; violet antiseptic (7)
14 Lack of interest (6)
16 Pester, hound (6)
19 Curved; mature; pursed (lips) (7)
21 Upper-class person (*derog.*) (4)
24 Birthplace of 1 *ac* (5)
25 Raised-dot writing (7)
26 Endure; final (4)
27 Naively trustful (4-4)

DOWN

1 Army settlement (4)
2 Officially permitted (5)
3 The Scottish play (7)
4 Liquid loss, shortfall (6)
6 The New World (7)
7 Follower of Soviet founder (8)
8 Unite (4)
13 Part-song (8)
15 (Especially US) old boy (7)
17 Insurance statistician (7)
18 Fit to consume (6)
20 Timber; issue cards (4)
22 Female foal (5)
23 Conduct; an element (4)

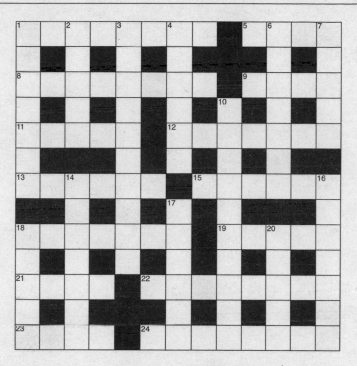

ACROSS

1 Animal panic (8)
5 Profound (4)
8 Rebellion (8)
9 A fish; conical hill (4)
11 Lump; temporary increase (5)
12 Very wicked (7)
13 Apart from (6)
15 Harass; interfere with (6)
18 Passage between seats (7)
19 Orig. name of St Peter (5)
21 (Run) in murderous frenzy (4)
22 More high-pitched (voice) (8)
23 Peel, trim (4)
24 Of the underworld (8)

DOWN

1 Stalks after harvest (7)
2 Of, heard by, the ear (5)
3 Man threatening to queen (6,4)
4 Inflatable boat (6)
6 A typical example (7)
7 Push, importune (5)
10 Ill-affordable little contribution (6,4)
14 Frankness (7)
16 Plant's twining shoot (7)
17 Constricting snake (6)
18 Hold firmly; come to understand (5)
20 Fruit; its *flower gaudy* for Browning (5)

ACROSS

1 One of many born after World War 2 (4,6)

7 A share (7)

8 Condemns (5)

10 Betrayal of country (7)

11 Come up (5)

12 Exhausted, decadent (6)

15 Modern name of Danzig (6)

17 Lampoon (5)

18 Accuse of 10 (7)

21 Sharp point (5)

22 Tiredness (7)

23 Frothy dessert, with marsala (10)

DOWN

1 Warren Hastings opponent; William Hare accomplice (5)

2 Rapture; English composer (5)

3 Fruit, unzip to eat (6)

4 Experienced person (3,4)

5 A wearing away (7)

6 Promotion to divine status (10)

9 Opportunist criminal (5,5)

13 The Sunshine State (7)

14 A thin, lustrous silk fabric (7)

16 Intentional (harm); obstinate (6)

19 Paved terrace (5)

20 Point of view; 5th century invader (5)

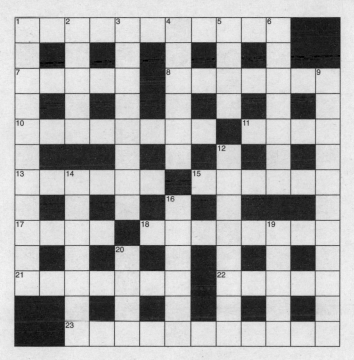

ACROSS

1 Definitely; whatever happens (7,4)
7 Hair grip; lose grip (5)
8 Vanity project (3-4)
10 Emotional closeness (8)
11 Part of fish, of mushroom; quarter pint (4)
13 Quick look (6)
15 Drums played on knees (6)
17 Per person (4)
18 Dilemma (8)
21 Be passive; relax (3,4)
22 Name; style (5)
23 Insidious Greek gift (6,5)

DOWN

1 Water source, takes coins (7-4)
2 Curl; Dickens boy (5)
3 Excessively (8)
4 Deep ditch (6)
5 Eden earldom; various rivers (4)
6 Hiding nefariously (7)
9 Rigid, light packaging (11)
12 First rate (3-5)
14 Very old (7)
16 Nepalese soldier (6)
19 Place of sacrifice (5)
20 Ring of light (4)

ACROSS

1 Tomorrow; sometime (Spanish) (6)
5 Broached (6)
8 Smart, genteel (4)
9 *Hail Mary* prayer (3,5)
10 Coupons (8)
12 Against; an opponent (4)
13 Fit to employ (6)
15 Penetrate (6)
17 Starch for puddings (4)
19 Renegade (8)
21 Give incentive to (8)
23 Baghdad its capital (4)
24 Invented; composed (quarrel) (4,2)
25 South Devon city (6)

DOWN

2 In loving mood (7)
3 For particular purpose (2,3)
4 Stupefaction (9)
5 Lyric poem (3)
6 Issue, proceed (from) (7)
7 Authoritative order (5)
11 Displace (9)
14 A sedative; a platitude (7)
16 Travesty; party-game act (7)
18 Wafted smell (5)
20 (Clock) sound; agree (with) (5)
22 Unit of current (*abbr.*) (3)

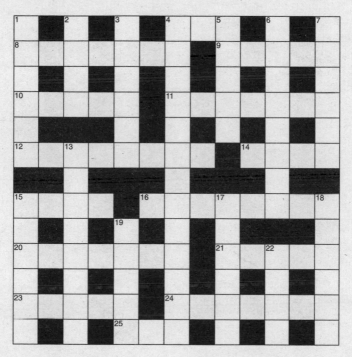

ACROSS

4 Turn up ground (3)
8 Normal course of events (7)
9 Divide in two (5)
10 Elector (5)
11 Bloat (7)
12 Have contrary view (8)
14 Low dam (4)
15 Bird; bit of fun (4)
16 US state; a musical (8)
20 Punish (7)
21 Return to civvy street (5)
23 A female relative (5)
24 Nine-sided figure (7)
25 Dowel; prevent (price) rise (3)

DOWN

1 Shown to be true (6)
2 Smallest piglet (4)
3 E.g. North Sea platform (3-3)
4 Blind navigation (4,9)
5 Phantom (5)
6 Bosom friend (5,3)
7 Supplier of funds (6)
13 Paper ribbon for throwing (8)
15 (Manuscript) gap (6)
17 Giving help (6)
18 Pigment-deficient creature (6)
19 Soak; unfairly expensive (5)
22 Caspar, Melchior, and Balthazar (4)

ACROSS

1 Company emblem (4)
3 Adolescent (8)
9 Newly made; cold (wind) (5)
10 Allspice (7)
11 A city; a US president (7)
12 Brought into existence (4)
14 China clay (6)
16 A showy perennial (6)
18 Capital of Norway (4)
19 Pablo —, 20th century artist (7)
22 Suitcases; a trollop (7)
23 Give one's view (5)
24 Wind from Continent (8)
25 I've spilled it! (4)

DOWN

1 Resembling the real person (8)
2 Global-warming air pollutant (10,3)
4 Lay out, use up (6)
5 Windhoek its capital (7)
6 President/supreme commander rank (13)
7 A bird; to swindle (4)
8 Go away! (4)
13 Noble lady (8)
15 Post-Bronze period (4,3)
17 Attraction; request to umpire (6)
20 Cut (e.g. wood); cut of pork (4)
21 A reed instrument (4)

ACROSS

6 Gardening skill (5,7)

7 Obvious; right to exploit invention (6)

8 Flashes of light; ship's radio officer (6)

9 One Zeus visited as swan (4)

10 Billboard; saving (8)

12 Transfer, surrender (4,4)

16 E.g. crocus "bulb" (4)

18 Storage compartment (6)

20 In unfeeling way (6)

21 Feeble, insipid (behaviour) (4-3-5)

DOWN

1 Ely outlaw, opposed Conqueror (8)

2 Grab quickly (6)

3 Spanish carnival (6)

4 Taj Mahal site (4)

5 Smashed; discontinuous (6)

6 Elegance; clemency (5)

11 Reduce by a tenth (8)

13 In fear (6)

14 *Romeo and Juliet* city (6)

15 Fame (6)

17 Governor (5)

19 Ship's track; funeral vigil (4)

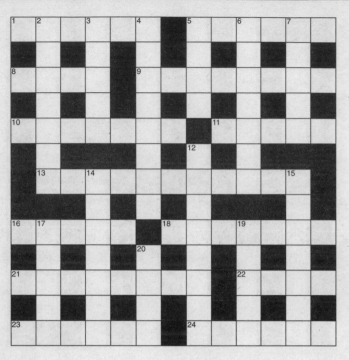

ACROSS

1 Start to grow (6)
5 Suit; turn into (6)
8 Jerky shock (4)
9 About to happen (8)
10 Loss of hope (7)
11 Throb, beat (5)
13 Travel widely (3,3,5)
16 European royal house once; some Operas (5)
18 Thoughtful (7)
21 Rudimentary (8)
22 His wife a countess (4)
23 Ski obstacle race (6)
24 Israeli money (6)

DOWN

2 Skill, daring (7)
3 Available whenever wanted (2,3)
4 Gloaming (8)
5 Small protuberance; exclude from plane flight (4)
6 Defeat (7)
7 Take-away (sign) (5)
12 Splinter-removing implement (8)
14 Marking an era (7)
15 Of many different types (7)
17 Make void (5)
19 One from Uppsala (5)
20 Windless (4)

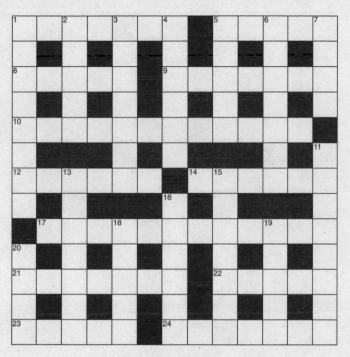

ACROSS

1 Place of activity, danger (3,4)

5 Reeking sunset ran into its Bay (*Browning*) (5)

8 Bird-dung fertiliser (5)

9 Mortification (7)

10 Fruit; Durrell Cyprus book (6,6)

12 Dull-witted; blunt (6)

14 Manage with what one has (4,2)

17 Way of ruinous indulgence (*Shakespeare*) (8,4)

21 Rope; artist (7)

22 Fairy-tale-writing brothers (5)

23 Swagger; strengthening bar (5)

24 Squirting implement (7)

DOWN

1 Intellectual (8)

2 Stretch of ground; pamphlet (5)

3 Declare (e.g. faith) (7)

4 Equipment; get to grips with (6)

5 Amulet; allure (5)

6 Send mad (7)

7 Defined area (4)

11 Geniality (8)

13 Asian primate; *it's rare (anagram)* (7)

15 One getting own back (7)

16 William —, 19th century designer; type of dancer (6)

18 Sacred choral piece (5)

19 Of birds (5)

20 (Musical) work (4)

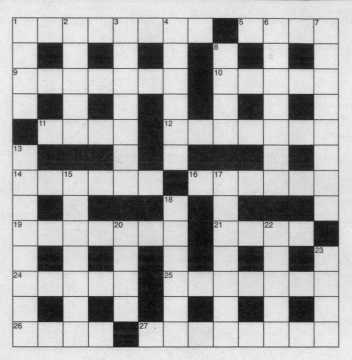

ACROSS

1 The Conqueror's book (8)
5 Speaker's platform (4)
9 Lowers (oneself) (7)
10 Aroma; atmosphere (5)
11 Rely (on) (4)
12 Fighting man (7)
14 John —, *Brief Lives* author (6)
16 Preoccupy (6)
19 One-horn beast (7)
21 Head-covering; US gangster (4)
24 Mindless (5)
25 Pet rodent (7)
26 Unit of heredity (4)
27 Keep safe; a special area (8)

DOWN

1 Lower part of wall (4)
2 Venomous African snake (5)
3 Coruscate (7)
4 Give help (6)
6 Torment oneself (7)
7 Unexpected event (8)
8 Young horse (4)
13 Becoming older, more developed (8)
15 The UK (7)
17 Island group north of Cuba (7)
18 Fix firmly (6)
20 Finished; on top of (4)
22 Target ring furthest from bull (5)
23 At liberty (4)

ACROSS

1 *Trout Quintet* composer (8)
5 Predatory animal; eat fast (4)
9 Musical form with repeats (5)
10 Portia's maid (*The Merchant of Venice*) (7)
11 Infringement penalty (7)
12 Container; sink (5)
13 Socially compulsory (2,7)
18 Monastic mountain (5)
20 Bar supporting fanlight (7)
22 Undeviating (imitation) (7)
23 Launcelot —, Shylock's servant (5)
24 Stagger; dance (4)
25 Candour (8)

DOWN

1 Conflict (6)
2 A number; part of county once (7)
3 A fellow (*slang*) (5)
4 Keep good discipline (3,1,5,4)
6 Refuge in trouble (*fig.*) (5)
7 Brandish gloatingly (6)
8 Boy singer (6)
14 Countryman (6)
15 Arousing contempt (7)
16 Thick (ship's) cable (6)
17 Print (characters) in relief (6)
19 Rise and fall (sea) (5)
21 An element; *groan (anagram)* (5)

ACROSS

1 Pointed (remark, wire) (6)
5 Bring up under pressure (4)
8 Practical joke (4)
9 Logic choppers (8)
10 Canadian east coast district (8)
11 Bunch (of hair) (4)
12 Short-sightedness (6)
14 A tree; smart (6)
16 Hole for e.g. coin (4)
18 One from Papeete (8)
20 Vault rib; base stone of arch (8)
21 Unexciting (4)
22 Fun; taunt (4)
23 Coy, modest (6)

DOWN

2 Out-of-line result (7)
3 Exponent of the *noble art* (5)
4 Drawback (12)
5 Indication, sign (7)
6 Distinctive (artistic) theme (5)
7 Spoils the child? (6,3,3)
13 Defender of one's country (7)
15 Thomas —, *Prayer Book* author (7)
17 Momentary slip; expire (5)
19 Symbolic animal (5)

ACROSS

2 Voltaire's optimist (*Candide*) (8)
6 Elegant cavalryman (6)
8 Loose collection (6)
9 Australian interior (7)
10 Cloister court; (Northern) yard (5)
12 Ranting speaker (3-7)
16 Fond of company (10)
18 Film for home viewing (5)
20 Rail tracks in yard (7)
21 Wood for furniture; edible wrinkled kernel (6)
22 Vigour (6)
23 Range of freedom (8)

DOWN

1 Heaped, white cloud mass (7)
2 Make (future event) impossible (8)
3 Cause of resentment (6)
4 Regularity; a taxonomic group (5)
5 To foam, be agitated (6)
7 Wrecking activity (8)
11 Guile, subterfuge (8)
13 (New Testament) hypocrite (8)
14 Trunks and cases (7)
15 Affirmation (6)
17 Strongly, healthily built (6)
19 Dutch town, its blue ware (5)

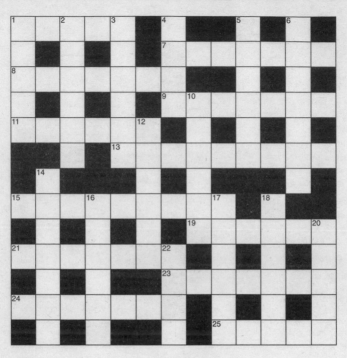

ACROSS

1 Skewered, grilled meat (5)
7 Mediaeval "chemistry" (7)
8 In keen fashion (7)
9 Slovenly dirtiness (7)
11 Deplore (6)
13 Only country to leave European Community (9)
15 One taken for ride (9)
19 Imitated (6)
21 Crowded, nestled together (7)
23 Pleasant, available service (7)
24 Range of hearing (7)
25 One from another planet (5)

DOWN

1 Tolling of bell (5)
2 Having too many wives (6)
3 A strait; sounds like *orientation* (6)
4 Paths; methods (4)
5 Servitude (6)
6 Seize and detain (7)
10 Canada's largest province (6)
12 Hypnotised state (6)
14 Japanese warrior (7)
16 Deliberate cruelty (6)
17 Ivanhoe's girl (*Sir Walter Scott*) (6)
18 Skimpy beachwear (6)
20 Senior member (5)
22 Items of information (4)

ACROSS

1 Come to bad conclusion (3,2,5)
8 Unacceptably different (7)
9 Dried coconut (5)
10 Fish; part of shoe (4)
11 Feeling sick; offensive (8)
13 Horse-rider (6)
15 Ornamental cave (6)
17 Blend, merge (8)
18 Studious pupil (4)
21 Rye-afflicting fungus (5)
22 In a perfect world (7)
23 Salvation; conversion into cash (10)

DOWN

2 Part of body; type of orange (5)
3 Mosque prayer leader (4)
4 Venetian painter, his auburn shade (6)
5 Pedigree (8)
6 Uphold, sustain (7)
7 *Forsyte* creator (10)
8 Book cover (4,6)
12 Down in dumps (8)
14 Bad error, especially when dropped (7)
16 (Church) division (6)
19 I shall obey (*radio*) (5)
20 Written material for study (4)

ACROSS

1 Cuts; journalists (5)

4 Temporarily inactive (7)

8 Lovingly bring up (7)

9 Area of expertise (5)

10 Table covering (5)

11 Such a Fleece, a Horde, a Gate Bridge (6)

13 Former Spanish dictator (6)

15 Pressure line on weather map (6)

18 A symbiotic plant (6)

20 Europe/US golf cup (5)

22 A horned beast (5)

23 Make aware (7)

24 Shyness (7)

25 Boat Race team (5)

DOWN

1 Secure (wrists) (8)

2 Argentina city; Moorish Spain capital (7)

3 Melting snow (5)

4 A seabed scoop (6)

5 Charity events; a gentleman burglar (7)

6 Sharp mountain ridge (5)

7 Fuss (2-2)

12 Salacious (8)

14 (In) league (7)

16 Starting to sprout (7)

17 Ill repute (6)

19 Covered in creeper (5)

20 Money in India (5)

21 (Glass) be very full (4)

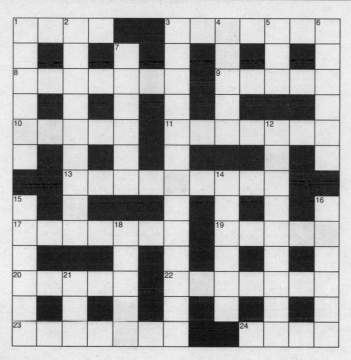

ACROSS

1 In which Po rises (4)

3 Surrey town, sounds like *marks* (7)

8 Busily active (2,3,2)

9 Samuel —, electric telegraph inventor (5)

10 Run away to marry (5)

11 Disappoint; lowered (3,4)

13 General agreement (9)

17 Make anxious (7)

19 Muslim saviour (5)

20 Tedium (5)

22 Attack (7)

23 Outrageous, corrupting (7)

24 Group of girls, of quail (4)

DOWN

1 Loved (6)

2 Policing vehicle (6,3)

3 The scapula (8,5)

4 Let in; confess (5)

5 And not (3)

6 18th century author; sounds like *severe* (6)

7 *Thick* on it *snow the leaves (Wenlock Edge)* (6)

12 Hop-kiln building (4,5)

14 Spicy fried pastry (6)

15 Mph indicator (*abbr.*) (6)

16 Very unclean (6)

18 Join in one (5)

21 Numbers (*abbr.*) (3)

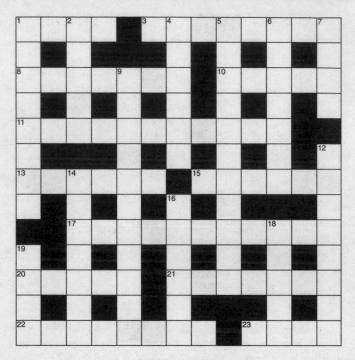

ACROSS

1 Nosegay (4)

3 Widely scattered (3-5)

8 Suffocate (7)

10 —jar; —life; —shade (5)

11 A deserved fall (4-7)

13 Delivery chit; certificate (6)

15 Wooster's battleaxe aunt (*Wodehouse*) (6)

17 Go separate ways (4,7)

20 Heraldic blue (5)

21 Keats *half in love with* such *Death* (7)

22 Evanescent (8)

23 Some ice; sounds like *move as liquid* (4)

DOWN

1 Essential part of address (8)

2 Force-ten wind (5)

4 Curt; steep (6)

5 Frivolous goings-on (3,3,5)

6 Ointment (7)

7 French rural holiday home (4)

9 Confinement to home (5,6)

12 Senior Service shade (4,4)

14 Seize (7)

16 Hide from view (6)

18 Terrifying; bad (*loosely*) (5)

19 Neglected child (4)

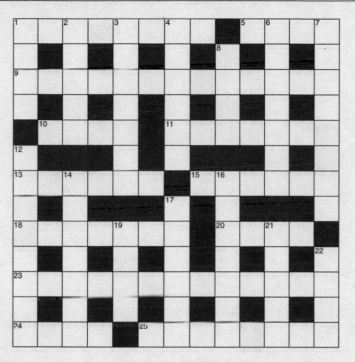

ACROSS

1 Boring, unvarying voice (8)
5 Wife of Zeus (4)
9 Cardinals collectively (6,7)
10 Had sensation (of); a material (4)
11 Brought into effect; asked (for) (7)
13 Horse gait; won easily, at this (6)
15 (Customs) permit (6)
18 That can be defended (7)
20 Small restaurant (4)
23 Phone-wire support (9,4)
24 Criminal's blunt weapon ... (4)
25 ... his sharp one (8)

DOWN

1 Deer secretion; type of rose (4)
2 Mother-of-pearl (5)
3 Playhouse (7)
4 What bees collect (6)
6 Dry summer Mediterranean wind (7)
7 Humorous story (8)
8 Collapse; disaster (4)
12 Transported with joy (8)
14 Perplex (7)
16 Intoxicant (7)
17 Withdraw (opinion) (6)
19 Insects; a cartoon Bunny (4)
21 Money in till; carnival vehicle (5)
22 Short note (4)

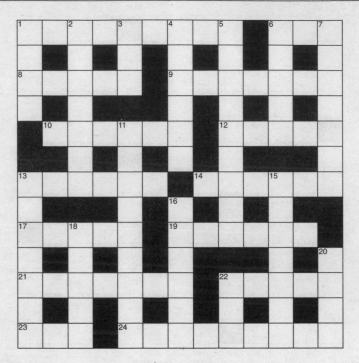

ACROSS

1 Cloak with pretence (9)
6 Dandy (3)
8 Travel over; lie on and hide (5)
9 Researcher (7)
10 Squat down (6)
12 Type of wheat; signified (5)
13 Franklin — Roosevelt (6)
14 Cartoon hero; servant (6)
17 A sense; a vision (5)
19 Affront (6)
21 Sir Winston L. — Churchill (7)
22 A snap (5)
23 Fail; one irrevocably cast (3)
24 Issued (drugs) (9)

DOWN

1 Cut; a remedial leaf (4)
2 Some, not many (7)
3 Part of body, of cereal (3)
4 Percy — Shelley (6)
5 New Testament book; Diana worshippers (9)
6 Untrue (5)
7 Stern, plain-living moralist (7)
11 Having escaped detection (9)
13 Obsolete (7)
15 Richard — Nixon (7)
16 Tree as lemon, lime (6)
18 Parson's land once (5)
20 Alfred, — Tennyson (4)
22 Food with crust (3)

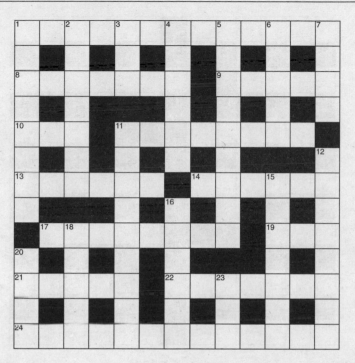

ACROSS

1 Early Dickens work (8,2,3)
8 Protective cover (7)
9 Prison; neglected state (5)
10 Dismissed; flowering (3)
11 Sticking condition (8)
13 Exculpatory reason (6)
14 (Clothes) not covering enough (6)
17 Splendid (8)
19 Professional charge (3)
21 Egyptian dam (5)
22 Infective organism (7)
24 Stealthy (13)

DOWN

1 Surgeon (*derog.*) (8)
2 Flexible (7)
3 National team place (3)
4 Uninhibitedly crude (6)
5 Vicious villain (*Oliver Twist*) (4,5)
6 Brainless beauty (5)
7 Move fast; change focus quickly (4)
11 Self-confidence; pledge of support (9)
12 Mountains Andorra lies in (8)
15 Sicilian gangster (7)
16 Hand over; carry out (crime) (6)
18 Further down (5)
20 Luggage; I claim! (4)
23 An animal; a boat (*abbr.*) (3)

ACROSS

1 Cloth; a structure (6)
5 University grounds (6)
8 Weaving machine; be near (4)
9 One implementing will (8)
10 Hilltop fire (6)
12 Sort, class (4)
15 Terrified (5-8)
16 Advantage; rim (4)
17 Items for meeting (6)
19 Confident; categorical (8)
21 Decline; basin (4)
22 Projecting rim (6)
23 Powerful shock, wound (6)

DOWN

2 Previously mentioned (9)
3 An animal; force down (3)
4 Least soiled (8)
5 Corner of sail; hammock thread; sounds like *hint* (4)
6 Face hair (9)
7 Strange celestial sight (*abbr.*) (3)
11 Yardstick (9)
13 Nom de plume (9)
14 Most general (8)
18 Heap; foundation beam (4)
20 Bird; loved Pussy-cat (*Lear*) (3)
21 — Fever (*Masefield*) (3)

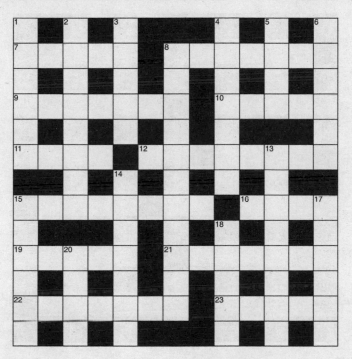

ACROSS

7 Non-clergy (5)

8 Visualise (7)

9 Enormous (7)

10 Tiniest amount (5)

11 Manifest (4)

12 Very bad (8)

15 Frozen sweet (3,5)

16 Slight problem (4)

19 England/Australia cricket trophy (5)

21 Set up ready for use (7)

22 Mutually decide about (5,2)

23 Release (knot) (5)

DOWN

1 Tongues of fire (6)

2 Cutting-edge sharpener (8)

3 Eagles' nest (5)

4 Posed scene (7)

5 Egypt princess, dies with Rhadames (4)

6 Legume seed, in soups etc. (6)

8 Drunkenness (11)

13 Painting, sculpture, etc. (4,4)

14 Flourish (7)

15 *Comfort ye, my people* prophet (6)

17 Ship's kitchen (6)

18 Number of magazine (5)

20 Animal, mad in spring (4)

ACROSS

5 One taken with incredible claim (1,5,2,4)

8 Sugared almond; cake-decoration ball (6)

9 Harass (6)

10 Actual event (4)

12 He's from Barcelona (7)

14 Wither (7)

15 Inter-family quarrel (4)

17 Handsome (Greek) youth (6)

18 One awkward at sea (6)

20 Dangerous person (4,8)

DOWN

1 Hangover-curing drink (4,2,3,3)

2 Call up; circle (4)

3 Hide (7)

4 Judge roughly (8)

6 Masticate (4)

7 Keep making new discoveries (4,3,5)

11 Smoke vents (8)

13 Temperature scale (7)

16 Boring; place to live (4)

19 Explosive weapon (4)

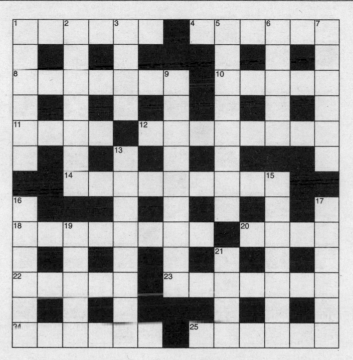

ACROSS

1 Naughty child; pile-driving hammer (6)
4 Teasing problem (6)
8 Punted canal boat (7)
10 Routine; boring instrument (5)
11 Single entity (4)
12 Equity (8)
14 Very tasty (9)
18 Diligence; manufacturing (8)
20 Impossible, forbidden (2-2)
22 Hebridean island, south of Uists (5)
23 Senior naval officer (7)
24 Erred; showed assent (6)
25 Headlong course (6)

DOWN

1 Double-size champagne bottle (6)
2 Over-fussily protected (7)
3 Cupid (4)
5 Less-fancied competitor (8)
6 Kinshasa its capital (5)
7 Join up (6)
9 The monkey puzzle tree (9)
13 Controlled slide; a ballet step (8)
15 Whip; one harassing (7)
16 *Decline and Fall* historian (6)
17 Egregious error (6)
19 Took a risk (5)
21 Jane Austen's Miss Woodhouse (4)

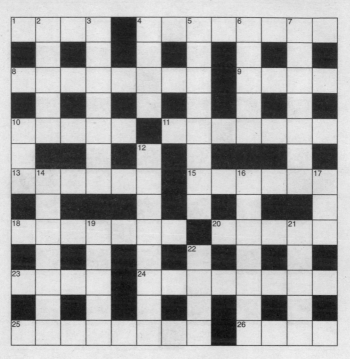

ACROSS

1 Slickly plausible (4)
4 US train system; unfairly compel (8)
8 Defensive gate-tower (8)
9 Reliable bet (4)
10 Queen — Antoinette (5)
11 Took lead role (in) (7)
13 Hold out enticingly (6)
15 Forward stampede (6)
18 Half-man half-horse (7)
20 Seize without right (5)
23 Daybreak (4)
24 Unable to meet debts (8)
25 Lifting power; influence (8)
26 Small (skirt, car) (4)

DOWN

2 Capital of Tibet (5)
3 Going up and down with waves (7)
4 Hard material; type of music (4)
5 Engine starter (8)
6 Competitive runner (5)
7 Stuffy, close (7)
10 Dirt; one's name, if unpopular (3)
12 Half-shadow area (8)
14 Mean, normal (7)
16 Dais (7)
17 A fruit; a joint (3)
19 Hint of colour (5)
21 North Yorkshire cathedral city (5)
22 Leg joint (4)

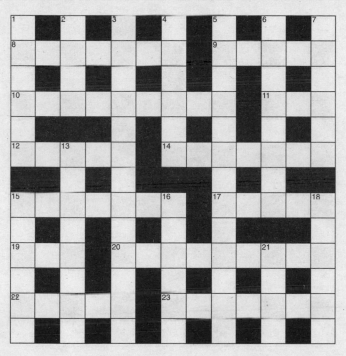

ACROSS

8 Not taking sides (7)
9 Stage (in process) (5)
10 One different from rest (3,3,3)
11 Hole-making tool (3)
12 Shed coat (5)
14 Nervousness (7)
15 *Podsnap, Heep* creator (7)
17 Breathes rapidly (5)
19 Part of fish; a deer (3)
20 Lasciviously excite (9)
22 Set of links (5)
23 Answer (7)

DOWN

1 Advise, tell (6)
2 Tobacco lump; pound (*slang*) (4)
3 Ostentatious remorse (6-7)
4 Not quite (6)
5 (Military) neatness (4,3,6)
6 One from Honolulu (8)
7 A raptor; a magician (6)
13 Personification of US (5,3)
15 Order; straight (6)
16 (Surgical) seam (6)
18 Regular (6)
21 Tiniest amount (*fig.*) (4)

ACROSS

1 Absolute hush (7)
5 Enormous (4)
8 Officer's side-arm (6)
9 Unsubstantiated report (6)
10 Author of *Emma Bovary* (8)
12 Guessing game (1-3)
13 Rules of behaviour (9)
17 A tree; part of hand (4)
18 An idealised rustic (8)
20 Too old, feeble (4,2)
21 Intermittent-motion transmitter (6)
23 Seed; bacillus (4)
24 Not deep (7)

DOWN

2 Frozen drip (6)
3 A newt (3)
4 Produce young; sounds like *slice meat* (5)
5 Clumsy (3-6)
6 Surly (6)
7 Twist in agony (6)
11 Final demand (9)
14 Mineral, its crystal in clocks (6)
15 Little savoury bite (6)
16 Summer-house (6)
19 Apprehend; trick; one worth marrying (5)
22 Friend, mate (3)

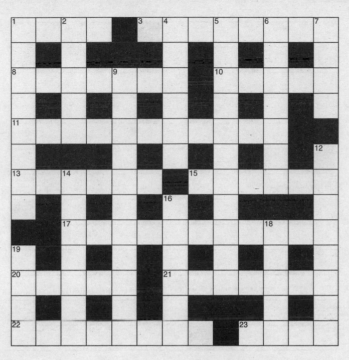

ACROSS

1 Male animal; one passed, to avoid blame (4)

3 Omnipresence (8)

8 Ancient Egypt monument (7)

10 Become liable for (5)

11 Madeleines; *so peck, Agnes (anagram)* (6,5)

13 Magic remedy (6)

15 Start (fire) (6)

17 Zest for living (4,2,5)

20 Gorse (5)

21 Decorate (food) (7)

22 Actor's, singer's test (8)

23 Stitched (4)

DOWN

1 Avoided, driven round (2-6)

2 Interesting, rare, item (5)

4 Upper part of dress (6)

5 Mercury (11)

6 Cut, scored (into) (7)

7 Tale; thread (4)

9 Splendid (11)

12 Charity-funding TV evening (8)

14 Wounded (7)

16 Slow (*music*) (6)

18 Opinion; ability to speak (5)

19 Dyke-building Mercian (4)

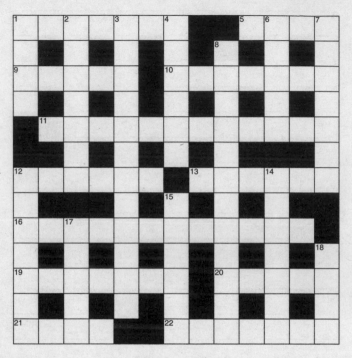

ACROSS

1 Large animals hunted (3,4)
5 Prime Minister once; flake off (4)
9 Pastoral lover (5)
10 Nauseously sweet (7)
11 Fired with keenness (12)
12 Roof of mouth (6)
13 A sly one; Toad Hall invader (*Grahame*) (6)
16 Transparently honest (7,5)
19 Gulf island sheikdom (7)
20 Write in capitals (5)
21 Religious teacher; expert (4)
22 Where King John lost crown jewels (3,4)

DOWN

1 Soak up sun, praise (4)
2 Hooked grabber; little anchor (7)
3 Shakespeare's wife (4,8)
4 Surfeit (6)
6 Have life (5)
7 Rational (7)
8 When (e.g. sun) disc vanishes (5,7)
12 (Lots of) incoming mail (7)
14 Power of endurance (7)
15 Baby swan (6)
17 Attendant (5)
18 Mormon state (4)

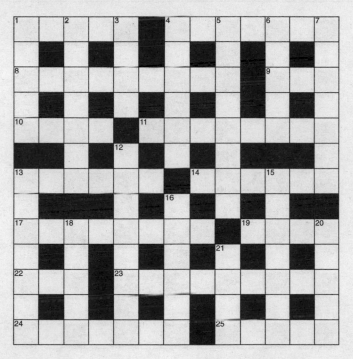

ACROSS

1 Big (plane, crossword) (5)
4 Live together (7)
8 Emily Brontë's *Heights* (9)
9 Flightless bird; a federal project (*abbr.*) (3)
10 Connecting piece (4)
11 Ran fast, naked (8)
13 Dull, boring (6)
14 Fuelling tanker (6)
17 Last round in knock-out (3,5)
19 Prima donna (4)
22 Spoil (3)
23 Robin Hood's jolly monk (5,4)
24 Devotion (7)
25 Wilkie Collins's *Woman in* it (5)

DOWN

1 Precious stone (5)
2 Type of performance, jacket, idol (7)
3 Cooker (4)
4 A patterned cotton (6)
5 A French Protestant (8)
6 Dickens's *House* (5)
7 Stormy peal (7)
12 Prolific; profitable (8)
13 In units of ten (7)
15 Spurs to action (7)
16 Thackeray's *Fair* (6)
18 A social; person (in lawsuit) (5)
20 Low leg joint (5)
21 Front of vessel (4)

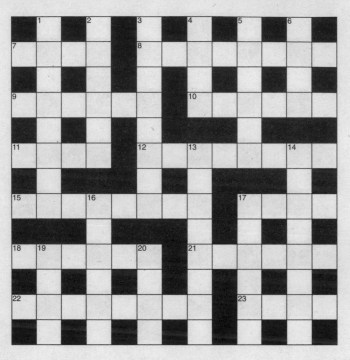

ACROSS

7 The blackthorn (4)
8 Persuasively spoken (8)
9 Boring person (*slang*); his coat (6)
10 Those accepting (e.g. bet) (6)
11 Churl (4)
12 Money earned on deposit (8)
15 Foreword (8)
17 Mountain-top (4)
18 Swift; punctual (6)
21 Beat (cornstalks) (6)
22 Dark (night) (8)
23 Charity bazaar (4)

DOWN

1 Commotion; loud resonance (8)
2 Native servant (6)
3 Feeble person (8)
4 Defensive water (4)
5 Follower of William Penn (6)
6 Trunk protuberance; grade (*reversed*) (4)
13 Formal academic work (8)
14 Sporadic, scattered state (8)
16 Thin plate (e.g. of mineral) (6)
17 To filter, cleanse (6)
19 Civil commotion (4)
20 Level, row (4)

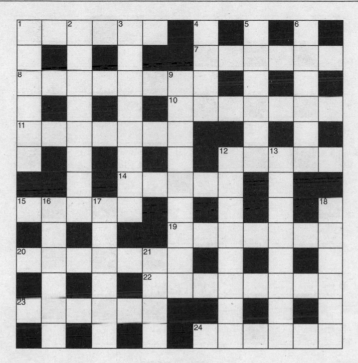

ACROSS

1 Confirm (6)
7 Cloud over, dim (6)
8 Impose control over (8)
10 Neck of land (7)
11 Sort of small peach (7)
12 South American range (5)
14 Scandinavian cave-dweller (5)
15 Unpleasant (5)
19 Diplomatic (7)
20 Exact copy (7)
22 (For) all time (8)
23 Behind (ship) (6)
24 One with blue pencil (6)

DOWN

1 In words (6)
2 Strict, unbending (8)
3 Great happiness (8)
4 Fifteenth (of Roman March) (4)
5 Ragged child (6)
6 Disprove (6)
9 Retributive action (3,3,3)
12 (Eating) not the set meal (1,2,5)
13 Scottish town; *firm sued (anagram)* (8)
16 Opposed (to) (6)
17 Steering handle (6)
18 Competitor in game (6)
21 Small coin; sounds like *given errand* (4)

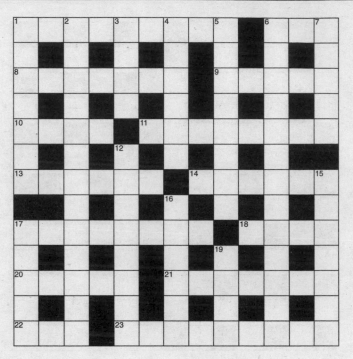

ACROSS

1 Painstaking (9)
6 Deep hole; part of theatre (3)
8 Reprove (7)
9 Slim and long-limbed (5)
10 Bend; cable (4)
11 Grotesque carving (8)
13 Venice business centre once (6)
14 Steppes; a US Presidential birthplace (6)
17 Sir John —, was Poet Laureate (8)
18 Mark of wound (4)
20 Nag; colic (5)
21 Mound-building insect (7)
22 Record; one put on fire (3)
23 Glare of publicity (9)

DOWN

1 Water-holding rock (7)
2 Making threatening gestures (5-8)
3 Double; sounds like *combat* (4)
4 Passé (3-3)
5 Conflict (8)
6 Parsimonious (5-8)
7 Oberon knew a bank where it blew (5)
12 Exquisitely delicate (8)
15 Snake; a deceiver (7)
16 A cock; a fighting weight (6)
17 Jewish roll (5)
19 Paperless exam (4)

ACROSS

1 Free-form effusion (8)
5 Study (university subject) (4)
9 Triple godhead (7)
10 Copying (5)
11 Jump; sort of year (4)
12 School (7)
14 It made Beerbohm insufferable (6)
16 Water-boiler (6)
19 Sink, fail (7)
21 Roman Catholic head; Greek parish priest (4)
24 Adhere; cane (5)
25 Contravene (rule) (7)
26 Rather wet (4)
27 One MP does not fear losing (4,4)

DOWN

1 Duty list (4)
2 Live (especially *with me*) (5)
3 A butterfly; a captain (7)
4 Solid carbon dioxide (3,3)
6 Urgent, pressing (7)
7 Poor verse (8)
8 Formal dance (4)
13 Muddled up (8)
15 School of e.g. Matisse (7)
17 Blow up (7)
18 Unimportant facts (6)
20 Top-rank nobleman (4)
22 Tranquillity (5)
23 Hamlet wished his *too-solid flesh* would (4)

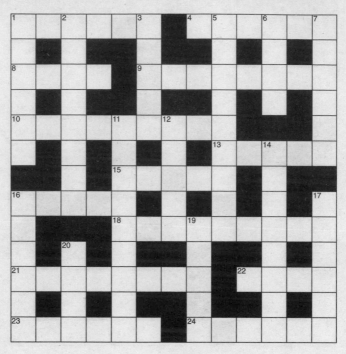

ACROSS

1 Drinking vessel (6)
4 One keeping tally (6)
8 Tree-trunk (4)
9 Bothered; anxious (8)
10 Combine into unity (9)
13 Recess for statue (5)
15 Portion (of cake) (5)
16 Part of body; piece of furniture (5)
18 Aus. monolith; *corker, say (anagram)* (5,4)
21 End of the line (8)
22 Watch-face (4)
23 Plump (6)
24 A cure (6)

DOWN

1 Malicious fairy (6)
2 Demean (8)
3 Private coach (5)
5 Vulgarity; undeveloped state (9)
6 Get under skin of (4)
7 Make smaller (6)
11 Period of development (9)
12 Similar (5)
14 George IV's queen (8)
16 Little Bighorn his last stand (6)
17 Thin gruel (6)
19 Vertical part of stair (5)
20 Be worried; fingerboard ridge (4)

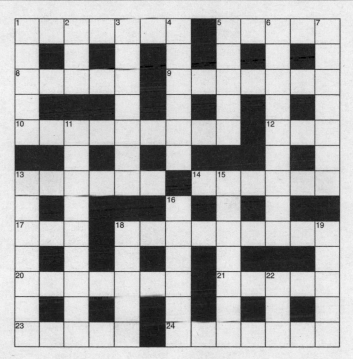

ACROSS

1 Aircraft engine cover (7)
5 Beam-bouncing detection method (5)
8 Bundle of corn (5)
9 (Disease) native to area (7)
10 An artificial language (9)
12 Sharp cutter (3)
13 Clergyman (6)
14 Protective clothes, have strings (6)
17 A constellation; various Popes (3)
18 In love; Titania was, *of an ass* (9)
20 Location; place of duty; post (7)
21 Feathered weapon (5)
23 Bring to bear (effort, pressure) (5)
24 Shake (7)

DOWN

1 (Hereditary) layer of society (5)
2 Misery (3)
3 Raging fire (7)
4 An elopers' Green (6)
5 Cowboy show (5)
6 Personal manner, bearing (9)
7 Dins; a game (7)
11 Vote in name of (another) (9)
13 Fur-lined cloak (7)
15 Secular; disrespectful to religion (7)
16 A gemstone; sounds like an Alf (6)
18 Turn out of home (5)
19 Use rod to find water (5)
22 To chafe (3)

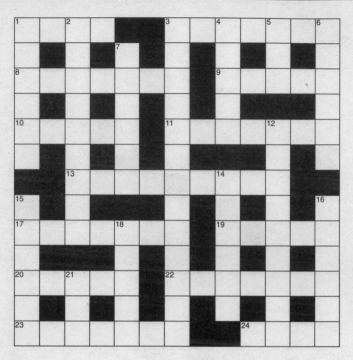

ACROSS

1 A lot of (4)
3 Vivid; type of arts (7)
8 Powdery woodcutting residue (7)
9 Joyful (5)
10 Find out (5)
11 French bean (7)
13 About 1092 yards (9)
17 Goods sent back (7)
19 Hidden store (5)
20 Celebrated (5)
22 French city, papal palace (7)
23 One under instruction (7)
24 Learned volume (4)

DOWN

1 Body tissue; strength (6)
2 Racecourse; card game (9)
3 Clearly understand (3,3,7)
4 Loathe (5)
5 Jump on one leg (3)
6 The prairie wolf (6)
7 Underground passage (6)
12 A loudening of sound (9)
14 Ploy (6)
15 Advantage (6)
16 Session with medium (6)
18 Inert gas, element 86 (5)
21 New Zealand extinct bird (3)

ACROSS

1 Competence to get around (8)
5 A tie; a surety (4)
8 The Mystery Cat (*T. S. Eliot*) (8)
9 Summon; ring (4)
11 Is it still for tea? (*Brooke – Grantchester*) (5)
12 E.g. gas, water supplier (7)
13 Grief (6)
15 (Face) showing distress (6)
18 Socks, stockings etc. (7)
19 Item of information (5)
21 Civil wrong (4)
22 Material used to fill (8)
23 Caution, care (4)
24 Streaked with grey (8)

DOWN

1 Ancient Egypt capital; Tennessee port (7)
2 Pig meat (5)
3 Revoltingly affectionate (5-5)
4 Disapproval expression (3-3)
6 Delirious applause (7)
7 Hold up; hang back (5)
10 *We're off to see* him (Garland film) (6,2,2)
14 Earmark; spare (7)
16 Super-human hero (7)
17 Mollusc, eaten by Walrus and Carpenter (6)
18 Tie up; a snag (5)
20 Judicial process (5)

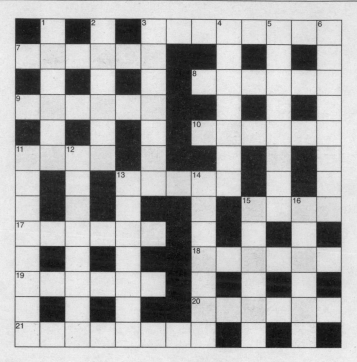

ACROSS

3 Friendly (8)

7 Nicked (6)

8 In the air; very quick (visit) (6)

9 Rich cake (6)

10 (Female) seclusion (6)

11 Knight's attendant (4)

13 Number of *cards* in the *trick* (5)

15 Young woman (4)

17 Eerie (6)

18 Sharpness (of intellect) (6)

19 Deed; battle (6)

20 Overweening pride (6)

21 Song of lament for the dead (8)

DOWN

1 Rock layers (6)

2 Bring charge (that) (6)

3 Emotional torment (7)

4 Work together (to deceive) (7)

5 Port in heel of Italy (8)

6 Type of porcelain; (paint) with sheen (8)

11 Liking, inclination (8)

12 Energetic, self-made type (2-6)

13 China seas cyclone (7)

14 Instinctive fellow-feeling (7)

15 Soiled, dirty (6)

16 Keep in possession (6)

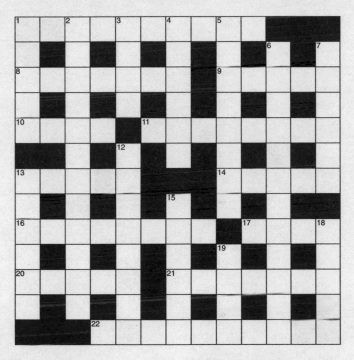

ACROSS

1 Violate code (10)
8 Ambushed (7)
9 A spread; an adhesive (5)
10 Disastrous defeat (4)
11 Uninvolved; separate (8)
13 Stoneworker (5)
14 Kingsley Amis's *Lucky* Jim — (5)
16 Very wet; fat from roast (8)
17 Twosome (4)
20 Colourful seed-eating songbird (5)
21 Concealing (7)
22 Wiltshire megalith group (10)

DOWN

1 Tall structure (5)
2 Radio panel discussion (3,9)
3 An East European (4)
4 Steering device (6)
5 A Spanish Jew (8)
6 Suffocation (12)
7 Muffle (sound) (6)
12 Simple photo (8)
13 Adjust (6)
15 Irregular, not smooth (6)
18 Scoundrel; mad elephant (5)
19 Desire (4)

ACROSS

1 Contribute opinion (4,4,3)
7 Military trumpet (5)
8 Hero's lover (*Much Ado about Nothing*) (7)
10 Repair, restore (8)
11 Feeble person (4)
13 Response (6)
15 Soapy froth (6)
17 One engaging eye (4)
18 Hawaii capital (8)
21 More prepared (7)
22 Sight; part of play (5)
23 Afternoon off (4-7)

DOWN

1 Sewing accessory dealer (11)
2 Non-animal-product user (5)
3 Summary (8)
4 Arouse (6)
5 Kill (4)
6 German/Jewish vernacular (7)
9 At advantageous time (11)
12 Noisy drinking bout (8)
14 An organ; to tolerate (7)
16 A quarter (6)
19 Tip over (5)
20 A beak; a statement (4)

ACROSS

1 Quibble (5)
7 Principled (7)
8 Woodblock (floor) (7)
9 Ham it up (7)
11 Saturate (6)
13 Restless desire (for) (9)
15 US Western film tough-guy (4,5)
19 Hearty laugh (6)
21 Prohibits (7)
23 Variant of element (7)
24 Reticule; Jack Worthing mislaid in one (7)
25 Call across Swiss valley (5)

DOWN

1 Love god (5)
2 Engulfing spiral (e.g. of whirlpool) (6)
3 Get (project) started (6)
4 Ban (4)
5 Looking-glass (6)
6 Railed platform; theatre area (7)
10 Norse raider; a sea area (6)
12 Risk, danger (6)
14 Washington DC river (7)
16 A nonentity; Pooter, for Grossmiths (6)
17 Speech of praise (6)
18 Provide; be able to purchase (6)
20 Execute turning movement (5)
22 Breathy gesture; the *Moor's Last*, Rushdie (4)

218

ACROSS

1 Tolerating (8)
5 Mound (4)
8 Castle mound (5)
9 *Onegin, Godunov* poet (7)
11 Chance; large amount (3)
12 An indigenous person (9)
13 Given name, new soundtrack (6)
15 One having to live abroad (6)
18 One taking the blame (9)
19 Hostelry (3)
20 (Look) sideways, disapprovingly (7)
21 Diver's breathing pack (5)
22 Speck; as opposed to *beam* (4)
23 Good-looking (8)

DOWN

1 Was clumsily inefficient (7)
2 Work for eight (5)
3 Mildly supervise (4,2,3,2)
4 Japan, for Japanese (6)
6 Vague notion (7)
7 Thrust forward (5)
10 Branded as bad (11)
14 Bed covering; comprehensive (7)
16 Hug (7)
17 Nine-day prayer cycle (6)
18 Throng; climb (up) (5)
19 Outermost planet (5)

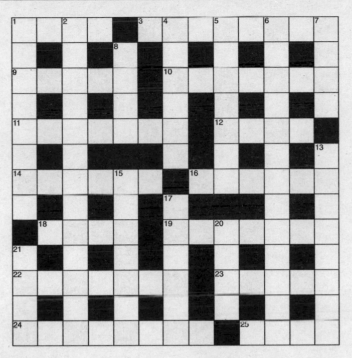

ACROSS

1 Tube; whistle (4)

3 Minor medical attention (5,3)

9 Hoarder of money (5)

10 Intention, aim (7)

11 To revel (7)

12 One hunted for food (4)

14 Genial (6)

16 Edible grain (6)

18 Sand drift (4)

19 Complete circuit (*baseball*) (4,3)

22 Briefings with the latest (7)

23 Crush, break violently (5)

24 In youthful way (8)

25 Norse thunder god (4)

DOWN

1 Welsh town; Oxford, Cambridge college (8)

2 Fourteen days before Easter (7,6)

4 Meaning; bring from abroad (6)

5 Tiny weight; moral doubt (7)

6 Unimpeachable (5,8)

7 Food regime; a parliament (4)

8 Badly-behaved child (4)

13 Decisive argument (8)

15 Ophelia's brother (7)

17 Wood-working tool (6)

20 Pressed grape juice; a necessity (4)

21 Type of plant; one giving light (4)

ACROSS

4 Soothsayer (5)

7 Impractically idealistic (8)

8 Water creature; metal plate (4)

9 Suicide (pilot) (8)

10 Rugged, solid (6)

13 Elephant driver (6)

14 Complaining, parrot, noise (6)

15 Highest point (6)

18 Pass, move across (8)

19 Look sullen, alluring (4)

20 Large bottle (8)

21 Beneficiary of cheque (5)

DOWN

1 Cross eyes (6)

2 Plucked-string instrument (6)

3 Unemphasised (3-3)

4 Excite, get going (8)

5 Restless pleasure-seeker (8)

6 One not accepted (6)

11 In unserviceable fashion (8)

12 A school; disadvantage (8)

14 (Persian) provincial governor; *as part (anagram)* (6)

15 *Aeneid* author (6)

16 Bird of prey (6)

17 Of horses (6)

ACROSS

1 Improvident (8)
7 Swim; apply water to (wound) (5)
8 Order, act of imprisonment (9)
9 White wine/cassis drink (3)
10 Pare; neat (4)
11 Take away; Billy Bunter's form (6)
13 Missing company (6)
14 A football club; a suit (6)
17 Knock about; a food coating (6)
18 Rough attempt; attack with knife (4)
20 A tree; sounds like *pelt* (3)
22 Remiss (9)
23 T. S. —, poet (5)
24 Intensify (8)

DOWN

1 Gem surface (5)
2 A perennial; Thomas —, poet/composer (7)
3 Beast's den (4)
4 One being painted; easy catch (6)
5 Amount bet (5)
6 Push down; make miserable (7)
7 A bad error; a loaf (7)
12 Brazenly overt (7)
13 Published handout (7)
15 Go back; a nook (7)
16 Scanty (6)
17 Plait; edge band of e.g. silk (5)
19 One passed on in relay race (5)
21 Ruler; a chessman (4)

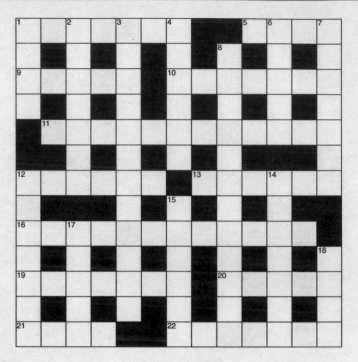

ACROSS

1 Tomahawk (7)
5 Unfocused sight (4)
9 Maintain right to (5)
10 Boasted (7)
11 Wearer of the Scarlet Letter (*Hawthorne*) (6,6)
12 Proverb (6)
13 Population count (6)
16 Teacher; *the classroom (anagram)* (12)
19 Exact opposite (7)
20 Put into coordination (5)
21 Number of tails, lives, of cat (4)
22 Lucerne plant (7)

DOWN

1 A wine; pawn (4)
2 Bad-end play (7)
3 Wolsey's London palace (7,5)
4 Alehouse (6)
6 Romance-language parent (5)
7 Richard —, *South Pacific* composer (7)
8 Six-foot-pole weapon (12)
12 Court, parliament, meeting (7)
14 Out of the ordinary (7)
15 Shape-changing protozoan (6)
17 Place of refuge (5)
18 Old Peruvian (4)

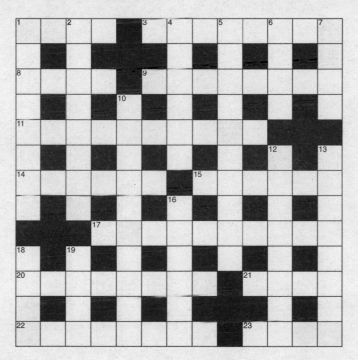

ACROSS

1 Conceal; skin (4)
3 Typical example (8)
8 Lateral part (4)
9 Rules expressed in symbols (*maths.*) (8)
11 Trickery; conjuror's incantation (5-5)
14 Courage; ghost (6)
15 Give satisfaction to (6)
17 Sea-plane (6,4)
20 Put a name to (8)
21 Reasonable; light-coloured (4)
22 (Inscription) on stone (8)
23 Head growth (4)

DOWN

1 Not to be talked about (4-4)
2 Imparting a lesson (8)
4 Particle of light (6)
5 Protective colouring, concealment (10)
6 A grinder (4)
7 Scottish turnip (4)
10 Swung from side to side (10)
12 Wide view (8)
13 University teacher (8)
16 Not be the same (6)
18 Satiate; wholly occupy (4)
19 (Liquid) trickle thinly (4)

ACROSS

1 Of education; pedantic (10)
8 One chasing (7)
9 Fraction of pound (5)
10 Cage for hen (4)
11 Keeping apart (8)
13 Pound with fists (6)
15 Potential; not yet manifested (6)
17 (Especially pre-Lent) festivity (8)
18 Collection of data; rasp (4)
21 A raptor; two-under score (5)
22 Lover of Cressida (7)
23 Seeing how far one can go (6,2,2)

DOWN

2 Freight (5)
3 Burden of responsibility (4)
4 Skilful (6)
5 Of equatorial regions (8)
6 1/100th franc (7)
7 Feeling no gravity (10)
8 Artful Dodger's trade (*Dickens*) (10)
12 Style of speaking; liberation (8)
14 Husband of one's dreams (2,5)
16 Package; *Two Cities* hero (*Dickens*) (6)
19 Ice house (5)
20 Hindu spiritual master; cartoon bear (4)

ACROSS

1 (Caught) in the act (3-6)
6 Lorry (*abbr.*) (1,1,1)
8 Bar door to (strikers) (4,3)
9 Bedroom at sea (5)
10 Cog-engaging lever (4)
11 (Water)birds one shoots (8)
13 Surviving (6)
14 Agreement; a trade union (6)
17 Without warning (8)
18 G. B. —, Irish dramatist (4)
20 In bad temper (5)
21 Communion cup (7)
22 Serious personal injury (*abbr.*) (1,1,1)
23 Traditional cuddly toy (5,4)

DOWN

1 Return to the bad (7)
2 Take suicidal risk (4,4,5)
3 Boat-hailing call (4)
4 Small particular (6)
5 In moral, artistic decline (8)
6 Only one to pick from (7,6)
7 Open to bribes (5)
12 Lewd (8)
15 January 1st its Day (3,4)
16 Unruffled (6)
17 Hurl; arm support (5)
19 Shy of effort (4)

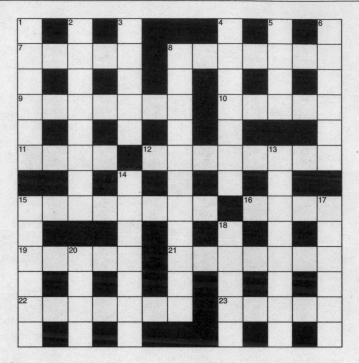

ACROSS

7 Avoid (capture) (5)
8 Rust away (7)
9 Clown (7)
10 A line dance (5)
11 Work over again (4)
12 Clearance; (at one's) discretion (8)
15 Corrupted (8)
16 Old Tory opponent (4)
19 Causing death (5)
21 Shorten (text) (7)
22 Inexplicable event (7)
23 Map book (5)

DOWN

1 Limb; one in club (6)
2 Conceited; inflated (6,2)
3 One diverting attention (5)
4 Rule, maxim (7)
5 Complain; low wind sound (4)
6 Happen (*arch.*) (6)
8 Polite, thoughtful (11)
13 Timetable (8)
14 William —, led Scots against Edward I (7)
15 To libel (6)
17 Slippery, fatty (6)
18 Snap; piece of good luck in career (5)
20 Lawn grass (4)

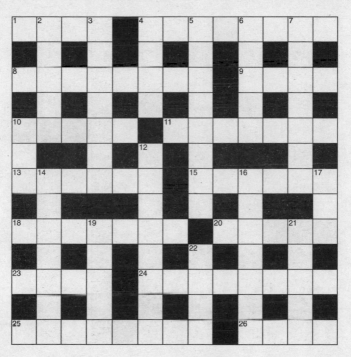

ACROSS

1 Stern; forceful (4)
4 Unthankful people (8)
8 Promiscuous women (8)
9 Take long strides (4)
10 US president after Washington (5)
11 25th March (4,3)
13 Illegible writing (6)
15 Hole (to thread cord) (6)
18 Fine glass (7)
20 Country of Sphinx (5)
23 Some lines of text; type of soldier (*both abbrs.*) (4)
24 Compass housing (8)
25 Sweet-smelling (8)
26 Ancient small harp (4)

DOWN

2 Pungent; caustic (5)
3 Unpalatable choice (7)
4 Press; an element (4)
5 Cobweb; fine gauze (8)
6 Put at rest (suspicion) (5)
7 Atone for (7)
10 Fathead (3)
12 Moorish palace, Granada (8)
14 Barbary pirate (7)
16 Decorate with notches; *realign (anagram)* (7)
17 Shoddy stuff (3)
19 Jargon (5)
21 Of the highest latitudes (5)
22 Biting little insect (4)

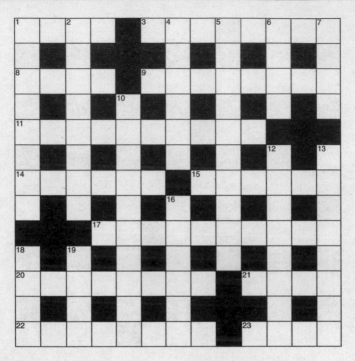

ACROSS

1 A tax; unavoidable task (4)
3 Ban (8)
8 Distinctive clothes (4)
9 Sting-in-tail creature (8)
11 Wooden spoon (5,5)
14 Gloomy, depressing (6)
15 In poor health (6)
17 Courtly-love singer (10)
20 One of ruling clique (8)
21 Manifestation (4)
22 Writer of short pieces (8)
23 Over-the-top publicity (4)

DOWN

1 A menial drudge (8)
2 Slowcoach; Mock Turtle's teacher (*Alice*) (8)
4 Officially write down (6)
5 Lying flat (10)
6 Morsel as lure (4)
7 Melody (4)
10 *Pygmalion* musical (2,4,4)
12 Savage violence (8)
13 Italian city; loving sister of Dombey (Son) (8)
16 Liquid secretions (6)
18 Prod; old bonnet (4)
19 Sound of static, of disapproval (4)

ACROSS

1 Radically severe (7)
5 Chairman's hammer (5)
8 Dryly amusing (5)
9 Real surname of Lenin (7)
10 Holiness (8)
11 Shivering fit (4)
13 Without restraint (2,5,6)
16 Bombast (4)
17 Badly wounded, ravaged (8)
20 Remark, observation (7)
21 Real surname of George Eliot (5)
22 Quiz team (5)
23 Rapture (7)

DOWN

1 Real surname of Lewis Carroll (7)
2 Fruit of oak (5)
3 A sneak (8)
4 Prefix used by noble's heir (8,5)
5 Teases; opposite of *Dolls* (4)
6 Acetic-acid preservative (7)
7 Court reception; US embankment (5)
12 Caution (8)
14 Executioner (7)
15 Line of kings (7)
16 Cover main points again (5)
18 Eucalyptus-eating marsupial (5)
19 Pseudonym of Brontës (4)

ACROSS

5 Tiny width (5-7)
8 Beam over door (6)
9 Overpaid businessman (3,3)
10 Piece of roof, floor covering (4)
12 Gracefully slim, like a tree (7)
14 Contradict (7)
15 Cut, carved with effort (4)
17 Eremite (6)
18 Capital of Canada (6)
20 Fates; *Macbeth* witches (5,7)

DOWN

1 Stocking-hanging time (9,3)
2 Shaft; one is *backed* to it (4)
3 Commerce; road vehicles (7)
4 Old Paris prison (8)
6 To brood (4)
7 What a lying excuse! (4,4,4)
11 Place-identifying feature (8)
13 Dream; genre of fiction (7)
16 Failure; damage (4)
19 Opponents of *us* (4)

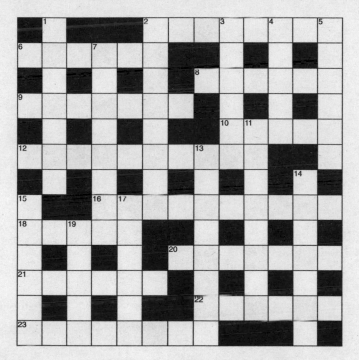

ACROSS

2 Aware; level-headed (8)
6 One of great knowledge (6)
8 Hard to make out; cunning (6)
9 Vegetable; one Walrus wanted to discuss (*Carroll*) (7)
10 Cancel; waste (5)
12 Kingsley novel; Devon town (8,2)
16 Ali Baba's spell (4,6)
18 Swiss-German border river (5)
20 Madman (7)
21 Hired group of clappers (6)
22 Start (journey); display, explain (3,3)
23 All of us (8)

DOWN

1 Low wall on roof (7)
2 Be still, fail to progress (8)
3 A US vegetable; a game (6)
4 One snapping teeth (5)
5 Privileged to be omitted (6)
7 Keenness to advance (8)
11 Unvarying (8)
13 Conceal (8)
14 Wicked (7)
15 Baby nursery (6)
17 Poverty (6)
19 Mental picture (5)

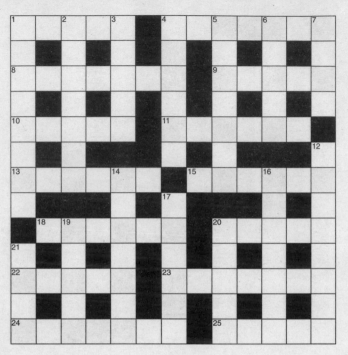

ACROSS

1 Berkshire racecourse (5)
4 Restricted (7)
8 Raise to peerage (7)
9 Praise highly (5)
10 Appointment book (5)
11 Get hold of (6)
13 One or the other (6)
15 Allay (6)
18 Excavate (stone); one hunted (6)
20 Welsh town; something hard, igniting (5)
22 Deposit; take accommodation (5)
23 Made void; denied (7)
24 (Spaceship's) return to atmosphere (2-5)
25 Belated, slow (5)

DOWN

1 The Granite City (8)
2 State of touching; useful acquaintance (7)
3 Rather fat (5)
4 Avoid attention (3,3)
5 Star conductor (7)
6 Everyone play (*music*) (5)
7 Dish out; a benefit (4)
12 (Argued) in emotional way (8)
14 Pledge; serious (7)
16 A cheat; (US) whirlwind (7)
17 New South Wales capital (6)
19 Excessive (5)
20 Battle (5)
21 Pronounce indistinctly (4)

ACROSS

1 Encroach (8)

5 Safety device; melt together (4)

7 Smelling salts (3,8)

8 Mercy, sympathy (4)

9 Move in from margin; place order (6)

10 Mafia conspiracy of silence (6)

13 Small hotel (3)

14 City of ancient Greece, Egypt (6)

17 Mass departure (6)

18 Narrow opening; gashed (4)

19 Bravura performance (4,2,5)

20 A bird; it flies straight (4)

21 Speak condescendingly; help pilot's descent (4,4)

DOWN

1 Vow-of-silence monk (8)

2 Totter; influence (4)

3 A commercial (13)

4 Makes pact with devil (5,4,4)

5 (Fine) condition (6)

6 Pick; specially picked (6)

7 Heavy pudding (6)

11 Poser; sieve (6)

12 German shepherd (8)

15 Virtue; a top card (6)

16 Underground lair; dig this (6)

18 Race along (clouds) (4)

ACROSS

7 Honest; accurate (4)

8 Come close to (8)

9 Prolific (6)

10 Symbol, badge (6)

11 Worthless, deplorable (4)

12 Construct anew (2-6)

15 Break (regulation) (8)

17 Avoid (question, bouncer) (4)

18 Treeless permafrost zone (6)

21 With eagerness (6)

22 A brew (8)

23 Stake; position (held) (4)

DOWN

1 One from Erevan (8)

2 Rubbish; decline (6)

3 Senior bureaucrat; type of 17 *ac* (8)

4 Domed recess in church (4)

5 Much more; a lookalike (6)

6 Dull pain (4)

13 Halting; verifying (8)

14 Tricky (problem); easily made to laugh (8)

16 Element 88, discovered by Curies (6)

17 A French Channel port (6)

19 Longer forearm bone (4)

20 Related, similar (4)

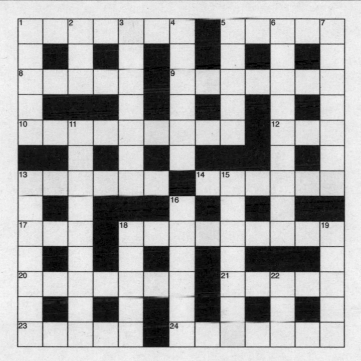

ACROSS

1 Four kings; a sweet flower (7)
5 Seating enclosure; resolute view (5)
8 Four-point ball (snooker) (5)
9 Manx town; type of fir (7)
10 Fruit; rude noise (9)
12 Mesh; fly-trap (3)
13 A spice; red (hair) (6)
14 Disordered mess (6)
17 Robert E. —, Confederate commander (3)
18 Decorum (9)
20 Made fizzy (7)
21 One bit of sand; wood texture (5)
23 Eight kings; unit of inductance (5)
24 Fugitives (7)

DOWN

1 Carl Maria von —, *Freischütz* composer (5)
2 Card game, a stake in it (3)
3 Base, unworthy (7)
4 Up to date (6)
5 Improper; impertinent (5)
6 Licit (9)
7 Put out of action (7)
11 New Testament Jewish council; *has dinner (anagram)* (9)
13 Giant David killed (7)
15 Honest; on one's feet (7)
16 Haiti cult, spell (6)
18 Short and sharp (5)
19 A long time (*informal*) (5)
22 Ottoman commander (3)

ACROSS

1 Promotion of kin (8)

5 Part of leg; baby animal (4)

9 Suspension of hostilities (5)

10 Obvious (7)

11 That which is left over (7)

12 Barbarian tribesmen (5)

13 Getting bald (4,2,3)

18 Challenging behaviour (5)

20 Offer; resist (4,3)

22 Warning; wariness (7)

23 Surface lustre (5)

24 Cleopatra its serpent (*Antony and Cleopatra*) (4)

25 Get together (8)

DOWN

1 Oath-giving official (6)

2 Drop like stone (7)

3 Greek *th* (5)

4 Amorous burble (5,8)

6 Watchful (5)

7 One irrationally worshipped (6)

8 Dwarf (6)

14 Humorously incongruous (6)

15 Saw (7)

16 French chorus-line dance (6)

17 Position, attitude (6)

19 Thin porridge (5)

21 Strong cotton fabric (5)

ACROSS

1 Permission; penalty (8)
5 Stylish (4)
9 Edible bulb; sounds like *Tennyson's Lady* (7)
10 Instrument, in cinema once (5)
11 Unable to move; able to speed (4)
12 Country home (7)
14 "Wilco" (navy) (3,3); lemur-like primate (3-3)
16 Bring to conclusion; prepare (e.g. toy) to start (4,2)
19 The tallest mammal (7)
21 Something owed (4)
24 Teller of life's tale (*Macbeth*) (5)
25 Type of reed Moses was found in (7)
26 A foodstuff; as sure as — is — (4)
27 A drink; *teenager (anagram)* (5,3)

DOWN

1 Neither good nor bad (2-2)
2 Spiral-horned antelope (5)
3 Creator of Anna Karenina (7)
4 Science of light, sight (6)
6 Gaunt; a captured hawk (7)
7 Derision (8)
8 Make secure; race off (4)
13 Optimistic; florid (8)
15 Deserving, receiving (7)
17 Gratify; pamper (7)
18 North African Muslim people, language (6)
20 Is just right; convulsions (4)
22 Pointed (remark); (blade) not sharp (5)
23 Flightless bird; Saturn satellite (4)

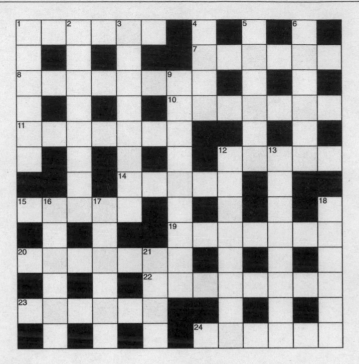

ACROSS

1 A covering, awning (6)

7 Peers; does as well as (6)

8 One full of vitality; one dangerous to touch (4,4)

10 Raise (7)

11 Imprisoned, locked away (7)

12 Put on clothes (5)

14 (Tsar's) edict (5)

15 "Men are — when they woo ..." (5)

19 One promising (money to charity) (7)

20 Home city of Agamemnon (7)

22 Obstinate (8)

23 Take (vehicle) at gunpoint (6)

24 With thick outsides (bread) (6)

DOWN

1 Channel port, English till 1558 (6)

2 "Damp, drizzly — in (Ishmael's) soul" (*Moby-Dick*) (8)

3 Strong; important (8)

4 Base of ship framework (4)

5 Tremble; weapon-holder (6)

6 Polish currency notes (6)

9 One rolled out for VIPs (3,6)

12 "... — when they wed" (*As You Like It*) (8)

13 Paltry, meagre (8)

16 Massage (*abbr.*) (6)

17 Polar cover (3-3)

18 Deranged fury (6)

21 Inquires, applies (for) (4)

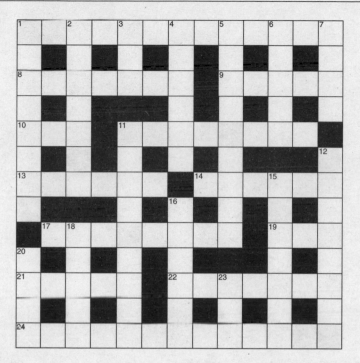

ACROSS

1 Zambezi cascade (8,5)
8 Summarise; corral (5,2)
9 Solar System occasional visitor (5)
10 Hazelnut; a horse (3)
11 Capital of Sardinia (8)
13 Inter-state pact (6)
14 Occurring intermittently (6)
17 Liquid slopped (8)
19 Unprocessed (3)
21 Surrounded by (5)
22 Appalling action (7)
24 Rudely challenged decision (6,3,4)

DOWN

1 Ravenousness (8)
2 Fall apart; pudding (topping) (7)
3 Unusual (3)
4 Call into question (6)
5 Exact copy (9)
6 Madagascar tree-dweller (5)
7 Paving block; burrow (4)
11 Product list (9)
12 Perfect (e.g. diamond) (8)
15 A mishmash (7)
16 To caper, frolic (6)
18 Pointed end of fork (5)
20 Celebration, festival (4)
23 Fasten; equal outcome (3)

ACROSS

1 Don't tell anyone! (4,3,4)
8 "Christmas — ..." (5)
9 Louis —, bacteriologist (7)
10 "... but — ..." (4)
11 Herbert —, World War 2 Home Secretary (8)
13 Non-boarding pupil (3,3)
14 Against (another team) (6)
17 American holiday (8)
19 "... a —, ..." (4)
22 Subdivision of genus (7)
23 Light-splitting glass (5)
24 Of brilliant appearance (11)

DOWN

1 Swaggeringly masculine (5)
2 Close imitation (7)
3 Job (4)
4 Give job to (6)
5 A paper; non-participant (8)
6 Pieces for two players (5)
7 "... And when it 8 *ac*, it — ..." (6)
12 Distinguished, important people (8)
13 Contrive (6)
15 Germ-free (7)
16 Relic of past age (6)
18 "... good —" (5)
20 Send (money); cancel (penalty) (5)
21 Twirl round (4)

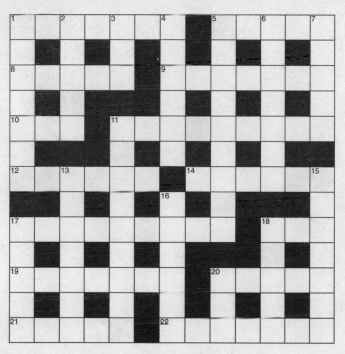

ACROSS

1 Wool-winding stick (7)
5 Stoke —, Gray's country churchyard (5)
8 Wakeful night (5)
9 Incorporate (in greater whole) (7)
10 Grassland; straight track (3)
11 Exactness (9)
12 Idiomatic expression (6)
14 Himalayan guide (6)
17 Performers' entrance (5,4)
18 Miserable (3)
19 Wide area, stretch (7)
20 Capital of Egypt (5)
21 Eskimo canoe (5)
22 Burial mound (7)

DOWN

1 Grow to maturity (7)
2 Soft and wet (5)
3 Sicken (3)
4 Nurse, encourage (6)
5 Book issuer (9)
6 More showy (7)
7 Coil of yarn (5)
11 Boris —, *Zhivago* author (9)
13 Try again (for job) (7)
15 Needing hard work (7)
16 Big wood (6)
17 Tale-teller (5)
18 Tumble quickly (out) (5)
20 Rotating-part projection (3)

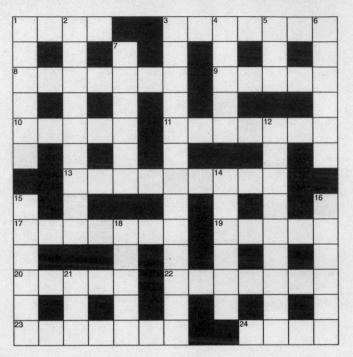

ACROSS

1 Fighting force (4)
3 Conspiracy to convict (*slang*) (5-2)
8 Sacred vocal piece (7)
9 Classical prophetess (5)
10 Small fish, herring (5)
11 "Some village- —" (*Gray*); a Glasgow Park (7)
13 Two dots over vowel (9)
17 Set of clothes etc. for baby (7)
19 Type of capital (*architect.*); of bond (*chem.*) (5)
20 Practise; a suite (5)
22 Top of boat's side (7)
23 Pressure position (3,4)
24 Limit; school period (4)

DOWN

1 Right of approach (6)
2 Robinson Crusoe's servant (3,6)
3 A boxer; *he fit, we gather* (*anagram*) (13)
4 India tea-growing state (5)
5 (Tide) go down (3)
6 Electrical cable supports (6)
7 Sanskrit sacred books; seen in *Bhutan, traditionally* (6)
12 Withdraw (9)
14 Too thin (6)
15 Side of bacon (6)
16 Shout in fear, laughter (6)
18 Taut, nervous (5)
21 Social insect, 1 *ac* variety (3)

ACROSS

1 Max —, quantum theorist (6)
4 One thousand kilos (5)
8 Complete amount (5)
9 Pain relieving drug (7)
10 All one can hold; more than one can manage (7)
11 Island east of Java (4)
12 Piece of advice (3)
14 Make gentle fun of (5)
15 Fossil resin (5)
18 Knock; a valve (3)
20 Japanese wrestling (4)
22 Went to bed (7)
24 Thug (7)
25 A spice; sliced through (5)
26 Fielding position; indicate (5)
27 Desisted (6)

DOWN

1 One casually fired (3,4)
2 Insect's feeler (7)
3 Failure of nerve (4,4)
4 Recording; long ribbon strip (4)
5 Emperor before Trajan (5)
6 Bored weariness (5)
7 Leap; underground chamber (5)
13 Work of art in mixed styles (8)
16 Arab hooded cloak (7)
17 One with ginger hair (7)
19 Practical joke (5)
20 Sugary liquid (5)
21 Civilian clothes (5)
23 Sieve minutely (4)

ACROSS

1 Bashful; embarrassed (10)

8 Reinforce; a pillow (7)

9 Cut with sweeping stroke (5)

10 Make fast; constrain (4)

11 Thin wire, fibre (8)

13 Food store (6)

15 Interwoven twigs; an acacia (6)

17 Sickening reverse (4,4)

18 Wickedness (4)

21 Available for rent (2,3)

22 Nimbleness (7)

23 See 7 (*D. H. Lawrence*) (10)

DOWN

2 Trojan War over her abduction (5)

3 Ship's officer; cornering of king (4)

4 (Nine-gallon) cask (6)

5 One shipwrecked (8)

6 Local variant of language (7)

7 Constance —, loved Mellors the 23 (10)

8 Foaming tub (6,4)

12 In the exact words (8)

14 Socialist symbol (3,4)

16 Return, retire (2,4)

19 A gauzy fabric (5)

20 Wait (one's time) (4)

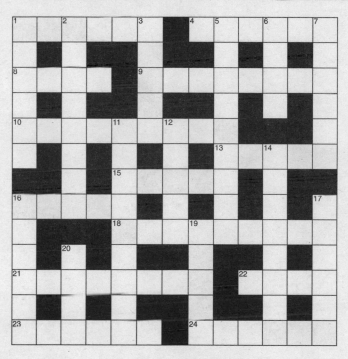

ACROSS

1 Marcel —, French author (6)
4 A vegetable; burgeon (6)
8 Warm and comfortable (4)
9 Detailed examination (8)
10 Wife of US president (5,4)
13 Grey; (face) pale with shock (5)
15 Fusion (5)
16 (Japanese) mattress/bed (5)
18 A disbelieved prophet of doom (9)
21 Cooking pot (8)
22 Cut up; cut of meat (4)
23 Rectangular (6)
24 Daze (6)

DOWN

1 Quieten (6)
2 Impede (8)
3 Fish by dragging net (5)
5 Mindlessly optimistic person (*after E. Porter*) (9)
6 Displace (from role) (4)
7 One from Florence region (6)
11 Policeman's baton (9)
12 First sign of zodiac (5)
14 Privation (8)
16 Humiliating failure (6)
17 Meddle (with e.g. mechanism) (6)
19 Skull cavity (5)
20 Replete (4)

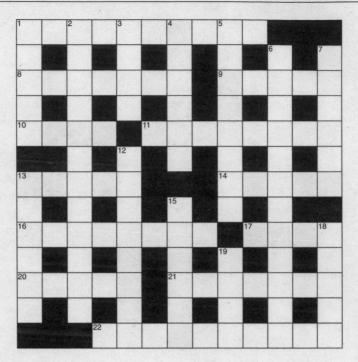

ACROSS

1 Player of records (4,6)
8 One calling from minaret (7)
9 Pride (oneself); resentment (5)
10 Cook (bread) (4)
11 Top-of-column summary (8)
13 Body of singers (5)
14 Implements (5)
16 He wins Portia (*Merchant of Venice*) (8)
17 A bird; a hardliner (4)
20 An animal; a deadly sin (5)
21 A dog; a voluntary soldier (7)
22 (Temperamental) leading lady (5,5)

DOWN

1 Discharge from army (5)
2 Wrongly anticipate (5,3,4)
3 Improvised music (4)
4 Have discussions (6)
5 Chase up, hurry along (8)
6 Ambiguous speech, hedging (12)
7 Niche; adjournment (6)
12 One in pulpit (8)
13 Picasso, Braque style (6)
15 One hurt, swindled (6)
18 Burden of one's past (*Buddhism*) (5)
19 Lattice (4)

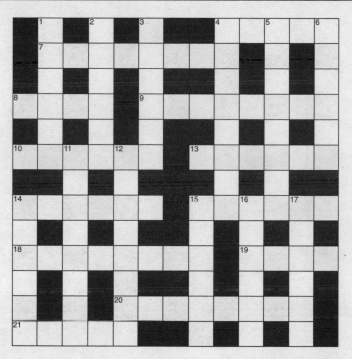

ACROSS

- **4** Go in; put down (5)
- **7** Compromise (5-3)
- **8** Period; prison sentence (4)
- **9** Of the fall (8)
- **10** Of the opposite season (6)
- **13** Rebecca de — (*du Maurier*) (6)
- **14** Steamed Chinese snack (3,3)
- **15** Liverpool river (6)
- **18** Change key (8)
- **19** Opinion; prospect (4)
- **20** Thin dressing-gown (8)
- **21** Dig (with energy) (5)

DOWN

- **1** Conflict (6)
- **2** Keel over (for de-barnacling) (6)
- **3** Memory; summon back (6)
- **4** Emotionally gushing (8)
- **5** Ringing in ears (8)
- **6** A wave; (e.g. paint-) spreader (6)
- **11** (Action) to repair damage (8)
- **12** Beaklike (nose) (8)
- **14** Insist on (6)
- **15** In acquiescent fashion (6)
- **16** Plunder, wreck (6)
- **17** *Legs* number (6)

ACROSS

1 Swivelling wheel (6)
5 Team; swagger (*slang*) (4)
8 Not make it (4)
9 Strange; *snug lair (anagram)* (8)
10 Temporarily lose (8)
11 Cowardly terror (4)
12 Wise guide (6)
14 Twin of 1 (6)
16 Metered form of transport (4)
18 Leg-covering garment (8)
20 Smallest tea-party member (*Alice*) (8)
21 Adore (4)
22 Fabulous story; false idea (4)
23 Complicated mess (6)

DOWN

2 Cupidity (7)
3 Bell-shaped spring flower (5)
4 One selling meals (12)
5 Expressing deep emotion (7)
6 Run-off channel (5)
7 With expressed unwillingness (5,7)
13 Huge success (7)
15 Come apart (7)
17 Torturing pain (5)
19 Literary gathering; beauty parlour (5)

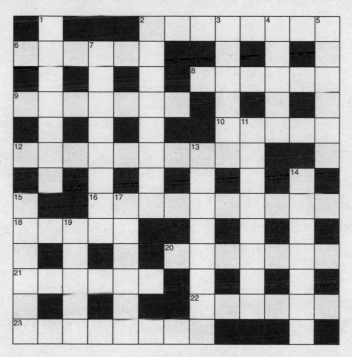

ACROSS

2 Easy conquest (4-4)
6 Indigent person (6)
8 Apprehend directly (6)
9 Corridor (7)
10 One playing a part (5)
12 Uncomplimentary (10)
16 A let-down (10)
18 Serving spoon (5)
20 Fine-weather timepiece (7)
21 Desperately sad (6)
22 Homily (6)
23 Awful place (4-4)

DOWN

1 Hubbub; boring fuss (7)
2 Expecting (8)
3 Aeroplane garage (6)
4 Boast (*arch.*) (5)
5 Sharp answer; lab. vessel (6)
7 Rural (poetry) (8)
11 Part of car; mathematical solid (8)
13 Naturally (2,6)
14 One exhibiting all virtues (7)
15 Part of car; some eggs (6)
17 Fairly recent (6)
19 Slow style of speech (5)

ACROSS

1 Of dark complexion (7)
5 Farewell; a glen (4)
8 One soliciting money (6)
9 Seductive appeal (6)
10 Haunt; common (8)
12 Burglar's haul (4)
13 Ballet duet (3,2,4)
17 Catherine —, survived Henry VIII (4)
18 Ammunition store (8)
20 Fish; got on by the hasty (6)
21 Bower (6)
23 Group of cooperating countries (4)
24 Pretended (7)

DOWN

2 Barge; passenger rowing boat (6)
3 Scrap; newspaper (*derog.*) (3)
4 Mongols' *Golden* throng (5)
5 *Rokeby Venus* painter (9)
6 Immature insects (6)
7 Winked (eye); faced bowler (6)
11 Equation with second power (9)
14 Patterned silk fabric (6)
15 A scavenger; his *Day*, Forsyth (6)
16 Hurt, wound (6)
19 Be discordant (5)
22 An insect; computer program error (3)

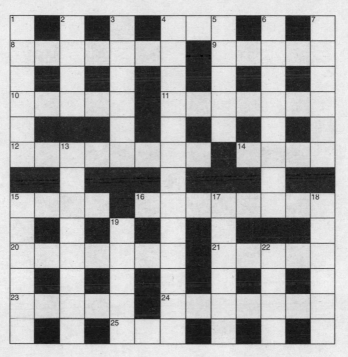

ACROSS

4 Animal enclosure (3)
8 One stockpiling (7)
9 Realms, domains (5)
10 The study of number, etc. (5)
11 Funeral procession (7)
12 One hiding aboard (8)
14 (US) school dance; (UK) concert (4)
15 Frustrate; thin metal sheet (4)
16 One insisting on (e.g. accuracy) (8)
20 Version (of paper, book) (7)
21 Desert beast of burden (5)
23 Titan (5)
24 Ten-year-siege victims; Berlioz subjects (7)
25 First woman (3)

DOWN

1 River at Henley (6)
2 Skin growth, may be charmed off (4)
3 Black Sea port; its *File*, Forsyth (6)
4 Put off till later (13)
5 Mother-of-pearl (5)
6 Intellectual (not emotional) (8)
7 Warm regard (6)
13 Newly devised; unchanged (8)
15 Acquire feathers (6)
17 Pupa's protection (6)
18 Thoroughly enjoy (6)
19 Skiing track (5)
22 Flesh; sounds like *come across* (4)

ACROSS

1 Arrogantly offhand (8)
5 Element, galvanises steel (4)
9 At an angle; indirect (7)
10 Chinese animal; police patrol (car) (5)
11 Boundary, side (4)
12 Employee list, cost (7)
14 Seniors (6)
16 Enumeration of inhabitants (6)
19 Take mazy path (7)
21 Mound; too old, if over it (4)
24 Quantity of drinks, sandwiches (5)
25 Plant for smoking (7)
26 Chief (4)
27 Well-meant falsehood (5,3)

DOWN

1 Jam up; item of footwear (4)
2 Having legal force (5)
3 Sweet alcoholic drink (7)
4 Given privileged freedom (6)
6 Volcanic (rock) (7)
7 King during Civil War (7,1)
8 Salmon river, sounds like *sterilise* (4)
13 Stain (e.g. reputation) (8)
15 The vampire count (7)
17 Show; one shown (7)
18 A prop (for the lame) (6)
20 Extinct Mauritius bird (4)
22 Of the neighbourhood (5)
23 Skin opening (4)

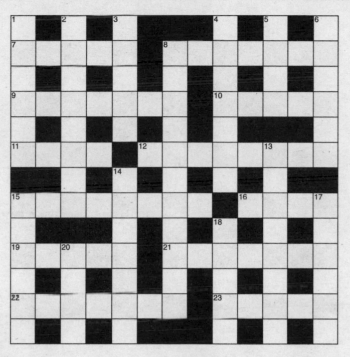

ACROSS

7 Faint sign; track down (5)
8 Irritable (7)
9 Mollify (7)
10 Regular radiation burst (5)
11 (Ship) arrive; cut short (4)
12 Grape orchard (8)
15 Very productive (8)
16 In low spirits (4)
19 Prop (up) (5)
21 With sharp corners; stiff, bony (7)
22 In, according to, law (7)
23 Madrid art gallery (5)

DOWN

1 A 6; a 19; to 17 (6)
2 A cold Spanish soup (8)
3 Take one's ease (5)
4 Cause puzzlement (7)
5 Young lady (4)
6 Spiral on screw (6)
8 Introductory (11)
13 Danger-over signal (3,5)
14 Luminous beetle (7)
15 Grinding tool, in mortar (6)
17 A colour; explosive signal (6)
18 With mouth open (5)
20 Wild party (4)

ACROSS

1 A seabird; *armful* (*anagram*) (6)
5 High on drugs; pelted (6)
8 (Mediaeval) Spanish Muslim (4)
9 Section of word (8)
10 Wrench (joint) (6)
12 A taunt (4)
15 Murder of public figure (13)
16 Unproductive (4)
17 Dally (6)
19 Variegates; a government house (8)
21 Minor panic (*slang*); beat (wing) (4)
22 Terrifying woman (6)
23 Cope with (6)

DOWN

2 Nem. con. (9)
3 Spoil (3)
4 Imprudence (8)
5 Dispose of (4)
6 Borneo ape (5-4)
7 Proverbially slippery fish (3)
11 Ballet position; flowing design (9)
13 Weapon; recoil unpleasantly (9)
14 America personified (5,3)
18 Not so much (4)
20 Embrace (3)
21 Part of fish; sounds like *a European* (3)

ACROSS

1 Bloom; (the) best part (of) (6)
5 Puzzle; frustrate (6)
8 Cold-meat counter (4)
9 Large-eyed primate, the galago (8)
10 Dignified, grand, and slow (7)
11 Tripoli its capital (5)
13 Oversee (11)
16 Calm; poteen apparatus (5)
18 A glazed earthenware (7)
21 Force majeure (8)
22 Russian river, mountain (range) (4)
23 Pithy (aphorism) (6)
24 Gentle; preoccupied; impractical (6)

DOWN

2 He kills Hamlet (7)
3 Narrow part of body (for some) (5)
4 Coarse banter (8)
5 Centre of operations; ignoble (4)
6 Feverish (7)
7 Hall; pressure group (5)
12 Crewless; bereft of courage (8)
14 Shrine visitor (7)
15 Read sonorously (7)
17 A rune; irritation (in side) (5)
19 (Musical) exercise piece (5)
20 Plate; record (4)

ACROSS

1 Killing the king (8)
7 A snap (5)
8 Future generations (9)
9 Droop (3)
10 Fight of honour (4)
11 Withdraw (heresy) (6)
13 London suburb; type of comedy (6)
14 Predator's target (6)
17 Elaborately decorated (6)
18 Witty remark (4)
20 Swindle; pain; college servant (3)
22 Government admin (street) (9)
23 Make straight (5)
24 Keep in mind (8)

DOWN

1 Swift (5)
2 Mrs. —, wrote *Cranford* (7)
3 Head of kitchen (4)
4 (Spout) rubbish (6)
5 Littoral; freewheel (5)
6 Approximately (7)
7 Thisbe's wooer (*MND*) (7)
12 Mysterious (7)
13 Mournful; type of couplet (7)
15 Edible plant; crowd-scene word (7)
16 (Formal) clothing (6)
17 Whence Masefield's quinquereme (5)
19 Of the earth's extreme regions (5)
21 Historian monk; sounds like *droplet* (4)

ACROSS

1 Giving good view (6)
5 Sprain; (hay)stack (4)
8 Pull; attract (4)
9 Fruitless; rudimentary (8)
10 Cream/wine/lemon dessert (8)
11 Wiles (4)
12 Seller (6)
14 Vigour (6)
16 Halt (4)
18 Hated (8)
20 (Text) supplement (8)
21 A spice; a staff (4)
22 Funeral fire (4)
23 Confederate opponent in Civil War (6)

DOWN

2 Thomas —, Victorian essayist/ historian (7)
3 Staircase post (5)
4 Hotel bedmakers (12)
5 Wearisome competitive struggle (3,4)
6 To envy (5)
7 Twofold setback (*slang*) (6,6)
13 Reduce in strength, number (7)
15 Where Campbells massacred Macdonalds (7)
17 Radio programme; present age (5)
19 St Paul such a citizen (5)

ACROSS

1 Regular (repeated) sequence (5)
4 Sly, stealthy (7)
8 Final knight check, king surrounded (9,4)
9 Political belief system (8)
10 Spurn (lover) (4)
12 Look with eyes screwed up (6)
13 Pass on (disease) to (6)
16 Part of tree; gruff noise (4)
17 (Insensitively) force through (8)
20 Intimidate, daunt (7)
21 Its queen visited Solomon (5)
22 Come as consequence (5)
23 Long journey; Greek poem (7)

DOWN

1 Brutus's colleague (*Julius Caesar*) (7)
2 Cramped position (5,8)
3 Breathing out (8)
4 Scout for food (6)
5 Work over again (4)
6 Conceive, picture (7)
7 Throw out (5)
11 Island over Menai strait (8)
14 Course of treatment (7)
15 US dinner-jacket (6)
16 Alcohol (*slang*) (5)
18 Broaches (5)
19 Ship's track; funeral party (4)

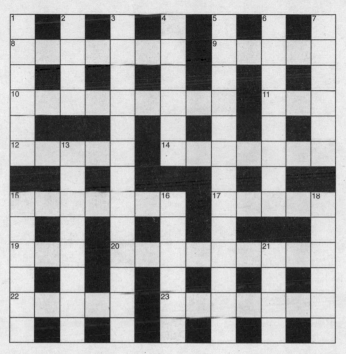

ACROSS

8 Capital of Kenya (7)
9 Club for superintelligent (5)
10 Bottom drawer contents (9)
11 Have debt (3)
12 Formal reasoning (5)
14 In irritable manner (7)
15 Make believe (7)
17 Cute Disney deer (5)
19 Beer cask (3)
20 A cuddly toy (5,4)
22 Greek island, off Albania (5)
23 Pen in (7)

DOWN

1 Gradually introduce, establish (6)
2 Bye-bye! (*Italian*) (4)
3 Conker tree (5,8)
4 Amuse; change course (6)
5 Spur-of-moment purchasing (7,6)
6 Speech of praise (8)
7 Table linen (6)
13 Decorative foliage (8)
15 Coup d'état (6)
16 Work out by 12 (6)
18 Country south of Lebanon (6)
21 Way out (4)

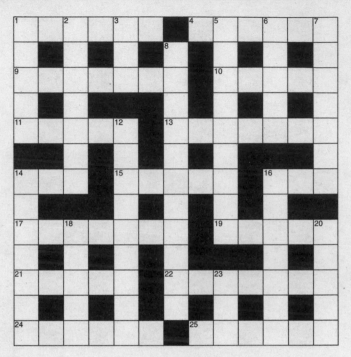

ACROSS

1 Gambling house (6)
4 Pictures; likenesses (6)
9 Gale; empty talk (7)
10 Damascus its capital (5)
11 Made smooth; tilted at angle (5)
13 Able to pay; one abused by glue-sniffers (7)
14 Drink (e.g. ale) (3)
15 Put forward (proposition) (5)
16 Electrically-charged atom (3)
17 Cooked rice dish (7)
19 Upright (5)
21 Ninth planet out (5)
22 To cheat, fool (7)
24 Flooding rain (6)
25 Extend; feast (6)

DOWN

1 Pole (for tossing) (5)
2 Posted (5,2); snooty (5-2)
3 (Cricket) practice (3)
5 White-berried parasite (9)
6 Ravine; eat hugely (5)
7 Unluxurious (7)
8 Argue, fight (with) (5,6)
12 Two-vowel syllable (9)
14 Marked with bands (7)
16 List in detail (7)
18 Oar; sounds like *head bone* (5)
20 Tyre rubber depth; walk on (5)
23 Drinking vessel (3)

ACROSS

1 Illumination (5)
4 Work team (7)
8 Disgracefully bad (9)
9 Residue from burning (3)
10 Fifty percent (4)
11 A terrier; *a shy male (anagram)* (8)
13 Alliance; club competition (6)
14 Further in same direction (6)
17 One from Zagreb (8)
19 A bird; a bar; complain (4)
22 Overweight (3)
23 Made bad mistake (9)
24 Forcibly subdue, put down (7)
25 Red Sea/Aden Gulf republic (5)

DOWN

1 Dog-lead (5)
2 The largest ape (7)
3 A nail; a sailing course (4)
4 Tamed; damaged (6)
5 Cheeky (8)
6 (Boat) flooded (5)
7 (Body) dug up (7)
12 Apt (8)
13 Satan; a match (7)
15 Letter mixture (7)
16 *All the world's a stage* speaker *(As You Like It)* (6)
18 With the advantage (2,3)
20 Encumbered (5)
21 Start of Europe liberation, 1944 (1-3)

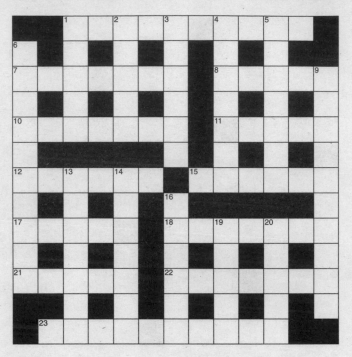

ACROSS

1 Welsh town; World War 2 general (10)
7 Result (7)
8 Skill; guile (5)
10 One from Myanmar; type of cat (7)
11 Item of information (5)
12 Surface glow; glory (in reputation) (6)
15 Waterproof jacket; a nerd (*slang*) (6)
17 Natural usage (language) (5)
18 Pioneering missionary (7)
21 Mouth of e.g. Nile, Mississippi (5)
22 Bitter bark extract, for malaria once (7)
23 One-room apartment (6,4)

DOWN

1 Vehicle engine (5)
2 Looped rope-end (5)
3 Hansel's sister (6)
4 Alexander the Great its king (7)
5 Nuclear-energy device (7)
6 Tubby (3-7)
9 One operating stopwatch (4-6)
13 Little pan (7)
14 Arthur —, French poet (7)
16 Macbeth saw his ghost (6)
19 Upstairs bay; its window (5)
20 Coil, distort (5)

ACROSS

1 The Ark builder (4)
4 Secondary job; to move away from influence (8)
8 Camouflage (8)
9 Single specimen of book; text for ad (4)
10 Pivoted bar (5)
11 An American marsupial (7)
13 Impostor; pretentious type (6)
15 (Taxes, troops) raised (6)
18 Thick, sticky (liquid) (7)
20 A benign growth; type of tiny sea creature (5)
23 Unrestrained, reckless (4)
24 Part of small intestine (8)
25 Unwillingly allow (8)
26 Ghana, Benin neighbour (4)

DOWN

2 Peace-symbol tree (5)
3 Healthy practices (7)
4 Rubbish bin; bound along (4)
5 Name-changing procedure (4,4)
6 (Technical) place; (math.) curve (5)
7 God of the sea (7)
10 Edge; cheek (3)
12 Unable to fly; based (8)
14 Cavity opening (7)
16 Using great force (7)
17 Decline; quick swim (3)
19 Apple drink (5)
21 Immature (5)
22 Half sleep (4)

ACROSS

1 Paper fastener; very important (6)
4 River crossing (4)
9 Have use of; like (5)
10 Near-plane-crash incident (3,4)
11 One cheating; a crab (7)
12 Brainless film strongman (5)
13 A putting back (11)
17 Light beer; a camp (5)
19 (Moon) not quite full; bulging (7)
22 Close colleague (7)
23 Excuse of being elsewhere (5)
24 Twofold (4)
25 Foul smell (6)

DOWN

1 Bundle of e.g. corn (5)
2 Give formal decision (7)
3 Faithful (5)
5 Repugnance (5)
6 Harsh tyrant (6)
7 One set off by tiniest pressure (4,7)
8 Internal decay (3,3)
14 Headdress of wound cloth (6)
15 One from home of lost causes (7)
16 Even-tempered, calm (6)
18 Third-class (mark) (5)
20 Strong wind, explosion (5)
21 Hissing, rustling noise; elegant (*slang*) (5)

ACROSS

6 Omen; be omen of (7)

7 Thermonuclear device (1-4)

9 Replete (5)

10 Asian wind; its rain (7)

11 Arched-roof tracery style (3,8)

14 Really tough (person) (4,2,5)

17 One read to the disorderly once (4,3)

19 Asian leaf for chewing; paan (5)

21 Ring-shaped roll (5)

22 Nelson's flagship (7)

DOWN

1 Confer (authority on); a garment (4)

2 Cagliari its capital (8)

3 Helena's rival (*MND*) (6)

4 Feeble; slender (4)

5 Ophelia's father (8)

6 Nuisance (4)

8 Kindly (6)

11 (Military) leave (8)

12 Very relaxed (4-4)

13 Angel; chubby child (6)

15 Indigenous (6)

16 Stratagem (4)

18 One on same side (4)

20 Priam its king (4)

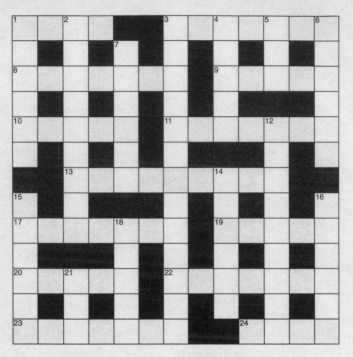

ACROSS

1 Regular solid; piece of sugar (4)

3 A vegetable; *chariot* (*anagram*) (7)

8 Of pivotal importance (7)

9 Nothing certain, but death and these (*?B. Franklin*) (5)

10 Become ready to pick, eat (5)

11 Get nearer; (weather) deteriorate (5,2)

13 International game (4,5)

17 The reindeer (7)

19 Path to take (5)

20 Jewish teacher (5)

22 Asked to come (7)

23 Six-sided figure (7)

24 Paradise garden (4)

DOWN

1 Roman author, orator (6)

2 Imminent-sailing flag (4,5)

3 The Eucharist (4,9)

4 A nostalgic fashion (5)

5 One steering oarsmen (3)

6 Herbal infusion (6)

7 Evil spirits (6)

12 Spent (9)

14 Prospered (6)

15 Burn with heat (6)

16 Flush with e.g. shame (6)

18 An entity, creature (5)

21 Fight; container (3)

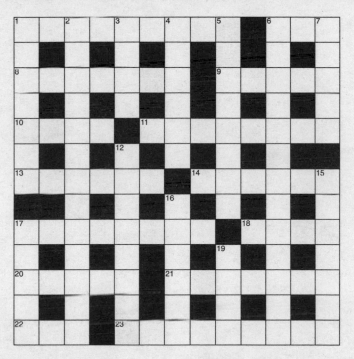

ACROSS

1 Risorgimento leader; a biscuit (9)
6 Centre of activity (3)
8 Definitely (2,5)
9 Provide (for) (5)
10 Almost shut (4)
11 Divination from thrown earth (8)
13 Large drink-pourer (6)
14 Dangerous moment (6)
17 E.g. Chinese, Japanese character (8)
18 On summit of (4)
20 Cunning, deceit (5)
21 All-change stations (7)
22 Label; child's game (3)
23 Lying down (9)

DOWN

1 Tolkien wizard (7)
2 Belated, nasty, realisation (4,9)
3 Spell (of fighting, illness) (4)
4 Bubbly froth (6)
5 Closed to public (2,6)
6 Start being really effective (3,4,6)
7 Powerfully built (5)
12 Tedious passage (8)
15 Specious arguer (7)
16 A gum; putty-like filler (6)
17 E.g. gold block (5)
19 Urban transport vehicle (4)

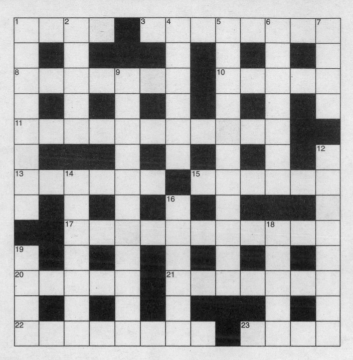

ACROSS

1 Asymmetrical; biased (4)
3 In professional training (8)
8 Evenly spaced (7)
10 Deprives of feeling (5)
11 (French) tiff (11)
13 Cut out; a duty (6)
15 Absence of social conscience (6)
17 Able to regulate body heat; ardent (4-7)
20 Friendship (5)
21 Giving ease (7)
22 (Human) statuette (8)
23 Disease-causing organism (4)

DOWN

1 Rim projection (8)
2 Scottish town; a collecting Lord (5)
4 Unusual item (6)
5 Humiliating (11)
6 Money as single payment (4,3)
7 Furniture to work at (4)
9 Our Father (5,6)
12 To-and-fro device (8)
14 Aircraft engine cover (7)
16 Husband of Titania (6)
18 *Journal of Plague Year* author (5)
19 Non-U (4)

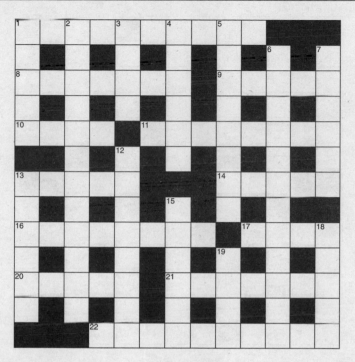

ACROSS

1 Copying others' work (10)
8 *Alice* illustrator (7)
9 To summarise (2,3)
10 *Peter Pan* pirate captain (4)
11 US lawyer (8)
13 Relative; pawnbroker (5)
14 In appropriate way (5)
16 A horse; an old joke (8)
17 Coffin stand (4)
20 Promise; be profane (5)
21 Chiselling, forcing, out (7)
22 Dominant position (10)

DOWN

1 Level of sound; steepness of slope (5)
2 Henry VIII's *Flanders Mare* (4,2,6)
3 An eye membrane (4)
4 Tell; be connected (6)
5 Incidental benefits (from discovery) (4-4)
6 Underfed condition (12)
7 Like sticky earth (6)
12 Dancers' stretchy garments (8)
13 Material thrown out; mine shaft (6)
15 Colourful cagebird (*abbr.*) (6)
18 A school; a game (5)
19 Store of earmarked money (4)

ACROSS

1 Manner of speaking (8)
5 Light (e.g. hair); fine (weather) (4)
9 Tall (5)
10 Heavy (e.g. responsibility) (7)
11 Frame (of car) (7)
12 Given nothing to eat (5)
13 Non-indulgent promotion of welfare (5,4)
18 Longest Iberian river (5)
20 Harvesting the sea (7)
22 Condition (attached) (7)
23 Thick-skinned beast (5)
24 Twilight (4)
25 Belief; side (table) (8)

DOWN

1 Principle of action; insurance document (6)
2 Bend (light-ray) (7)
3 Bottomless pit (5)
4 (MP) change sides (5,3,5)
6 Cold and distant (5)
7 Dwell (6)
8 Gas-cooker setting scale (6)
14 (Remark) kept to oneself (6)
15 Omission of vowel (7)
16 Unintelligent (6)
17 Pay no attention to (6)
19 Sheen; comment in margin (5)
21 A scrap; cut into tiny bits (5)

ACROSS

1 Arab souk (6)

5 South Pacific canoe (4)

9 Parliamentary record (7)

10 Healthy energy (6)

11 Sculptor's preliminary model (8)

12 Disprove (6)

15 Ask for review; be attractive (6)

18 French stick; cut gem (8)

20 Capital of Canada (6)

22 Portia's maid (*Merchant of Venice*) (7)

23 Inquisitive (4)

24 Stick and ball game (6)

DOWN

2 (Hindu) religious community (6)

3 Proclaim (8)

4 Cook in oven (5)

6 Circus arena; one round Saturn (4)

7 Fine-tune (6)

8 Word modifying adjective (6)

13 Relating to court of law (8)

14 Goneril's husband; New York capital (6)

16 A clog (6)

17 Machine-gun from air (6)

19 Circumference (5)

21 Reference line; centre of rotation (4)

ACROSS

6 Giving an assurance (12)

7 Angry outcry (6)

8 (Design) set into surface (6)

9 Competition; group of people (4)

10 Action involving new point of law (4,4)

12 Canvass personally; thick slice of bread (8)

16 Rapid narrows current; ginger root (4)

18 Little spasm; temporary difficulty (6)

20 Plush fabric; antler cover (6)

21 Say (word) wrong (12)

DOWN

1 Wrecker (8)

2 Natural skill (6)

3 Moral principles (6)

4 Calf meat (4)

5 Is jealous (6)

6 Yellow-rind cheese (5)

11 George IV's queen (8)

13 Father of Horus (*Egyptian myth*) (6)

14 Walk delicately, silently (6)

15 Russian dog-reflex scientist (6)

17 Cheshire town; sounds like *operators* (5)

19 Egyptian Christian (4)

ACROSS

3 Staring wide-eyed (8)
7 In profusion (6)
8 Absolute (truth) (6)
9 Precious stone; sounds like *sitcom Alf* (6)
10 Merchants' associations (*hist.*) (6)
11 Element Au (4)
13 Parson's land (5)
15 Jewels (4)
17 A Bight; a shepherd; type of measles (6)
18 Petrifying monster (6)
19 Pile of papers awaiting attention (2-4)
20 Graham —, *Brighton Rock* author (6)
21 Helpful advice (8)

DOWN

1 The bushbaby (6)
2 *Faust* composer (6)
3 Affectedly respectable (7)
4 Small round drop (7)
5 Rude (8)
6 Overshoes (8)
11 Awkwardly long-limbed (8)
12 Opera texts (8)
13 Alhambra city (7)
14 Impedimenta (7)
15 Poor attic room (6)
16 (Cow) calling (6)

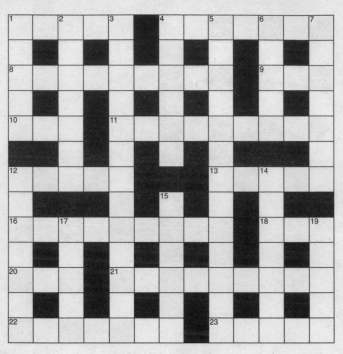

ACROSS

1 Part of farm; retrieve ball (5)
4 Shy (7)
8 Tackle, gear (9)
9 Go (for) (3)
10 Christen (3)
11 Command (9)
12 Federico García —, Spanish dramatist (5)
13 Is it still for tea? (*Brooke*) (5)
16 Triumph over odds (4,2,3)
18 "Play it again, —" (*Casablanca* misquote) (3)
20 Cambridgeshire cathedral (3)
21 Cook's Aussie landfall (6,3)
22 Great pleasure (7)
23 Keen (5)

DOWN

1 Devil (5)
2 EU food-additive code (1-6)
3 Container waved through Customs (10,3)
4 An ore; sounds like *mixture* (6)
5 Refuse to commit oneself (3,2,3,5)
6 Look displeased (5)
7 Random draw (7)
12 "Hear" being deaf (3-4)
14 Feeder worn by horse (7)
15 It sang "Willow" (*Mikado*) (3-3)
17 Faithful (5)
19 Corporation head (5)

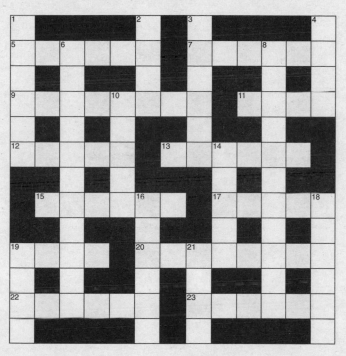

ACROSS

5 Off one's rocker (6)

7 South-west African republic (6)

9 From where Jesus taught; of Jupiter's four big moons (8)

11 Stream; one with *call* (4)

12 Run not off bat (5)

13 Representational sign (6)

15 Tin-alloy (e.g. tankard) (6)

17 Computer pointer; shy type (5)

19 Drama; 17 will, in cat's absence (4)

20 Throwing device (8)

22 The universe (6)

23 Style; sounds like *big house* (6)

DOWN

1 Pickwick scoundrel; bell sound (6)

2 Ballet leap (4)

3 Cheerful, debonair (6)

4 Knave; one that lifts car (4)

6 Concede position (4,3,4)

8 *Season of mists* poem (*Keats*) (3,2,6)

10 Smallest amount (5)

14 A venomous snake (5)

16 Reason given in apology (6)

18 Obtain by menaces (6)

19 Perfunctory kiss; quarter-bushel (4)

21 Dry, heavy volume (4)

ACROSS

1 Pause doubtfully (8)
5 Norway capital (4)
9 —of Windsor, *Shakespeare* (3,5,5)
10 Brave man (4)
11 Thin; small (chance) (7)
13 Officer's side-arm (6)
15 Feeble-minded; easy (6)
18 Of little depth (7)
20 Young attendant (4)
23 The first and the last (5,3,5)
24 Scream (4)
25 Capital of Finland (8)

DOWN

1 Great dislike (4)
2 Riddle (5)
3 Rapid-reiteration-of-note effect (*music*) (7)
4 Spotted-breast bird (6)
6 Laid money aside (for) (5,2)
7 One watching, monitoring (8)
8 Cutely precious (4)
12 Repudiation of belief (8)
14 Surgeon's knife (7)
16 Wicked, godless (7)
17 Brief pain (6)
19 Clay/sand soil (4)
21 Pick up (scraps) (5)
22 H. H. Munro pen-name (4)

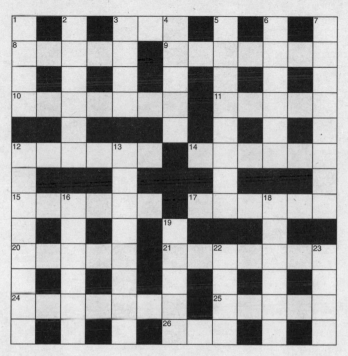

ACROSS

3 Buddy (3)

8 Green felt (5)

9 Reluctance to move (7)

10 Inebriated (7)

11 Hurt (5)

12 Skilled painter (6)

14 Interfere (6)

15 Vigorous struggle (6)

17 Leave without wind (6)

20 Hilarity (5)

21 Tetanus (7)

24 Acrobat; a glass (7)

25 From the country (5)

26 "—for one, one for —" (*Dumas*) (3)

DOWN

1 Down for the night (4)

2 Card game; a patrol (6)

3 Make (coffee); job benefit (4)

4 Trailing rain-forest plant (5)

5 Lawyers' jargon (8)

6 Eaten out by acid (6)

7 Reverie (8)

12 Robots (8)

13 Samuel Smiles *how to get on* book (4-4)

16 Be parsimonious (6)

18 Swear to leave alone (6)

19 Very (5-); an extremist (5)

22 Twist, twine (4)

23 Join (heated metals) (4)

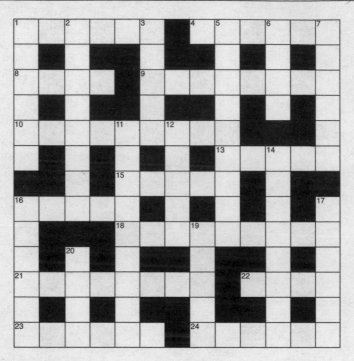

ACROSS

1 Scottish national dish (6)
4 Commit crime; upset (6)
8 Point of perfection (4)
9 Offer, burn as sacrifice (8)
10 Shrewish woman (9)
13 Bounty captain (5)
15 Muslim-paradise beauty (5)
16 Extra card in pack (5)
18 Without single answer, definite conclusion (4-5)
21 US President, killed; *gad, rifle! (anagram)* (8)
22 Competent (4)
23 Meal; a mess, if dog's (6)
24 Look up adoringly to (6)

DOWN

1 A toast; well-being (6)
2 Attractive but flimsy (8)
3 Oscillate (5)
5 Cold damage to extremities (9)
6 Brio (4)
7 Soak (6)
11 Goddess of Love (9)
12 Heraldic, sky, blue (5)
14 Unfit to eat (8)
16 With rough, sharp edges (6)
17 Stick (to) (6)
19 Lowest point (5)
20 Grain husks (4)

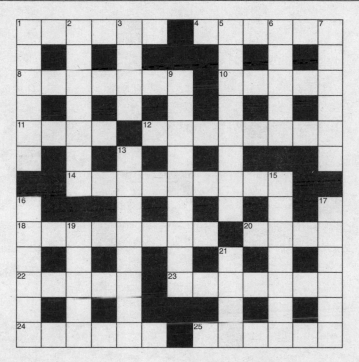

ACROSS

1 Put up with (6)
4 Shock absorber (6)
8 Dead body for meat (7)
10 Warm and sticky (5)
11 Unfriendly, severe (4)
12 Without worries (8)
14 Exuberantly cheerful (9)
18 Disruptive change (8)
20 Highest noble rank (4)
22 Broad comedy; ludicrous event (5)
23 Tanned skin (7)
24 Distant (6)
25 (House) floor (6)

DOWN

1 Leave (e.g. union) (6)
2 A strengthening metal tip (7)
3 Formal test (4)
5 Ignored (8)
6 Thigh bone (5)
7 Recover from pawn (6)
9 Paper, not electronic, post (*slang*) (5,4)
13 Capital of Hungary (8)
15 More difficult, rugged (7)
16 Dunce (6)
17 Be disloyal to (6)
19 Collection of wives (5)
21 James —, steam engine pioneer (4)

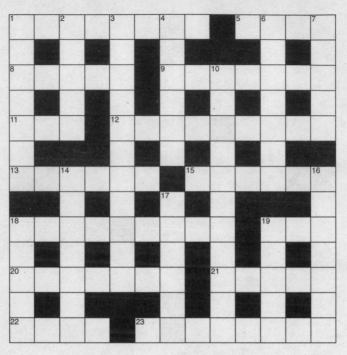

ACROSS

1 Inhabitants (8)

5 Gaiter; small quarrel (4)

8 Delay bedtime; look surprised (3,2)

9 (Part of) fortification; home of reaction (*fig.*) (7)

11 Expression of disgust (3)

12 With hardened tissue; unresponsive (*fig.*) (9)

13 Catch in web (6)

15 Wispy cloud (6)

18 Of marriage (9)

19 Belgian Formula 1 track, mineral-water town (3)

20 Getting bigger (7)

21 Island near Naples (5)

22 Baby's biscuit (4)

23 Return of output to input (8)

DOWN

1 (Especially physical) attitude (7)

2 (Repair with) piece of material (5)

3 Deep blue gemstone (5,6)

4 Whitish metal; a blue colour (6)

6 Computer output device (7)

7 Sleeveless robe; uniform jacket (5)

10 Prudish (6-5)

14 Delicate, thin (7)

16 Suffering on the waves (7)

17 Mix; circulate (at party) (6)

18 One for smoking (5)

19 Brown pigment (for photos once) (5)

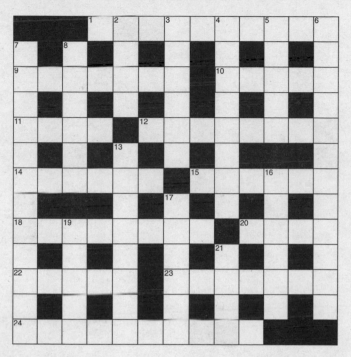

ACROSS

1 Vicious critical attack (7,3)
9 Sporting engagement (7)
10 Inca knot system (5)
11 Norse thunder god (4)
12 Apparent solar path (8)
14 Bring about; restrict (inheritance) (6)
15 Battle site, 1066 (6)
18 Scrooge's first name (8)
20 Make a to-do (4)
22 Provide; proposal (5)
23 Endanger (7)
24 Drudgery (6-4)

DOWN

2 Fit of fever (4)
3 Close fist round (6)
4 Asked (8)
5 Structural beam (5)
6 Inflatable children jump on (6,6)
7 Unofficially (3,3,6)
8 Urge strongly (6)
13 Linden (4-4)
16 Slat in door (6)
17 Notice; a 1, possibly (6)
19 Small and delicate (5)
21 Desultory fight; various minerals (4)

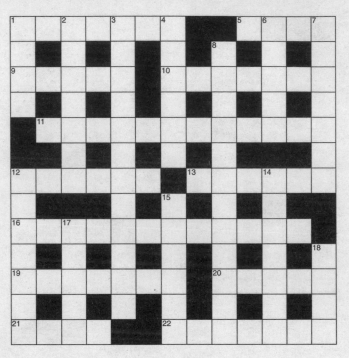

ACROSS

1 Speak with impediment (7)
5 Having footwear (4)
9 Boring paperwork (5)
10 Large, smooth stone (7)
11 Its artist his own subject (4-8)
12 First principles; back to them, for the ignorant (6)
13 Wanting to sit on eggs (6)
16 One not extinct after all (6,6)
19 Concern, necessitate (7)
20 Triatomic oxygen (5)
21 Open-air pool (4)
22 Bridge bid (4-3); remove; obtain (licence) (4,3)

DOWN

1 Influence; totter (4)
2 Without purpose (7)
3 In very generous style (12)
4 One cut at formal opening (6)
6 Monster Hercules killed; tiny water creature (5)
7 *Wizard of Oz* girl (7)
8 Disorientation in (e.g.) new country (7,5)
12 Oxford college; two Scottish kings (7)
14 Colombia/Venezuela river (7)
15 Consequence (6)
17 Clear and bright (5)
18 One's grand family home (4)

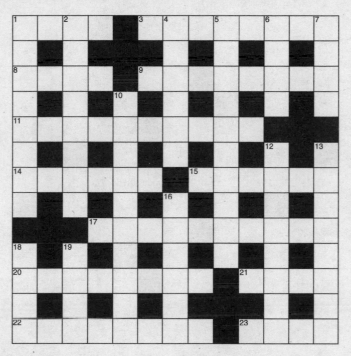

ACROSS

1 Go on horseback (4)
3 Crossword creator (8)
8 Young sow; a security (4)
9 Splendid, wonderful (8)
11 Political upheaval (10)
14 Hullabaloo (6)
15 Stimulus, boost (6)
17 An African ape (10)
20 Medium of communication (8)
21 Thin mist (4)
22 Cowboy and Indian films (8)
23 Icelandic saga (4)

DOWN

1 Demanding; logically faultless (8)
2 Salvation; consignment (8)
4 Devotee to religious life (6)
5 Journal (10)
6 Weaving machine; impend (4)
7 Take a chance on (4)
10 Dickens *Jarndyce* novel (5,5)
12 Snowstorm (8)
13 Items of passing interest (8)
16 Cymbeline heroine (6)
18 Shine; well-being feeling (4)
19 Purposes (4)

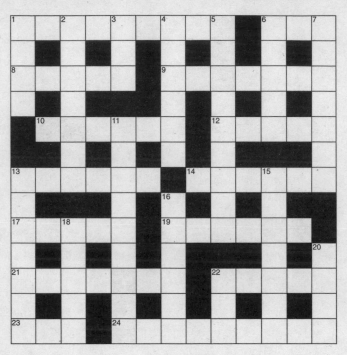

ACROSS

1 Angry (*slang*); covered in condensation (7,2)

6 Unavailable; spoiled (3)

8 Gradually decrease; a safe (5)

9 A 20th-century composer Lord; sounds like *stoves* (7)

10 Occurred (*literary*) (6)

12 Join, board; develop friendship (with) (3,2)

13 Dickens's Nell, outlaw John (6)

14 Clever; shining (6)

17 Constellation, has Belt (5)

19 Used tongue on; defeated (6)

21 Sporting ground (7)

22 Painted cherubs (5)

23 See other side (*abbr.*) (1,1,1)

24 Auld Reekie (9)

DOWN

1 Concessions; soaked bread pieces (4)

2 Beg (7)

3 Russian space station; sounds like *no better than* (3)

4 Take desultory interest (in) (6)

5 Old soothing medicine (9)

6 Done openly (5)

7 Open mesh (stocking) fabric (7)

11 The sweet-brier; *inelegant* (*anagram*) (9)

13 Gazes starwards; gives admiration (to) (5,2)

15 More important (7)

16 Former pupils (especially US) (6)

18 Adult insect stage (5)

20 (E.g. telescope) bowl; scupper (4)

22 The local (3)

ACROSS

1 Evacuate; drop (7)
5 Sparkling vigour (5)
8 Roughly (*Latin*) (5)
9 Day of Christmas on which drummers sent (7)
10 Lazy (8)
11 Indistinct sight (4)
13 Comprehensive reference book (13)
16 Month named for J. Caesar (4)
17 Miserable, pitiable (8)
20 Kabul monetary unit (7)
21 Make more interesting (5)
22 Smooth, unctuous (5)
23 Vital, defining quality (7)

DOWN

1 Assign authorship (to) (7)
2 Unpleasantly pungent (5)
3 Impasse (8)
4 Absolutely no way! (3,2,4,4)
5 Change direction (clockwise) (4)
6 Discomposed (7)
7 Imaginary interstellar medium (5)
12 Capt. Nemo's submarine (*Verne*) (8)
14 German city; toilet water (7)
15 Still firm (when cooked) (2,5)
16 Denims (5)
18 Port of safety (5)
19 Soak up sun (4)

ACROSS

1 Come to understand; six feet (6)
5 German POW camp (6)
8 West African fetish (4)
9 Mrs. Patrick —, English actress (8)
10 Outstanding instrumentalist (8)
12 State betting system (4)
13 Soft felt hat (6)
15 Scottish cloth (6)
17 John —, Angry Young Man; old cart (4)
19 Of the home (8)
21 Sudden emotional display (8)
23 A floor-covering (*abbr.*) (4)
24 Church reading; school period (6)
25 Change channels (6)

DOWN

2 Rude, insulting (7)
3 Place of frequent resort (5)
4 First Labour prime minister (9)
5 Total (3)
6 A judge (7)
7 Assign (shares) (5)
11 (Poetry) line with eight feet (9)
14 Multi-episode edition (7)
16 Southern French city, Papal home once (7)
18 Sharp (5)
20 Broken; a break (5)
22 Consecutive sequence; hurry (3)

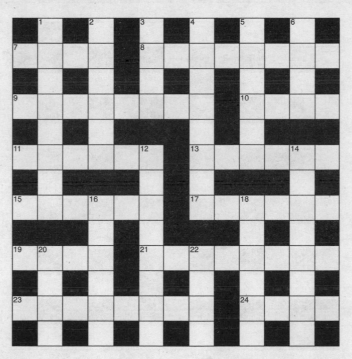

ACROSS

7 Blood (shed) (4)
8 Sluggishness (8)
9 *Porgy and Bess* composer (8)
10 Benefit cheque (4)
11 Remained; prevented (6)
13 Yearbook (6)
15 Apply (design) in relief (6)
17 Tending to sag (6)
19 Poke (4)
21 A shrub; *so rare – my!* (*anagram*) (8)
23 Impediment (8)
24 Against; an opponent (4)

DOWN

1 Impetus of movement (8)
2 Having spirited determination (6)
3 Run smoothly (4)
4 A classic ballad; flag (8)
5 Wait; hold tightly (4,2)
6 Borodin's Prince (4)
12 Divert attention (8)
14 Roughness of temper (8)
16 Quirk (6)
18 Military, German pub band sound (6)
20 Formal gown (4)
22 Killed; slide out of control (4)

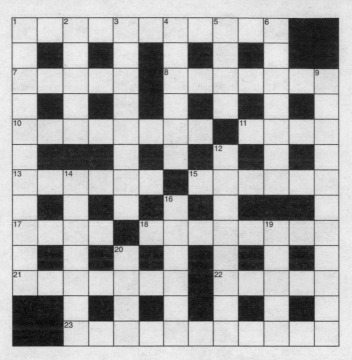

ACROSS

1 Action ensuring failure (4,2,5)
7 One imputing worst motives (5)
8 A creamy dessert (7)
10 Incidental skirmish (8)
11 New Zealander (*informal*) (4)
13 Securely fasten (6)
15 Of blooms (6)
17 Long, sharp (e.g. walrus) tooth (4)
18 Absolutely clearly; tangibly (8)
21 Motorists (7)
22 Farewell (5)
23 *Jude, Tess* author (6,5)

DOWN

1 Got going by foot thrust (4-7)
2 Church assembly (5)
3 Special time, event (8)
4 Put in position for action (6)
5 Yorkshire river; sounds like *song* (4)
6 More dense (7)
9 Common-law right; G. & S. operetta (5,2,4)
12 Hurried and careless (8)
14 Moral quibbler (7)
16 Sick feeling (6)
19 A rose; a pipe (5)
20 A fiddling emperor (4)

ACROSS

1 Pastoral; of country life (7)
5 Marvellous (*slang*); an extra (5)
8 Prestige (5)
9 Quivering with energy (7)
10 (Learned) in painless fashion (7,5)
12 Flippancy (6)
14 Clandestine; a thicket (6)
17 Covered in bruises (5,3,4)
21 Zog its king once (7)
22 Factory; install (e.g. spy) (5)
23 Smarten, admire oneself (5)
24 Cockney area of London (4,3)

DOWN

1 Derbyshire town, its pudding (8)
2 Trainee; junior family (branch) (5)
3 Suffice, endure, to end (4,3)
4 Hole (in e.g. tooth) (6)
5 Cavalryman's sword (5)
6 US open plain (7)
7 (Habitual) repetition (4)
11 Bore witness (to) (8)
13 With much to say (7)
15 He married his mother (*Greek myth*) (7)
16 Wild, violent (6)
18 Principle; genuine oeuvre (5)
19 (Permission to) go (5)
20 Speak gratingly; a tool (4)

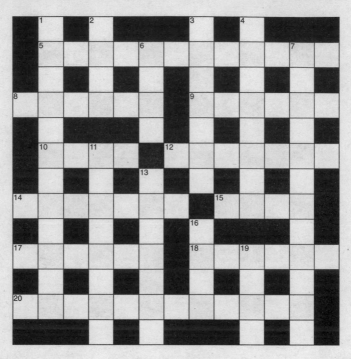

ACROSS

5 The skill of gardening (12)
8 High-spirited romp (6)
9 A hat; Svengali's subject (6)
10 Language of Pakistan (4)
12 Fabric hanging in folds (7)
14 Specially hire (e.g. aircraft) (7)
15 Sudden loud noise; right (on time) (4)
17 Its young fed on milk (6)
18 Fugitive from justice (6)
20 Habitual, almost automatic, trait (6,6)

DOWN

1 Main road (12)
2 Spoken (4)
3 A break (7)
4 Former Abyssinia (8)
6 Part of foot; small island (4)
7 Poet and *I, Claudius* author (6,6)
11 A National Park; a prison (8)
13 Gaelic social (7)
16 Duty list (4)
19 Ruffian (4)

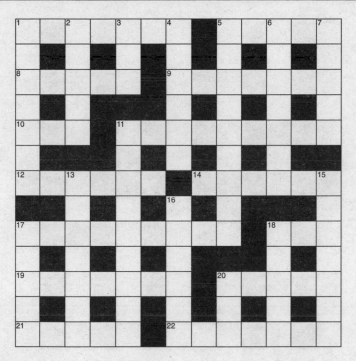

ACROSS

1 Serrated-beaked bird, the merganser (7)
5 Tiny particle, patch of colour (5)
8 Excessive (5)
9 (Groves of) scholarly retreat (7)
10 Divinity (3)
11 Untruth (9)
12 Do it again! (6)
14 Gripping tool (6)
17 One given something (9)
18 Watch-chain; palm (off) (3)
19 A road surfacing (7)
20 Florida resort city (5)
21 Rhythm of poetry; unit of distance (5)
22 Outermost; very unusual (7)

DOWN

1 Bring in contraband (7)
2 Walked through water (5)
3 Anger (3)
4 Answerable (6)
5 A flute; a bean (9)
6 Ugly building (7)
7 Work, mould, with hands (5)
11 Hearth, grate (9)
13 Pilot's cabin (7)
15 Retreat, go down (7)
16 Acquire dentition (6)
17 Build up weapons again (5)
18 Signal light (5)
20 Protective pad; tangle of hair (3)

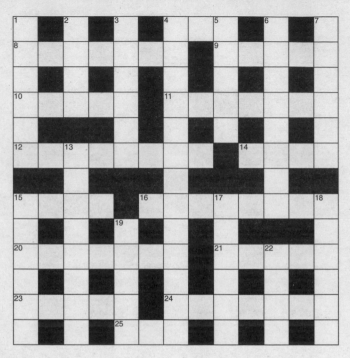

ACROSS

4 Shack (3)
8 Have anguish (over) (7)
9 Illicit spirit ... (5)
10 ... Russian spirit (5)
11 Gradually unfreeze (7)
12 Get over (embarrassment) (4,4)
14 Grain store; missile chamber (4)
15 Connection (4)
16 Sloppy; in broken-down shoes (once) (8)
20 Close-together group (7)
21 Give permission for (5)
23 Chief city of Piedmont (5)
24 Swiss city, 1925 Pact (7)
25 A hair preparation (3)

DOWN

1 Wonder (at) (6)
2 Fill (lorry); a burden (4)
3 Wonder-worker (6)
4 Serious punishment awaits (5,4,4)
5 Stealing (5)
6 Single big stone; faceless organisation (8)
7 Minority (slum) area (6)
13 Leading force (8)
15 Find position of (6)
17 A fish; sounds like 15 down (6)
18 Ernest —, *Cynara* poet (6)
19 Nettle, bee attack (5)
22 Ancient stringed instrument (4)

ACROSS

1 Weakness (after illness) (8)
5 Mongolian desert (4)
9 Incandescent with fury (7)
10 A bird; it *quoth Nevermore* (5)
11 Rude rebuff (4)
12 Prepare to fence! (2,5)
14 Series of games; a tree product (6)
16 Astute (6)
19 Bigwig (7)
21 Sit (for artist); set (puzzle) (4)
24 Warning signal (5)
25 Explosive, has pin (7)
26 Ballet costume (4)
27 Look for (gold); outlook (8)

DOWN

1 Attracted; sketched (4)
2 Element no. 5 (5)
3 Able to be read (7)
4 Made neat (6)
6 Head side of coin (7)
7 Obliquely suggestive remark (8)
8 Sailor's rum (4)
13 Boastful person (8)
15 Shamelessly unconcealed (7)
17 Unfortunate (7)
18 Account book (6)
20 Dispose of without ceremony (4)
22 Vibrate (5)
23 Outstanding achievement (4)

ACROSS

1 Indications (5)

4 Covetous (7)

8 "Never glad confident —again" (*Browning*) (7)

9 Skin preparation; copier powder (5)

10 Small stream; tolerate (5)

11 Land round house (6)

13 Lack of employment, exercise (6)

15 Pollen-holding part of stamen (6)

18 Clothes maker (6)

20 Stalin aide; Leningrad ballet (5)

22 Town announcer once (5)

23 Plant support up wall (7)

24 Bertrand —, philosopher and mathematician (7)

25 Repentant (5)

DOWN

1 Portable frames for sleeping on (4,4)

2 Extirpates (7)

3 (A little too) polished; trail of oil (5)

4 Take on (staff, opponent) (6)

5 Old campaigner (7)

6 Part of pound (5)

7 A small island; Burns's *cutty* shirt (4)

12 Parodied version (8)

14 Throw (money) around (7)

16 Jumping runner (7)

17 Sub-humanly violent (6)

19 (Things going) wrong (5)

20 Retains; castle strong-points (5)

21 Mark of old wound (4)

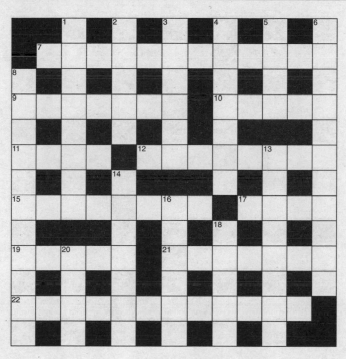

ACROSS

7 Concede to majority (4,4,4)
9 Powerful; fervent (7)
10 Long narrow top (5)
11 Drink carrier; sounds like *feature* (4)
12 Sunken continent (8)
15 Deep (ice) fissure (8)
17 Ring of light (4)
19 To deposit; gatehouse (5)
21 Loss of memory (7)
22 Hurry up! (*slang*) (4,2,6)

DOWN

1 Phoenician city, Rome rival (8)
2 Side (of animal, army) (5)
3 Swarm damagingly in (6)
4 Diary; magazine (7)
5 Intelligence; object to (4)
6 Final e.g. hymn; Kipling poem (11)
8 Subversive group (5,6)
13 Wing of church (8)
14 Athlete's spear (7)
16 Thinly scattered (6)
18 Relative by marriage (2-3)
20 Embankment; ditch (4)

ACROSS

7 Override yes-vote (4)

8 —Swinburne; —Moncrieff (*Wilde*) (8)

9 With unusual talent (6)

10 Resounds (6)

11 Bad-luck bringer (4)

12 Immature (behaviour) (8)

15 Fearless (8)

17 Throw violently (4)

18 Pursued; engraved (6)

21 Speculative ploy (6)

22 Realisation (of plan) (8)

23 Advance (2,2); fool, (US) thug (4)

DOWN

1 Act undermining state (8)

2 Grey matter (of brain) (6)

3 Disadvantage (8)

4 Frightening monster (4)

5 Bee, fly, lady, monkey flower (6)

6 Folk wisdom (4)

13 Poor (8)

14 One who pulls through (8)

16 Biggest-land-area country (6)

17 Public respect (paid) (6)

19 Damage (4)

20 Platform for e.g. high table (4)

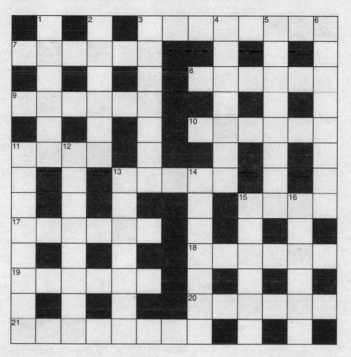

ACROSS

3 Tension of waiting (8)

7 International distress call (6)

8 A chess piece; a Sir (6)

9 Second-smallest continent (6)

10 Become less hard (6)

11 Stretches of water; sounds like *grab* (4)

13 Palm-like tree, gives e.g. sago (5)

15 Await attention (4)

17 (Music) not using key system (6)

18 French champagne, coronation, city (6)

19 Jinx (6)

20 Unexpected, quick (6)

21 Huge statue (at Rhodes once) (8)

DOWN

1 Gesture of respect (6)

2 Loathsome (6)

3 Whole-greater-than-parts effect (7)

4 Animal pound; Gilbert —'s ordeal, *Waugh* (7)

5 Pessimistic; minus (quantity) (8)

6 Prolonged (8)

11 Of highest angel order (8)

12 Basic plane-wing structure (8)

13 An antelope; a leather (7)

14 At which one lives (7)

15 False (6)

16 To count; a total (6)

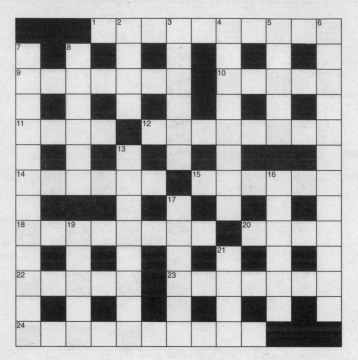

ACROSS

1 It joined England and Scotland (3,2,5)
9 Manifest (7)
10 It divides England and Scotland (5)
11 Swearword (4)
12 Top of ship's sides (8)
14 Caress; a blow (6)
15 Sun-turning latitude line (6)
18 Fought off; offended (8)
20 Burst of laughter, thunder (4)
22 Tarnish; flaw (5)
23 Old trumpet; loud and inspiring (7)
24 Pay (for work) (10)

DOWN

2 (Cock) called; ship's operators (4)
3 (E.g. factory) production (6)
4 Adverse, improper (8)
5 Perfect (5)
6 Naturist camp (6,6)
7 Laboratory worker; one on protest (12)
8 Group of young; portable bed (6)
13 Rigid framework; minimum (staff) (8)
16 Summary (of writing) (6)
17 Sword-fighter (6)
19 Light-splitting device (5)
21 One known to be true (4)

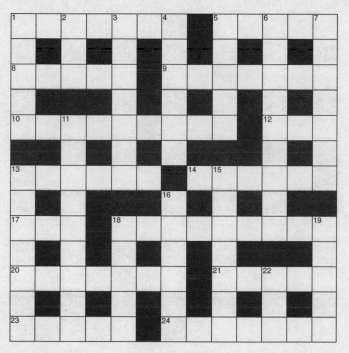

ACROSS

1 Royal domain (7)
5 Plain architecture order (5)
8 Money penalties (5)
9 Edgar's disguise (*Lear*) (4,3)
10 Finding of innocence (9)
12 Unwell (3)
13 Woodworker (6)
14 Curving outwards (6)
17 Dickens' pseudonym (3)
18 Entirety of staff (9)
20 It is provoked and unprovoked by drink (*Macbeth*) (7)
21 Capital of Ghana (5)
23 Shining success, distinction (5)
24 Rouged, unkempt (7)

DOWN

1 Franz —, Czech novelist (5)
2 (Indian) bread; grandmother (3)
3 Hold in contempt (7)
4 Capital of Mozambique (6)
5 Drivel; show huge pleasure (over) (5)
6 Type of dog; one fetching (9)
7 Intricate; group of related buildings (7)
11 Showing amused bafflement (9)
13 Special anniversary (7)
15 Curt, impolite (3-4)
16 Request to deity (6)
18 Pull away forcefully (5)
19 The largest antelope (5)
22 A pass through ridge (3)

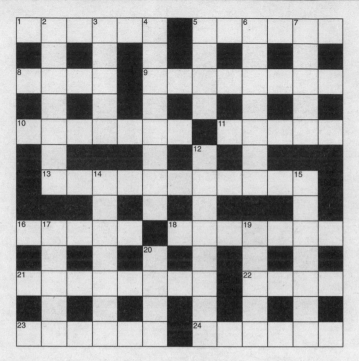

ACROSS

1 Committee's minimum attendance (6)
5 Airless space (6)
8 A long-necked wader (4)
9 Supporter of Old Pretender (8)
10 Baby's room (7)
11 Cambridge college; Irish county (5)
13 Realistic, practical (4-2-5)
16 Fit with glass (5)
18 Number in Rugby Union team (7)
21 Brisk (pace); splendid (8)
22 Lacking warmth (4)
23 North-east France battle, 1916 (6)
24 Range, size (6)

DOWN

2 Free, like Shelley's Prometheus (7)
3 Flowers; —, all the way (*Browning*) (5)
4 Greater part; adult age (8)
5 Wickedness; a gripper (4)
6 A craftsman; an iced drink (7)
7 Complete; pronounce (5)
12 Crisp sugar/egg confection (8)
14 Shrivelled with age (7)
15 US folk-dance party (7)
17 A slip; to expire (5)
19 Understood, unspoken (5)
20 Phineas, Huck —(*Trollope, Twain*) (4)

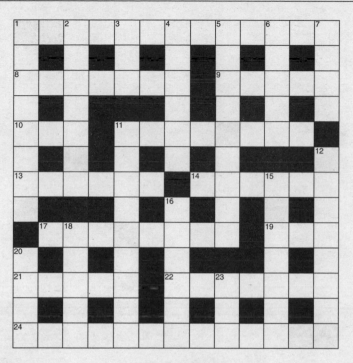

ACROSS

1 Mann story, Britten opera (5,2,6)
8 Important; prominent (7)
9 Secret store (5)
10 Fish eggs (3)
11 Dipping into books (8)
13 Anticlimax (6)
14 Play false shot (6)
17 (In) limbo (8)
19 Before (*poet.*) (3)
21 Less wet (5)
22 One-way-motion-only device (7)
24 Weighted truncheon (4,9)

DOWN

1 Explain, portray (8)
2 Minor illness (7)
3 Garden tool; Plymouth feature (3)
4 People of one country (6)
5 Undue (9)
6 Old Peruvian (5)
7 Level; yet (4)
11 One to catch the unwary (5,4)
12 One picking team (8)
15 *Seagull* author (7)
16 False (6)
18 Short; one's instructions (5)
20 False god (4)
23 Start of golf hole (3)

ACROSS

1 French astrologer/ prophet (11)
8 Uncanny (5)
9 Toronto its capital (7)
10 Eldest son of Rebekah (*Genesis 27*) (4)
11 Detroit in this state (8)
13 Little dent in chin (6)
14 Camelot king (6)
17 Better (8)
19 Mosquito-like fly (4)
22 Element S (7)
23 Beginning (5)
24 Citizens (in one place) (11)

DOWN

1 Mother's granddaughter, perhaps (5)
2 Mocking irony (7)
3 Smell appallingly (of) (4)
4 Casually visit (4,2)
5 Beautiful female spy (4,4)
6 Indifferent gesture (5)
7 Where boxer rests; a free-kick (6)
12 Four-line comic verse (8)
13 Abstain (6)
15 Gunman's surrender call (5,2)
16 Nuffield family name (6)
18 One directing plane (5)
20 Old ten per cent tax (5)
21 Little burrowing rodent (4)

ACROSS

1 Unwilling to speak (8)
5 Smile broadly; timber support (4)
8 Centre spot (8)
9 Stagger; spool (4)
11 Little poem (5)
12 Bear somewhat (unpleasantly) (on) (7)
13 Neglected, threadbare (6)
15 Hardened (to) (6)
18 Upstairs platform (7)
19 Impressive range (5)
21 Definite (4)
22 Falstaff's red-nosed companion (8)
23 Slowly leak (4)
24 Mused; was amazed (8)

DOWN

1 Comments (7)
2 Hot, sweet, spirit drink (5)
3 Subject one cannot understand (6,4)
4 Papal ambassador (6)
6 Henry II's, Edward I's queen (7)
7 Brawl (5)
10 Generous (4-6)
14 Not yet under arrest (2,5)
16 Without getting footwear wet (3-4)
17 Electrical generator (6)
18 Foundation (5)
20 Straight-edge (5)

ACROSS

1 NT book; *seen a ship? (anagram)* (9)

6 Baby's bed (3)

8 Dirty mark (5)

9 Working surface; oppose (7)

10 Small, slim (woman) (6)

12 Joseph —, classical composer (5)

13 Careless; *Our Mutual Friend* character (6)

14 Arrogant (6)

17 A superstructure; a fortress (5)

19 Restive; so lies a crowned head (*Henry IV Part 2*) (6)

21 Cancel out (7)

22 Snake (round); string (5)

23 Type of lettuce; an Aegean island (3)

24 Soviet St Petersburg (9)

DOWN

1 Otherwise (4)

2 Hauling cry (5-2)

3 Wickedness (3)

4 German Aix-la-Chapelle (6)

5 Amundsen there first (5,4)

6 Spiteful (5)

7 Oppressive rule (7)

11 Not biased (9)

13 Devilish (7)

15 Document collection (7)

16 John —, wrote *Pilgrim's Progress* (6)

18 Cardiff its capital (5)

20 Make (one's way) (4)

22 Darken in sun (3)

ACROSS

6 Honoured position (5,2,5)
7 Warning, proviso (6)
8 Public speaker (6)
9 Turn over; egg-nog (4)
10 Handbag (once) (8)
12 Pass, send across (8)
16 Collapse in heap; failure (4)
18 One keeping tally (6)
20 Inspiration (*literally*) (6)
21 That's enough from you! (3,1,4,2,2)

DOWN

1 Delicate (fabric) (4-4)
2 Character; missive (6)
3 On the sea (6)
4 Earnest request (4)
5 Move text up and down (screen) (6)
6 Oyster gem (5)
11 Stimulant in tea, coffee (8)
13 Fixed grin (6)
14 Ploughing trench (6)
15 Chide (6)
17 Work for eight (5)
19 Genuine (4)

ACROSS

1 Narrow stretch of water (6)
5 A forearm bone (4)
9 Island of Napoleon's birth (7)
10 Vague idea (6)
11 List of terms with explanations (8)
12 Order of business (6)
15 Fat stomach (6)
18 Rotating element of electric motor (8)
20 Stockholm its capital (6)
22 Give in, give up (7)
23 Noah's eldest son (4)
24 (English) 18-year-olds' exam (1,5)

DOWN

2 Deal with; equipment (6)
3 (Skin) scrape (8)
4 Forest, south of tundra (5)
6 Endure (4)
7 Out of the country (6)
8 Indian multi-trunk tree (6)
13 How the agreed see (3,2,3)
14 Involving risk (6)
16 Every time (6)
17 Horizontal band of e.g. sculpture (6)
19 Italian Formula 1 track (5)
21 Stupor (4)

THE SOLUTIONS

1

2

3

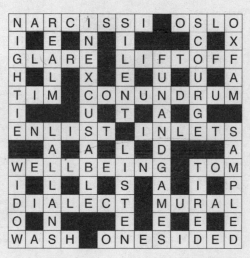

4

5

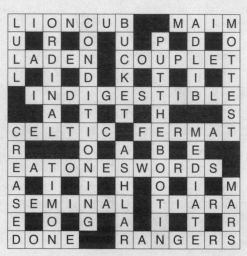

6

7

8

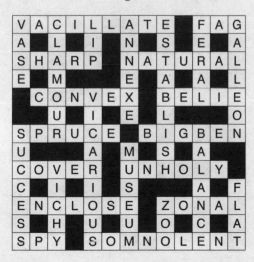

9

10

11

12

13

14

15

16

17

18

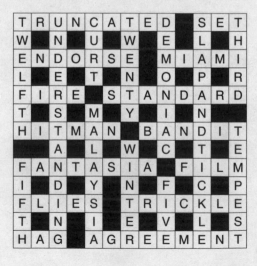

19

20

21

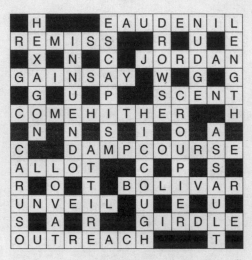

22

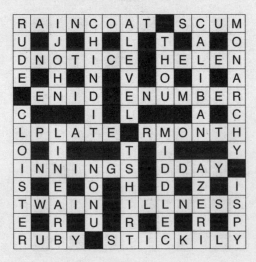

23

24

25

26

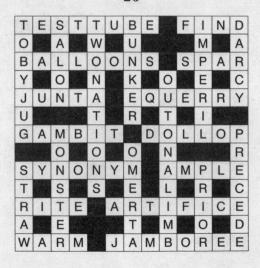

27

28

29

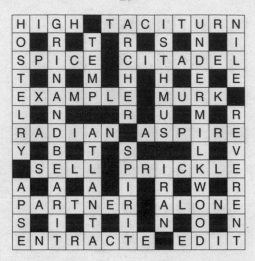

30

31

32

33

34

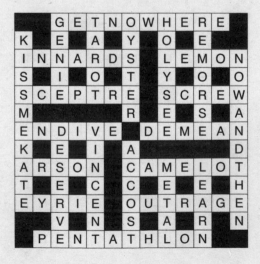

35

36

37

38

39

40

SOLUTIONS

41

42

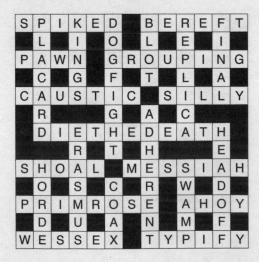

43

A	R	I	D		F	A	R	C	I	C	A	L
R		N		S		R		H		O		O
C	A	C	T	I		T	R	A	W	L	E	R
H		O		L		E		T		L		E
A	M	M	E	T	E	R			T	O	O	L
I		M			Y		E		Q			P
S	T	U	P	I	D		A	L	L	U	R	E
M		N		N		G				I		D
	L	I	S	T		U	N	H	E	A	R	D
G		C		E		N		A		L		L
A	N	A	G	R	A	M		H	A	I	T	I
N		D		I		A		A		S		N
G	L	O	A	M	I	N	G		S	M	U	G

44

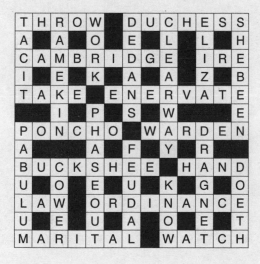

T	H	R	O	W		D	U	C	H	E	S	S
A		A		O		E		L		L		H
C	A	M	B	R	I	D	G	E		I	R	E
I		E		K		A		A		Z		B
T	A	K	E		E	N	E	R	V	A	T	E
		I		P		S		W				E
P	O	N	C	H	O		W	A	R	D	E	N
A			A		F		Y		R			
B	U	C	K	S	H	E	E		H	A	N	D
U		O		E		U		K		G		O
L	A	W		O	R	D	I	N	A	N	C	E
U		E		U		A		O		E		T
M	A	R	I	T	A	L		W	A	T	C	H

45

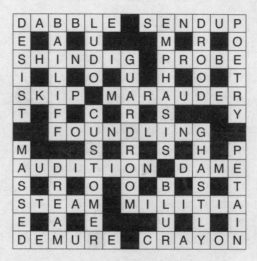

46

47

48

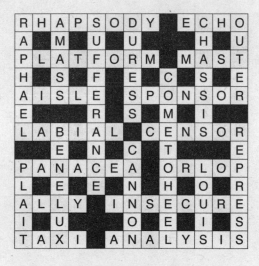

49

50

51

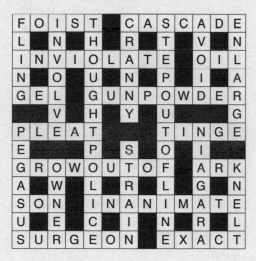

52

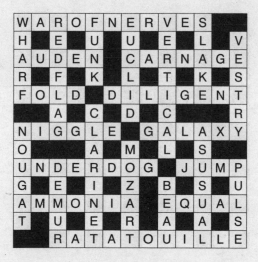

53

54

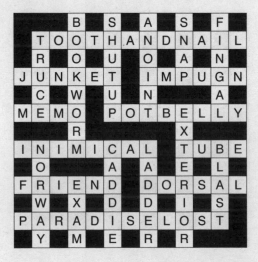

55

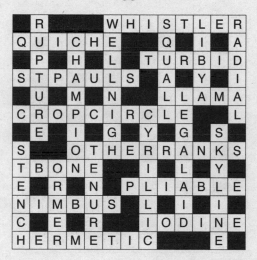

56

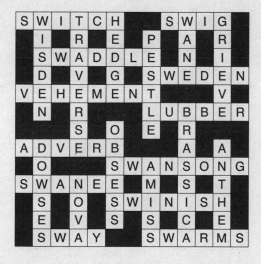

57

58

59

60

61

62

63

64

65

66

67

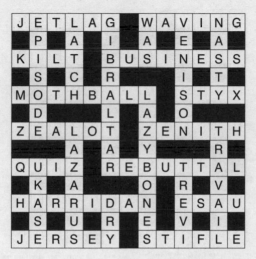

68

69

70

71

72

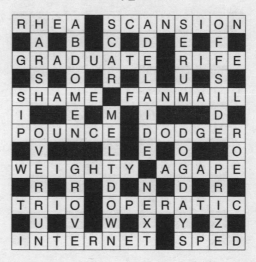

73

74

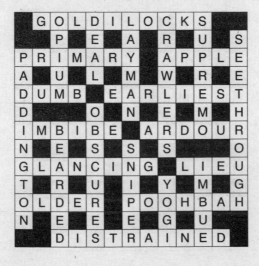

75

76

77

78

79

80

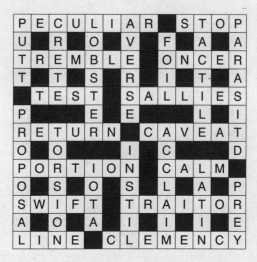

81

82

83

84

85

86

87

C	H	A	F	F		W	I	S	H	F	U	L

88

89

90

91

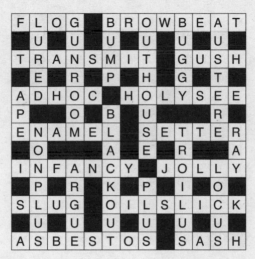

92

93

94

95

96

97

98

99

100

101

102

103

104

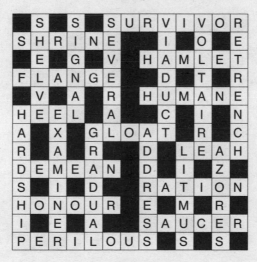

105

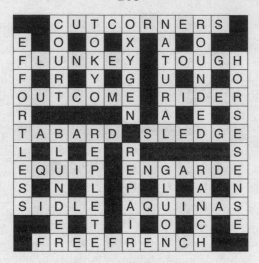

106

107

V	I	V	I	D		E	X	P	I	A	T	E
A		E		R		X		H		O		L
P	A	T	R	I	M	O	N	Y		R	O	E
I		E		P		D		S		T		C
D	A	R	K		J	U	B	I	L	A	N	T
		A		M		S		Q				O
W	I	N	C	E	D		B	U	Z	Z	E	R
I				D		D		E		A		
S	U	L	L	I	V	A	N		S	M	O	G
T		E		O		R		P		B		R
F	A	T		C	O	W	A	R	D	I	C	E
U		O		R		I		O		A		E
L	A	N	T	E	R	N		W	A	N	E	D

108

	P				P	R	O	B	A	B	L	E
S	A	F	A	R	I			A		R		I
	L		P		C		F	L	Y	I	N	G
B	E	S	P	O	K	E		Z		N		H
	R		A		E		A	R	G	O	T	
I	M	P	R	U	D	E	N	C	E			H
	O		E		U		O		S		O	
S			N	I	P	A	N	D	T	U	C	K
Q	U	I	T	S			S		R		T	
U		B		A		G	E	T	A	W	A	Y
A	S	S	A	I	L		N		I		G	
W		E		A		S	E	N	I	O	R	
S	U	N	S	H	I	N	E				N	

109

110

111

112

113

114

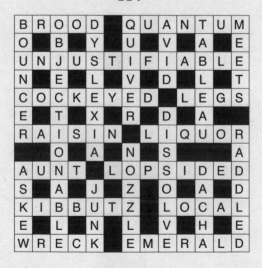

115

116

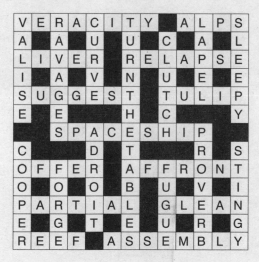

117

118

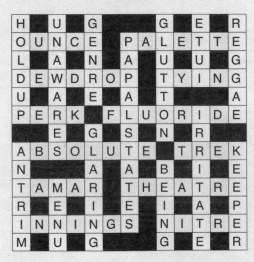

119

120

121

122

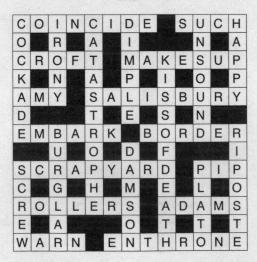

123

124

125

126

127

B	I	T	S	A	N	D	P	I	E	C	E	S
E		R		S		E		N		O		H
C	R	O	C	H	E	T		F	O	R	C	E
O		O			A		U		P		D	
M	O	P		B	A	C	K	L	A	S	H	
I		E		R		H		L				T
N	O	R	M	A	L		S	C	R	A	P	E
G			S		F		R		R		R	
	E	M	I	S	S	A	R	Y		T	O	M
S		E		B		L			D		I	
L	L	A	M	A		L	E	C	T	E	R	N
I		N		N		O		U		C		U
P	U	T	S	D	O	W	N	R	O	O	T	S

128

	E		A		S		T		E		R
	A	F	F	E	C	T	I	O	N	A	T	E
A		F		S		A		L		R		C
B	O	U	D	O	I	R		S	A	L	V	O
E		S		P		V		T				N
R	A	I	L		B	E	H	O	L	D	E	N
Y		V		A			Y		R		O	
S	V	E	N	G	A	L	I		S	U	F	I
T			I		I		G		D		T	
W	H	E	E	L		V	O	Y	A	G	E	R
Y		M		I		I		P		E		E
T	W	I	S	T	O	N	E	S	A	R	M	
H		T		Y		G		Y		Y		

129

130

131

B	R	A	N	D	N	E	W			B		T
O		V		U		D		D	R	A	P	E
G	R	E	Y	F	R	I	A	R		N		R
U		R		F		T		E		J	A	M
S	I	N	G		H	O	O	D	O	O		I
		U		I		R		G				T
V	I	S	H	N	U		G	E	N	T	L	E
I				S		B		R		O		
E		C	H	E	R	R	Y		B	U	L	L
W	A	R		R		U		G		R		O
I		U		T	O	N	S	O	R	I	A	L
N	E	E	D	S		E		N		N		L
G		L			P	L	U	G	U	G	L	Y

132

	M		S		S		S		T	
	C	L	O	C	K	W	A	T	C	H	E	R
	H		V		E		M		A		R	
S	I	L	E	N	T		S	O	M	B	R	E
	L		M		C		O			O		
S	L	O	E		H	O	N	O	R	A	R	Y
			N				E					
B	A	C	T	E	R	I	A		S	L	U	M
	P			A		S		E		N	
K	I	T	B	A	G		S	U	M	M	I	T
	E		R		G		E		B		T	
A	C	C	I	D	E	N	T	A	L	L	Y
	E		E		D		S		E	

133

134

135

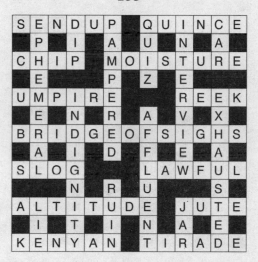

136

137

138

139

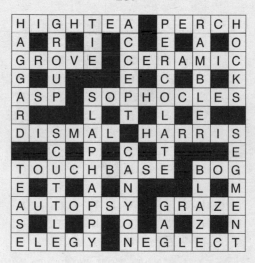

140

141

B	O	D	Y	B	L	O	W		C	O	R	D
A		O		O		P				V		O
B	A	N	K	R	U	P	T		D	E	F	Y
Y		O		E		U		T		R		E
L	U	R	I	D		G	R	E	M	L	I	N
O				S		N		R		A		
N	E	G	A	T	E		P	R	O	P	E	L
		R		I		B		A				I
S	O	U	F	F	L	E		F	R	A	N	C
T		M		F		A		I		R		E
R	O	B	E		E	V	E	R	Y	M	A	N
U		L				E		M		E		C
T	E	E	S		O	R	G	A	N	D	I	E

142

C	A	S	U	A	L		F	L	O	R	E	T
A		Y		A		A		A		A		A
V	I	L	E		S	O	U	T	H	P	A	W
O		L		S		E		T		D		D
R	H	A	P	S	O	D	I	C				R
T		B		U		I		O	D	D	L	Y
		U		B	U	X	O	M		O		
B	A	S	I	S		I		E		W		V
I				C	L	E	A	R	A	N	C	E
G		F		R		R			P			S
C	A	U	T	I	O	U	S		P	O	R	T
A		M		P		O			U			R
T	R	E	A	T	Y		N	E	A	R	B	Y

143

144

145

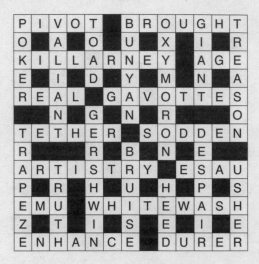

146

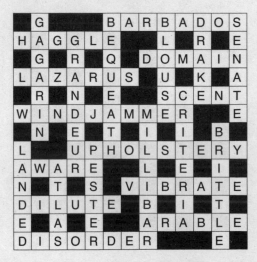

147

148

149

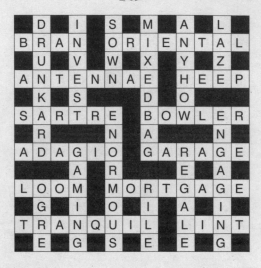

150

151

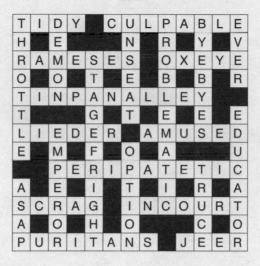

152

153

154

155

156

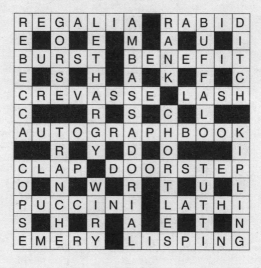

157

158

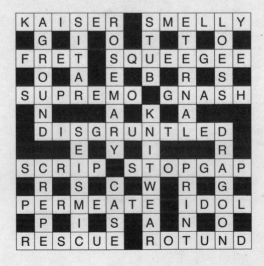

159

N	A	I	L			A	D	J	U	T	A	N	T
A		N		S		A		N		L		A	
V	I	T	A	L		C	O	B	B	L	E	R	
I		H	A	T		O		I		N		N	
G	R	E	A	T	L	Y		W	I	N	K		
A		S			L		E		G		E		
T	R	A	N	C	E		O	D	I	O	U	S	
E		M	U		U			O		P			
	B	E	A	R		P	I	C	A	D	O	R	
F		B		S		B		O		T		E	
E	M	O	T	I	V	E		C	H	I	P	S	
T		A		V		A		K		M		S	
E	N	T	R	E	A	T	Y		P	E	T	O	

160

M	U	T	E	S	W	A	N		N	U	T	S
A		E		T		N		T		N		O
I	C	E	B	E	R	G		O	T	T	E	R
M		T		A		O		S		R		O
	C	H	A	R		L	U	S	T	I	E	R
P			I		A			E		I		
R	E	M	A	N	D		R	E	E	D	I	T
E		E			E		N					Y
S	A	T	C	H	E	L		S	T	I	R	
U		O		A		A		U		R		I
M	I	N	O	R		P	O	I	S	O	N	S
E		Y		T		S		T		N		I
D	E	M	O		R	E	L	E	A	S	E	S

161

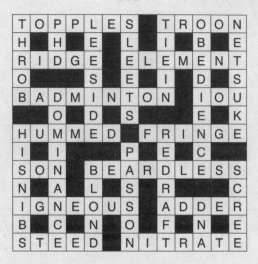

162

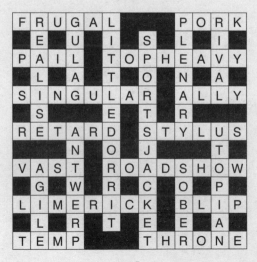

163

164

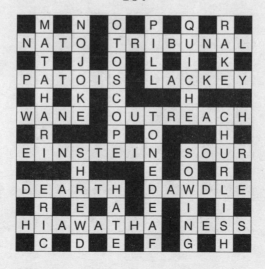

165

166

167

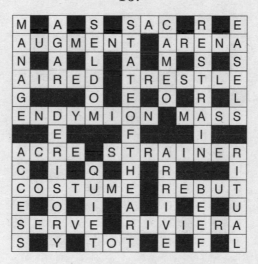

168

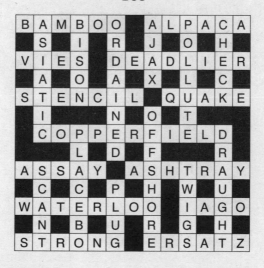

169

170

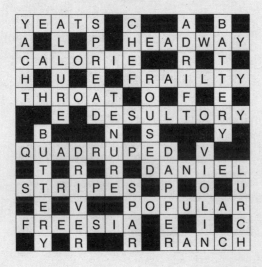

171

172

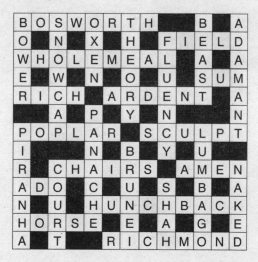

173

174

175

176

177

178

179

180

SOLUTIONS

181

182

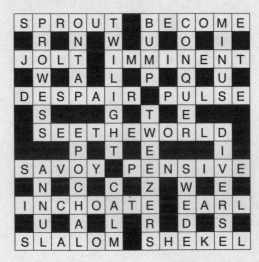

183

184

185

186

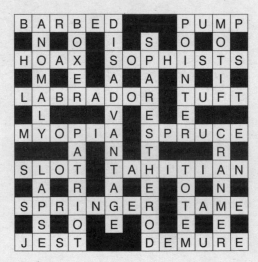

187

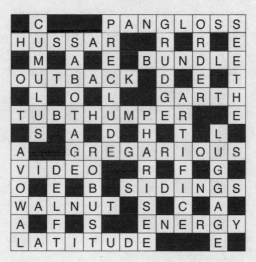

188

189

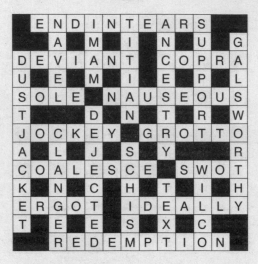

190

191

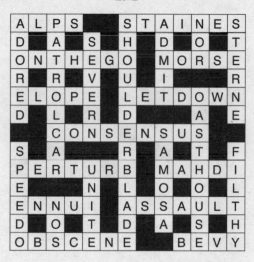

192

193

194

195

196

197

198

199

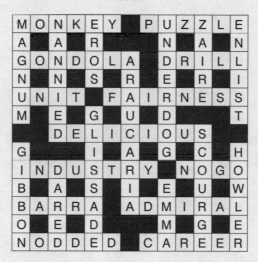

200

201

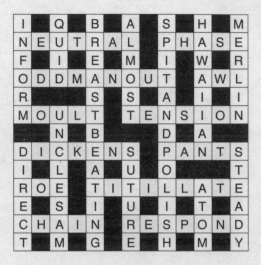

202

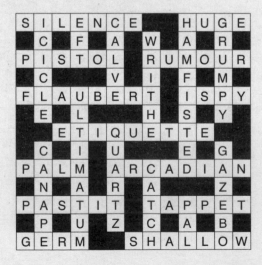

203

204

205

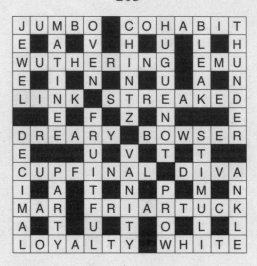

206

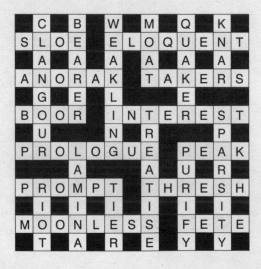

207

208

209

210

211

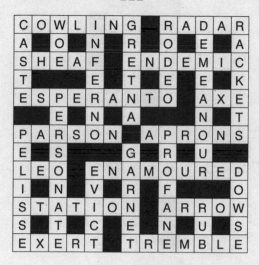

212

213

214

215

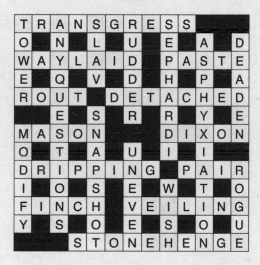

216

217

218

219

P	I	P	E		F	I	R	S	T	A	I	D
E		A		B		M		C		B		I
M	I	S	E	R		P	U	R	P	O	S	E
B		S		A		O		U		V		T
R	O	I	S	T	E	R		P	R	E	Y	
O		O				T		L		R		C
K	I	N	D	L	Y		C	E	R	E	A	L
E		S		A		C				P		I
	D	U	N	E		H	O	M	E	R	U	N
B		N		R		I		U		O		C
U	P	D	A	T	E	S		S	M	A	S	H
L		A		E		E		T		C		E
B	O	Y	I	S	H	L	Y		T	H	O	R

220

	S		Z		L			A	U	G	U	R
	Q	U	I	X	O	T	I	C		A		E
	U		T		W			T		D		J
F	I	S	H		K	A	M	I	K	A	Z	E
	N		E		E			V		B		C
S	T	U	R	D	Y		M	A	H	O	U	T
		N		O				T		U		
S	Q	U	A	W	K		V	E	R	T	E	X
A		S		N			I		A		Q	
T	R	A	N	S	F	E	R		P	O	U	T
R		B		I			G		T		I	
A		L		D	E	M	I	J	O	H	N	
P	A	Y	E	E				L		R		E

221

222

223

224

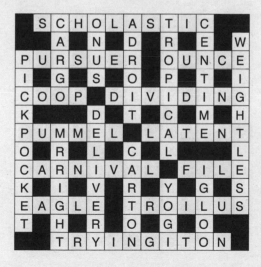

225

226

227

228

229

230

231

232

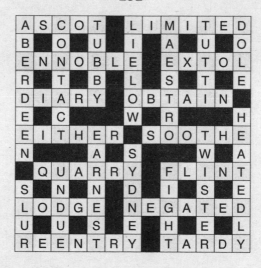

233

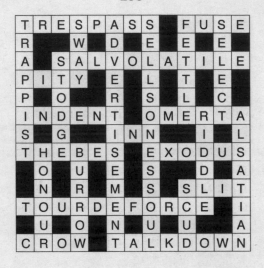

234

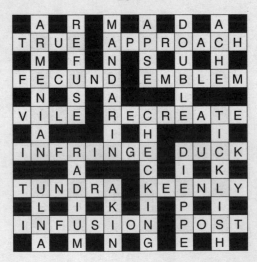

235

236

237

238

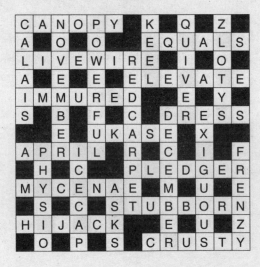

239

240

241

242

243

244

245

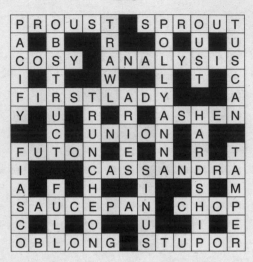

246

247

248

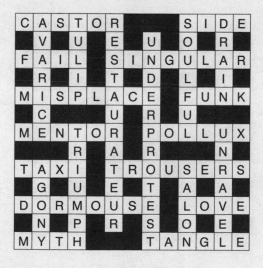

249

250

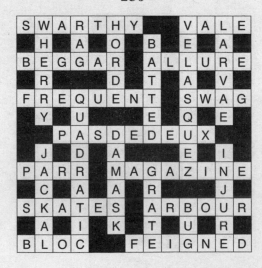

251

252

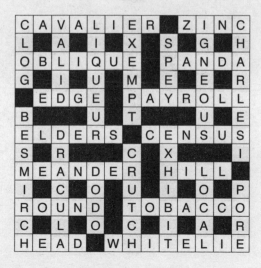

253

254

255

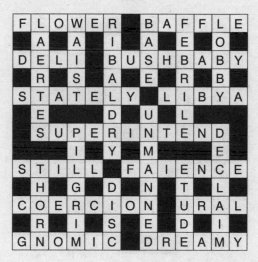

256

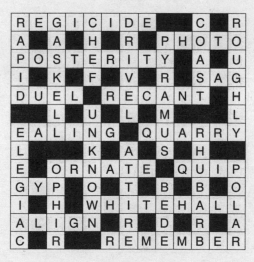

257

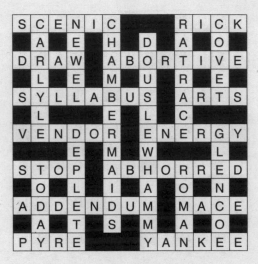

258

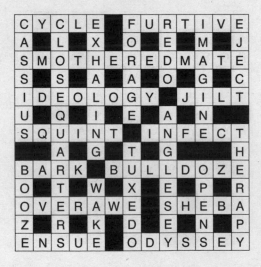

259

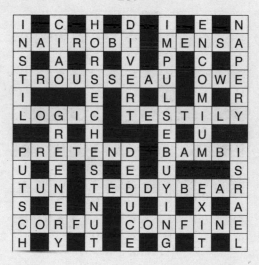

260

261

262

263

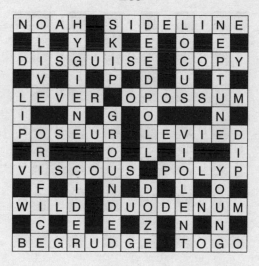

264

265

266

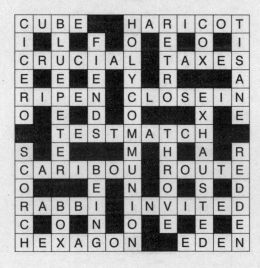

267

268

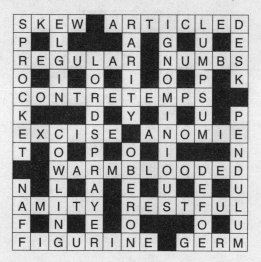

269

270

271

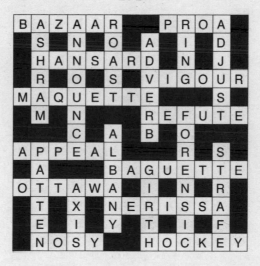

272

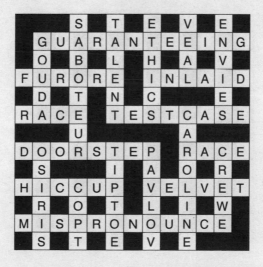

273

274

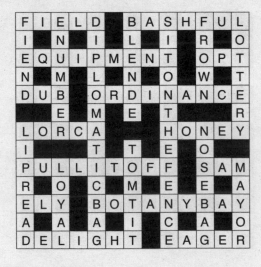

275

276

277

278

279

280

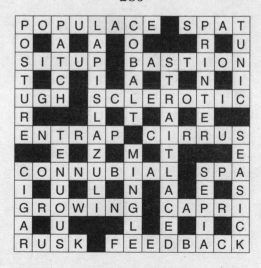

SOLUTIONS

281

282

283

284

285

286

287

288

289

290

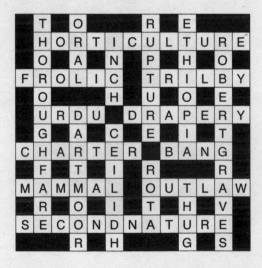

291

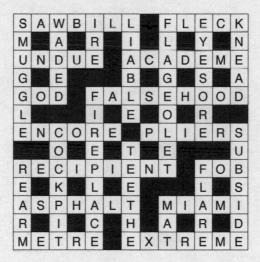

292

293

294

295

296

SOLUTIONS

297

298

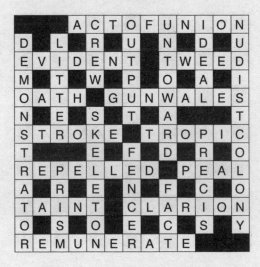

299

300

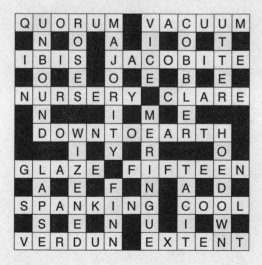

301

302

303

304

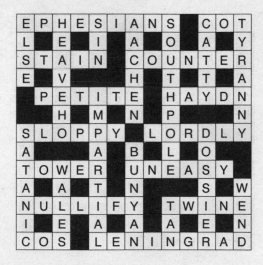

305

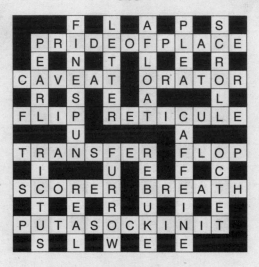

306